OTHER BOOKS BY COLETTE ROSSANT

A Mostly French Food Processor Cookbook
Cooking with Colette

Translation
Paul Bocuse's French Cooking

Colette Rossant's
After-Five
Gourmet

Colette Rossant's After-Five Gourmet

COLETTE ROSSANT

Illustrations by James Rossant

Random House
New York

Library of Congress Cataloging in Publication Data

Rossant, Colette.
Colette Rossant's After-five gourmet.

Includes index.
1. Cookery. I. Title. II. Title: After
five gourmet.
TX652.R6718   641.5'55   80–6014
ISBN 0–394–50506–9   AACR2

Manufactured in the United States of America

98765432

FIRST EDITION

For J. M. Kaplan with love
L'amitié est un don des dieux

Contents

Introduction

There is an old French saying: "If there is curiosity in the kitchen, a good meal is on the way." I am a curious cook, and curiosity leads to invention. This book is a collection of my recipes, some traditional, others less so, and I think you'll find them inventive—after all, they are mostly mine! I have compiled them to teach you how to think about food in a new way and to be able to prepare a sumptuous meal in less time than you might expect.

There is no reason why a working woman or man cannot turn the kitchen into a place for high adventure and experimentation, a laboratory to develop taste and to discover what is delicious. Throughout the writing of this book I continued to teach French literature and to chair the foreign language department at an independent school. At the same time that my work on the book progressed my job also seemed to expand. I was not only teaching from nine to three every day but also organizing a trip to France and directing a play with my students. I do not have extra hours to spend in the kitchen, and I don't believe too many other people do, either. I have written this book for the cook who also works, who wants to take the boredom out of food preparation and still have time for family, friends and other projects—but, most of all, who wants to have great results in the kitchen.

I have never adopted the American habit of shopping once a week. Instead, every day on my way home from work I stop at the supermarket, the butcher and the greengrocer in my neighborhood and select the foods I want to prepare that evening. With a little organization, these stops can be made in half an hour, and I have found no equal to this method for obtaining fresh, seasonal ingredients. I do purchase staples once a week, both to save time and to reduce the load I have to carry back from the store. I suggest that you shop the same way. A few years ago this method of shopping might have been impossible except in the major metropolitan areas, but now, with the burgeoning interest in natural foods, you can buy fresh fruits and vegetables almost everywhere. I urge you, whenever you can, to use fresh produce. If a recipe calls for a vegetable or a fruit that is out of season and you can't get the ingredient, forget the dish. Make a mental note—or better yet, write it down—to prepare the dish when the time is right.

I am home from market by five, giving myself roughly two hours for putting dinner on the table for my family. On weekends I allow more than two hours, but not too much longer, to prepare meals for guests. I entertain often to be with friends, not to spend my time in the kitchen while they sit at another end of the house.

Cooking—preparing even simple everyday dishes—should never be boring. Cooking, when you are really cooking, turns into an adventure. I love to experiment with combinations of ingredients, to play with the appetite. I guess this is another way of saying that I love to cook. Everyone loves to play; given the time and a little experience, I think you'll find you love to play in the kitchen too. Using these recipes will show you how.

For me, a major part of good cooking is the transformation of a simple meal into the unexpected. I like to consider every aspect of a dish: color, texture, overall presentation as well as the star attraction, taste. Imagine a whole lemon turned amber from being cooked stuffed with finely chopped and spiced meat, the entire surprising object edible. Or the taste and appearance of deep green Swiss chard with its bright red veins folded over beef marrow—yes, beef marrow. It's delicious and truly good for you.

I'm going to teach you how to be imaginative. For example, how can you transform a simple omelette into something intriguing? You might try, as I do, to make the omelette fold gracefully around a fan of asparagus spears while its center hides a tart vinaigrette. Or for a speedy touch of elegance, a surprise of a quite different flavor, try filling the omelette with red lumpfish caviar.

Here is a test for your imagination: Think about what you would do with fennel—a wonderful licorice-flavored vegetable the Italians call *finocchio,* and the French *fenouil*—which is available in most markets during its season. See if you can develop a curiosity about this vegetable that would lead you to be creative. Get some and try it!

And on the subject of seasons: one of the keys to making cooking an adventure is to use foods in season. Even though we do not really have seasons for food in the United States (you can get strawberries in January, though at great expense to both taste and purse), there are regional specialties and seasonal growth patterns that affect the quality of the food available to us. In the neighborhood around my home in New York City the produce brought in from farms in nearby states is always the best. Nothing compares with the taste of a New Jersey tomato at the peak of its flavor in midsummer, of fresh-picked corn in July, or of fresh baby lamb in the spring. Therefore, think about what is in season whenever you're planning a meal.

I've already suggested that some of the finest cooking is absolutely simple and traditional: for example, the sizzling steak topped with a crown of tarragon butter, the chopped meat that blends many flavors, the succulent roast of a pork loin. There are many different ways of achieving the same goals; cooking can be unusual and fun without being complicated and time-consuming, though most of my recipes will involve a tiny bit more effort than just broiling a steak. The emphasis is on organization, arrangement and surprise. Remember, *Menu mal fait, diner perdu.*

When you plan a menu, you need not select a complicated recipe for every course. Instead, choose a pivotal point for the menu, select a dish *you* really want to eat. Let this be the star of the meal; accompany it with good bread, a salad, a vegetable and fruit. With careful attention to planning your menu, you will save time shopping and cooking.

I always prepare first the dishes that require the most time. To do this, you should read through each recipe before you begin cooking and plan ahead. If your dessert requires baking or refrigeration time, prepare it first, of course, so that you can cook the rest of the meal while waiting. If the main course you choose must cook for an hour or more, use that time to prepare a vegetable and dessert. Those of my recipes that must be prepared the night before are best saved for a weekend when you may have more time.

With this book, you can learn to invent your own combinations. Become more aware of what pleases you. As you become liberated, so, too, will the palates of your friends.

Remember the fennel? For a start, how about stuffing it with

a purée of string beans?
ricotta mixed with herbs?
chopped pork spiced with sesame oil?
Italian sausage?
beef marrow?
mussels or clams?
smoked salmon or fish?
Or . . .
Read on!

The Well-Equipped Kitchen

In order to save time and cook well you must have a well-equipped kitchen. Take stock of your own kitchen. What do you have, and what do you use most? Using the proper utensils will reduce preparation time. The following are some of the tools I consider necessary for great cooking in little time:

—A food processor. This need not be expensive, and will perform four essential functions: slicing; chopping; mixing and making dough.

—Good knives:

    1 chef's knife, 8-inch-long blade

    1 paring knife, 4-inch-long blade

    1 all-purpose knife, 5¼-inch-long and 1-inch-wide blade

    1 boning knife, 6½-inch-long blade

    1 slicer, 14-inch-long and 1½-inch-wide blade

—Wooden spoons. These are simple utensils that are indispensable for making sauces.

—A good measuring cup, one that is large and easy to read for liquid measures.

—Measuring cups for dry measures. These come in ¼-cup, ⅓-cup, ½-cup and 1-cup sizes, and the best are made of stainless steel.

—Measuring spoons. These come in ¼-teaspoon, ½-teaspoon, 1-teaspoon and 1-tablespoon sizes.

—A steamer. I prefer Chinese bamboo steamers. These are available with two or three layers and range from 6 to 12 inches in diameter. One with a diameter of 9 or 12 inches is the best choice. These layers cut cooking time and allow you to prepare vegetables, meat and fish easily and healthfully. If you cannot find a Chinese steamer, the metal steamer that is sold everywhere and fits into a pot will do very well.

—An electric beater.

—A wire whisk.

—High-quality pots and pans:

    Saucepans: 2-cup, 1-quart, 2-quart and 8-quart sizes

    Skillets: 7-inch, 10-inch and 12-inch sizes with lids

    Flameproof casseroles: 3-quart and 6-quart sizes

    Double boiler

    Baking dishes

    Pie pans

—Strainers, small and large

—Colander

—Mixing bowls in several sizes

—A stainless-steel utensil set: spatula, ladle, 2-tined fork, slotted spoon, dull-edged knife.

Pots and pans and measuring spoons are not the only items you'll need in your well-equipped kitchen. There are staples no kitchen should be without and that you should always have readily at hand. High on the list are spices and herbs, which should be of high quality, and stored in tightly covered jars and away from heat in order to retain their perfume:

Allspice
Basil
Bay leaf
Cinnamon
Cloves
Coriander
Dill
Fennel
Ginger
Marjoram
Mint

Nutmeg
Oregano
Paprika
Parsley
Pepper
Rosemary
Sage
Salt
Sorrel
Tarragon
Thyme

I always keep the above items (and many more) at hand, as well as a mixture called four-spices, which I make myself. Since so many of the recipes in this book call for that mixture, I advise you to prepare it too, and keep it ready at all times. Here's the recipe:

FOUR-SPICES

1 tablespoon each thyme, bay leaf, sage
½ teaspoon each coriander and mace
1½ tablespoons freshly ground pepper

Combine the spices in a blender or coffee grinder, run through a sieve and place in a tightly closed jar. Keep away from heat.

Three other ingredients are essential to an efficient kitchen, and can be prepared in advance to save time and duplication of effort:
—Fresh parsley can be chopped, several bunches at a time, and re-
   frigerated for future use.
—Garlic can be chopped in advance and will keep for several weeks if
   stored in a tightly covered jar in the refrigerator.
—Onions can be prepared the same way as garlic.

You should also always have on hand the following. They can flavor almost any vegetable and chicken, fish or other meats:
—Soy sauce (good quality)
—Sesame oil
—Fresh ginger

Last, you should consider making crème fraîche, that quintessential French delight you can make inexpensively and simply, and keeping it in your refrigerator at all times. This is the recipe:

CRÈME FRAÎCHE*

2 pints heavy cream
5 tablespoons buttermilk
1 tablespoon sour cream

Pour all the ingredients in a glass jar. Close tightly and shake vigorously for *1 minute.* Place in a turned-off oven (if it has a pilot light) or next to a source of heat for 16 hours. Shake from time to time. Refrigerate for 24 hours. The crème fraîche is then ready to use. It will keep in the refrigerator for at least 10 days.

*Actually, this is a substitute for the real thing, which is cream that has been allowed to "mature." The true crème fraîche is the result of the action of lactic acids and natural fermentation.

How to Plan Your Imaginative Meals

To help you prepare exciting meals without spending your life in the kitchen, I have indicated both preparation time and cooking time for each recipe. If a dish takes 30 minutes to cook and 15 minutes to prepare for cooking, then, of course, you have to allow 45 minutes for it. But if you are also planning on something else that takes an hour, you should begin with that dish, and while it is cooking you can prepare and cook the 45-minute dish.

To make your menu planning even easier, I have worked out ten sample menus. These range from a simple family dinner to a repast fit for your most important guests. You will see that I go through planning and preparation step by step, showing you how to organize your time in the kitchen. Read through my menus to get a sense of the timing needed to make a complete meal in half an hour, an hour, or perhaps two hours. Learn how to choose a meal with all the dishes working well together in the kitchen as well as on the table. But remember, my menus are only suggestions.

FAMILY DINNERS

Eggs in Chantilly Cream (p. 5)
Calf's Liver with Bacon (p. 106)
Snow Peas with Pine Nuts (p. 196)
Fresh apples

String the snow peas.

Prepare the sesame oil and pine nuts.

Preheat the oven for the liver.

Cook the eggs and prepare them on a platter.

Twenty minutes after starting the sauce, cook the liver. Remove to a warm platter set on top of a saucepan of hot water, and begin cooking the bacon. Beat the egg whites with the Perrier. Keep the bacon warm in the turned-off oven.

Finish the egg dish.

Steam the snow peas and pour the sauce over them.

Finish the liver.

Cold Avocado Soup (p. 45)
Braised Roast with Shallots (p. 72)
Spaghetti Squash with Clam Sauce (p. 205)
Brussels Sprouts Salad with Sesame Seed (p. 222)
Fresh fruit in season

Preheat the oven. Prepare the roast according to the recipe and put in the oven.

Place the squash in a saucepan covered with water and cook it.

Prepare the Avocado Soup and set in the refrigerator to chill well.

Prepare the clams for the sauce.

Remove the squash from the saucepan and continue with the recipe.

Wash the Brussels sprouts and steam. Make the dressing.

Serve the soup.

Carve the meat and finish the sauce. Reheat the squash and serve with the meat. Serve the salad after the meat, followed by fresh fruit.

DINNERS FOR GUESTS

Pears and Kiwis with Prosciutto (p. 35)
Stuffed Saddle of Lamb (p. 86)
Glazed Carrots (p. 182)
Rhubarb Mousse with Strawberry Sauce (p. 252)

Peel the pears and refrigerate.

Cook the spinach. Preheat the oven. Prepare the lamb and the stuffing. Continue the lamb recipe and put in the oven.

Cut the rhubarb into small pieces and cook.

While the rhubarb is cooking, prepare the carrots in the food processor.

Refrigerate the rhubarb. Cook the carrots following the recipe.

Prepare the strawberry sauce and refrigerate. Prepare the pears. Finish the rhubarb mousse and refrigerate.

Coeurs de Palmier à la Provençale (p. 3)
Rolled Beef with Bacon (p. 75)
Steamed Broccoli (p. 179)
Raspberries with Peaches (p. 251)

Trim the broccoli and put in a steamer; set aside.
  Prepare the lemon butter.
  Prepare the coeurs de palmier (hearts of palm) and refrigerate.
  Prepare the beef and set aside.
  Prepare the peaches and purée the raspberries; refrigerate.
  Just before serving the first course, steam the broccoli. Your guests will have to wait for the second course, as the beef must be broiled at the last possible moment.

Smoked Salmon with Asparagus and Celery Root (p. 38)
Roast Chicken in Beer (p. 122)
Spring Cabbage Purée (p. 181)
Cold Kiwi Soufflé (p. 244)

Preheat the oven for the chicken.
  Prepare the dessert and refrigerate until serving time.
  Prepare the chicken and put in the oven.
  Steam the cabbage and asparagus in two layers in a steamer (or one at a time). Refrigerate the asparagus. Prepare the Cabbage Purée and keep warm over very low heat.
  Prepare the Smoked Salmon with Asparagus.

Cold Tomato Soup with Cucumber (p. 47)
Veal Scaloppine with Grapefruit (p. 95)
Glazed Carrots (p. 182)
Fresh fruit

Prepare the carrots and steam. Set aside.
  Prepare the soup.
  Glaze the carrots and set over very low heat to keep warm.
  Peel the grapefruit. Cook the veal and keep warm while adding the grapefruit.

Avocado with Red Caviar (p. 24)
Filets of Fluke with Green Peppercorns (p. 148)
Braised Endives
Green Salad
Apple Mousse (p. 236)

Start with the dessert and refrigerate until serving time.
   Wash and cook the endives; wash the salad greens.
   Prepare the dressing for the salad.
   Prepare the avocado.
   Start cooking the fish just before serving the first course.

   Sorrel Soup (p. 60)
   Rib Steak with Vinegar and Herbs (p. 67)
   Paul Bocuse's Potato Pancake (p. 197)
   Celery, Apple and Walnut Salad (p. 223)
   Bowl of cherries

Prepare the soup.
   While the soup is simmering, peel and grate the potatoes.
   Prepare the salad.
   While the steaks are cooking, make the potato pancake and keep
warm in the oven. When the steaks are done, the potato pancake will
be ready.

   Yogurt Soup (p. 52)
   Charcoal-Broiled Lamb Chops with Sauce Piquante (p. 85)
   Sautéed New Potatoes (p. 200)
   Brioches with Ice Cream (p. 271)

Make the yogurt soup and refrigerate.
   Clean the potatoes and steam.
   Prepare the sauce for the lamb chops and set aside.
   Sauté the potatoes and heat the broiler.
   Prepare the brioches.
   Serve the soup while the lamb chops are broiling.
   Serve the potatoes with the chops.
   Add ice cream to the brioches at the last moment and serve.

   Mushrooms with Mussels and Clams (p. 9)
   Broiled Marinated Steak (p. 68)
   Purée of Watercress with Bean Curd Sauce (p. 210)
   Zabaglione with Fruit (p. 256)

Prepare the marinade and add the London broil. Set aside; occasionally
turn the steak.
   Wash and soak the mussels and the clams. Wash the mushrooms.
   Cook the clams and mussels.
   Wash the watercress, prepare the purée, and keep warm.
   Heat the broiler.
   Finish the mushroom-mussel-clam dish.
   Wash the fruit for dessert.

Put the steak on to broil while your guests are eating the hors d'oeuvre.

Make the zabaglione at the end of the meal.

When you sit down to plan a meal, first determine the amount of time you can spend in the kitchen. Then go to the tables on the following pages where the preparation and cooking times are given for dishes in various categories—hors d'oeuvre, soups, meats and so forth—and select the dishes that will fit your own schedule.

I use several time frames for preparing a dish from start to finish: less than 15 minutes, less than 30 minutes, less than 1 hour, more than 1 hour and overnight. All of the times are generous estimates and will vary according to your skill in the kitchen and the equipment you have access to.

Thus, if you have half an hour and want to make a chicken dish, look under "Poultry: Less than 30 minutes." After choosing your main course, go on to decide on the rest of the meal in the same manner. Remember that you need not prepare several complicated courses: choose one important dish and a few simple accompaniments.

HOT HORS D'OEUVRE

Less than 15 minutes
Eggs with Yogurt
Grenouillettes de Veau

Less than 30 minutes
Asparagus Omelette
Chicken Livers with Port
Hot Prosciutto with Fresh
   Tarragon and Shallots
Omelette with Goat Cheese and
   Mint
Omelette with Red Lumpfish
   Caviar
Eggs in Chantilly Cream
Parmesan Puffs

Less than 1 hour
Boudin Blanc with Hazelnuts
Coeurs de Palmier à la
   Provençale
Snail Stew with Walnuts
Four-and-Twenty Asparagus
   Quiche
Sweetbread Mousse
Mustard Pie
Eggplant in Oil
Baked Eggs with Sorrel
Jerusalem Artichokes with
   Mozzarella
Mushrooms with Mussels and
   Clams
Pâtés de Romarin
Broiled Mussels with Ham and
   Bacon

More than 1 hour

Cucumber Stuffed with Clams

Phyllo Stuffed with Bay Scallops
and Spinach

Mushroom Flan

Artichokes Stuffed with Ricotta

Talmousses

Fried Samosas

COLD HORS D'OEUVRE

Less than 15 minutes

Pears and Kiwis with Prosciutto

Tapenade for Crudités

Ricotta with Fines Herbes

Less than 30 minutes

Eggplant with Peppers

Sweetbread Salad with Raw
Mushrooms and Fennel

Crème de Foies de Volaille au
Calvados

Avocado with Red Caviar

Mousse de Roquefort

Prosciutto Stuffed with
Watercress

Smoked Salmon with Asparagus
and Celery Root

Basket of Crudités

Less than 1 hour

Cold Chicken Balls

Mousse de Caviar

Salmon Rillettes

More than 1 hour

Marinated Sole Filets

Cold Fish Pâté with Peppercorns

Rabbit Pâté

Pâté with Herbs

Terrine of Turkey

Overnight or more

Marinated Salmon

Pickled Summer Vegetables

Vegetable Pâté in Aspic

SOUP

Less than 15 minutes

Cold Beet and Tomato Soup

Yogurt Soup

Less than 30 minutes

Soupe de Petits Pois

Tapioca and Asparagus Soup

Watercress Soup

Green Soup

Chilled Peanut Soup

Cold Tomato Soup with
Cucumber

Oyster Stew

Shrimp Soup

Less than 1 hour

Cold Avocado Soup

Lentil Soup

Carrot Soup

Mushroom Consommé

Portuguese Soup

Tomato Soup

Brussels Sprouts Soup

Sorrel Soup

Beef Soup with Marrow

Soupe de Poissons de Décembre

Spring Soup

More than 1 hour

Tomato Soup with Fennel

Cream of Fennel Soup

Cabbage Soup with Blue Cheese

Mussel Soup

Codfish Soup from Cardiff

Potage à la Viande

Overnight or more

Dried Lima Bean Soup

Potage Emeraude

BEEF

Less than 15 minutes

Cold Roast Beef with Mushroom Sauce

Less than 30 minutes

Hamburger with Crème Fraîche

Rib Steak with Vinegar and
   Herbs

Steak with Coffee Sauce

Pan-Broiled Steak with Onion
   Sauce

Hamburger Tartare

Rolled Beef with Bacon

Less than 1 hour

Beef with Lingonberries

Broiled Marinated Steak

Hamburgers with Anchovy
   Potatoes

Stuffed Lemons

Filets Mignons with Artichoke
   Hearts

Broiled Steak with Black Olive
   Sauce

More than 1 hour

Beef Bracioli Stuffed with Swiss
   Chard

Roast Beef with Fresh Herbs

Roast Beef with Cranberries

Braised Roast with Shallots

Rolled Beef with Carrots

Potée

Filet of Beef with Stuffed Prunes

LAMB, VEAL AND PORK

Less than 15 minutes

Baby Lamb Chops with Lemon

Poached Calf's Liver

Less than 30 minutes

Calf's Liver with Bacon
Broiled Lamb Steaks with Garlic
Butter

Calf's Liver with Oranges
Veal Scaloppine with Marinated
Italian Artichoke Hearts

Less than 1 hour

Pork Cubes with Cherrystone
Clams
Ham Steaks with Shallots
Veal Scaloppine with Grapefruit
Veal Scaloppine with Lemon and
Avocado Purée
Whole Calf's Liver in White
Wine
Pork Liver en Croûte

Charcoal-Broiled Lamb Chops
with Sauce Piquante
Sautéed Sweetbreads
Veal Kidneys en Bateau
Veal Scaloppine with Clams
Charcoal-Broiled Lamb with
Laurel
Veal Hamburgers

More than 1 hour

Roulades de Porc
Roast Pork with Black
Peppercorns
Spring Lamb with Sorrel
Spring Leg of Lamb with
Tarragon
French Winter Lamb Stew
Sautéed Lamb with Yogurt Sauce
Sautéed Spring Lamb with
Salsify
Veal Loaf

Sautéed Veal with Small White
Onions
Pork Filet with Prunes
Roast Pork with Pommes de
Terre Boulangère
Roast Pork with Cherries
Baked Veal Chops with Ham
Stuffed Saddle of Lamb
Hot Lamb Pâté
Roast Pork

Three hours or more

Veal Roast in Milk

POULTRY

Less than 30 minutes

Chicken Breasts with Avocado

Chicken-Breast Shish Kebab

Less than 1 hour

Chicken Breasts with Mangoes
and Green Grapes
Sautéed Chicken Livers with
Egyptian Rice
Chaud-Froid of Chicken Breasts
with Walnut Sauce
Chicken Breasts with Straw
Mushrooms and Avocado

Chicken Sautéed with Beets
Gratin of Chicken with Endives
Spicy Chicken with Vinegar
Turkey Scallops with Asparagus
Chicken Fricassee
Chicken Giblets with Garlic and
Cream
Turkey Fondue

More than 1 hour

Roast Chicken in Beer
Salt Chicken with Ginger Sauce
Braised Duck with Green
  Peppers
Chicken Stuffed with Boudin
Roast Chicken with Juniper
  Berries
Stew of Goose Giblets with
  Dried Fruit
Turkey Pie with Fresh Clams
Canard aux Oignons
Chicken Dodoma
Christmas Goose with
  Sauerkraut
Cornish Hen with Glazed
  Turnips
Poulet à l'Ail

Duck with Apple
Gratin of Turkey
Michel Warren's Duck with
  Cucumber
Sautéed Chicken with Celery
Sautéed Chicken with Madeira
  and Tomatoes
Stuffed Chicken with Lemon
  Sauce
Stuffed Goose Neck
Capon Stuffed with Chestnuts
Chicken Breasts with Figs and
  Watercress
Fricassee of Goose
Chicken with Cherries
Chicken Stuffed with Garlic
  Cloves

FISH AND SHELLFISH

Less than 30 minutes

Filets of Fluke with Green
  Peppercorns

Broiled Filets of Sole with
  Lemon-Butter Sauce

Less than 1 hour

Noodles with Stingray and
  Capers
Fresh Tuna in White Wine
Mullet with Lime
Poached Shad with Beurre Blanc
Striped Bass with White Wine
Tilefish with Prawns
Trout with Garlic Cream
Broiled Prawns
Halibut with Avocado
Prawns with Asparagus

Red Snapper with Peaches
Shrimp Beignets
Mackerel with Aïoli
Filets of Flounder with
  Marjoram
Fresh Bluefish with Pistachios
Gratin of Shad Roe with Sorrel
  Purée
Phyllo Stuffed with Bay Scallops
  and Spinach

More than 1 hour

Clafoutis de Moules
Salmon Baked in Champagne
Filets of Flounder with Swiss
  Chard
Filets of Sole in a Shrimp-Filled
  Boat

Fish Stew with Garlic Bread
Prawns with Vegetables
Profiteroles with Shrimp
Poached Filets of Flounder with
  Morels

Grilled Sardines with Lemon
Saumon en Croûte
Mussels Cooked in Hard Cider

Tilefish with Capers
Tuna with Aïoli

Overnight
Baked Dried Cod

Cold Sardines or Smelts

VEGETABLES

Less than 15 minutes
Snow Peas with Pine Nuts
Steamed Eggplant with Ginger
    Sauce

Steamed Spinach with Lemon
    Sauce

Less than 30 minutes
Sautéed New Potatoes
Steamed Broccoli
Brussels Sprouts with Bacon and
    Pine Nuts
Mushrooms with Cider
Paul Bocuse's Potato Pancake
String Bean Purée

Purée of Watercress with Bean
    Curd Sauce
Steamed Cauliflower with
    Beaumont Cheese
Eggplant Gratiné
Green Peas with Romaine
Fresh Tagliatelle with Walnuts

Less than 1 hour
Fennel with Sherry
Macaroni with Anchovies
Broiled Eggplant
Purée of Mushrooms
Lentils with Bacon
Baked Potatoes with Anchovies
Cauliflower Cake with Pesto
Fresh Noodles with Leek Sauce
Glazed Carrots
Purée of Celery Root
Spaghetti Squash Rémoulade
Spring Cabbage Purée
Stuffed Tomatoes with Fresh
    Mint
Broccoli with Blue Cheese Sauce
Carrot Soufflé

Five-Layer Vegetable Cake
String-Bean Pancakes with Ham
Galettes de Pommes de Terre
Green Pudding
Hot Pumpkin Mousse
Potato Pancakes with
    Mushrooms
Sorrel Purée
Stuffed Onions
Swiss Chard with Beef Marrow
Baked Tomatoes with Bacon
String Beans with Anchovies
Spaghetti Squash with Clam
    Sauce
Baked Potatoes with Ricotta

More than 1 hour
Ail Au Four
Baked Macaroni
Fricassee of Fennel
Braised Onions

Celery Root with Smoked Bacon
Chestnut Stew
Red Cabbage wth Granny Smith
    Apples

Cabbage Pie
Braised Fava Beans and
  Artichokes
Roulade d'Epinards

Stuffed Endives
Swiss Chard Pie
Stuffed Spinach Roll
Braised Artichokes

SALAD

Less than 15 minutes

Fresh Spinach Salad with
  Hard-Boiled Eggs
Beet Salad with Walnuts

Celery, Apple and Walnut Salad
Endive Salad with Kiwis
Okra Salad

Less than 30 minutes

Brussels Sprouts Salad with
  Sesame Seeds
Hot Leek Salad
Carrot Salad
Chinese Duck Salad
Endive Salad with Fresh Peas

Radish and Fennel Salad
Carrot, String Bean and
  Cucumber Salad
Walnut-Ball Salad
Pomegranate Salad

Less than 1 hour

Rice Salad with Prawns and
  Tuna
Asparagus Salad with Mussels

String Bean and Mussel Salad
Crab and Rice Salad

DESSERT

Less than 15 minutes

Barbecued Bananas
Chocolate-Orange Cookies
Brioches with Ice Cream

Chestnut Ice Cream
Fresh Pineapple with Pineapple
  Sauce

Less than 30 minutes

Caramel-Cream Pears
Zabaglione with Fruit
Cantaloupe with Watermelon
  and Pine Nuts

Fruit Salad in Frosted Oranges
Coconut Balls
Les Chichis

Less than 1 hour

Nectarines with Fresh Figs
Hot Compote of Dried Fruits
Apple and Apricot Tart
Cecile's Tahini Cookies

Tarte au Sucre
Apple Mousse
Banana Cake with Raspberry
  Jelly

Chocolate Pears
Profiteroles Stuffed with Coffee
　Ice Cream
Raspberries with Peaches
Gâteau aux Amandes
Peach Soufflé
Persimmon Pie
Strawberry Soufflé
Almond Crescent Cookies
Easter Nests
Poached Pears with Green
　Grapes

Banana Pudding
Cherry Soup
Chocolate Sabayon with Grapes
French Toast
Calvados Cream with Mangoes
Cold Kiwi Soufflé
Date Pudding
Rhubarb Mousse with
　Strawberry Sauce

More than 1 hour

Kiwi Sherbet with Fresh
　Raspberry Purée
Lemon Squares
Rachel's Cheesecake
Tomato Jam
Beggar's Pie
Apple Roll
Gâteau de Petit Beurre

Cherry Fondant
Crème de Marrons au Chocolat
Prune Turnovers
Strawberry Pie
Green Grape Tart
Pear Tart
Pistachio Cake
Tarte aux Betteraves

More than 2 hours

Anne's Almond Cookies
Mollie's Spritz Cookies
Honey Cream with Kiwis

Coconut Flan
Crème aux Pêches

SAUCES

Less than 15 minutes

Aïoli
Black Olive Vinaigrette
Garlic Sauce
Ginger Sauce
Green Sauce
Mayonnaise
Mayonnaise with Yogurt
Pesto

Béarnaise Sauce
Tomato and Yogurt Sauce
Yogurt Sauce
Pink Sauce
Rouille
Basil and Cream Sauce
Lemon-Butter Sauce

Less than 30 minutes

Béchamel

Green Peppercorn Sauce

Less than 1 hour
Tomato Sauce

Overnight
Crème Fraîche

DOUGH AND BATTER

Less than 15 minutes
Beer Batter for Crêpes
Pâte Brisée

Appetizers

Hot Hors d'Oeuvre

Coeurs de Palmier à la Provençale
(Hearts of Palm Provençal Style)

PREPARATION: 10 MINUTES   COOKING: 20 MINUTES

2-pound can Italian peeled
  tomatoes
2 tablespoons olive oil
Salt and freshly ground pepper
2 tablespoons chopped fresh
  basil
1 can hearts of palm

4 tablespoons butter
1 medium-size onion, minced
2 cloves garlic, crushed
5 ounces pitted black olives
1 tablespoon chopped parsley
1 head Boston lettuce

Drain the tomatoes, squeezing all the water out. In a large skillet, heat the olive oil, add the tomatoes and sprinkle with salt and pepper. Add the basil, reduce the heat and simmer for 10 minutes.

Drain the hearts of palm and slice. In a large skillet, melt the butter. When the butter is hot, add the onion and garlic, sauté for 5 minutes, then add the hearts of palm, salt and pepper. Lower the heat and simmer for 5 minutes.

Add the olives to the tomatoes.

When the hearts of palm are cooked, add them to the tomatoes. Pour into a serving bowl, sprinkle with parsley and serve on a bed of lettuce.

This dish can also be served cold the next day.

6 servings

Artichokes Stuffed with Ricotta

PREPARATION: 25 MINUTES   COOKING: 45 MINUTES

I first had this dish when people in my neighborhood decided one day to improve the street by planting trees. As the trees were very expensive, we thought of having a block party to raise the money. We had stands with games and stands with food. Everyone made something. One neighbor made great stuffed artichokes, and her stand collected the most money. Today the tree in front of her house is also the tallest!

12 small artichokes	½ pound ricotta
3 or 4 lemons	¼ cup chopped fresh parsley
1 tablespoon flour	Pinch of paprika
¼ cup chopped fresh basil	1½ tablespoons butter
1 tablespoon dried tarragon	Salt and pepper

Strip off the tough outer leaves of the artichokes. Remove the chokes with a teaspoon and trim the hearts so that they are all even. Rub the artichokes with a lemon cut in two, then put them in a saucepan and cover with water. In a small bowl, mix the flour with ½ cup water, add the juice of two lemons and pour the mixture over the artichokes.

Cook the artichokes, keeping the water boiling over medium heat for 15 to 20 minutes, depending upon their size. To test if the artichokes are done, remove one leaf: it should come off easily when done. Drain the artichokes and cool them while preparing the cheese stuffing.

Preheat the oven to 375°.

Put the basil, parsley and tarragon in a food processor or blender. Run the machine for 30 seconds, or until the herbs are chopped. Add the cheese, paprika, salt and pepper. Run the machine for 30 seconds more, or until the herbs are well mixed with the cheese.

Stuff each artichoke with the cheese mixture, making a mound. Butter an ovenproof dish and place the artichokes in it side by side. Put a small piece of butter on each artichoke. Bake for 20 minutes. Serve piping hot.

6 servings

Cucumbers Stuffed with Clams

PREPARATION: 25 MINUTES   COOKING: 45 MINUTES

The subtle taste of cucumbers mixed with clams makes an elegant and delicious hors d'oeuvre.

24 cherrystone clams or 7-ounce can whole clams	1¼ teaspoons thyme
	1 clove garlic, chopped
4 medium-size cucumbers	Juice of 2 limes
1 stick (¼ pound) butter	2 tablespoons bread crumbs
Salt and pepper	2 tablespoons chopped fresh
½ cup Béchamel (see p. 201)	parsley (Chinese or regular)

Preheat the oven to 325°. If you are using fresh clams, wash and scrub them, and soak in cold water. Peel the cucumbers, then halve the cucumbers lengthwise and remove the seeds. Pat dry with paper towels.

Butter a gratin dish and place the cucumbers in it side by side. Melt the remaining butter; with a pastry brush, brush some butter on the cucumbers. Sprinkle with salt and pepper. Bake for 30 minutes.

Meanwhile, place the clams in a large kettle. Cook, covered, over high heat until the clams open. Remove them to a bowl to cool and drain the cooking liquid through a very fine sieve.

Make the béchamel using the liquid instead of milk.

Remove the clams from their shells (or from the can) and chop them coarsely. Add the clams to the béchamel, then add the thyme and garlic. Mix well and correct the seasoning. Add freshly ground pepper and the lime juice to taste.

Fill the cucumbers with the clams. Sprinkle the clams with bread crumbs and brush with the remaining melted butter. Broil for a few minutes, or until golden brown. Sprinkle with parsley and serve.

4 servings

Eggs in Chantilly Cream

PREPARATION: 15 MINUTES   COOKING: 6 MINUTES

One muggy summer night in New York I was suddenly faced with six unexpected guests. What I had in great quantity were eggs, heavy cream and Perrier water. I wanted something light and refreshing, and I came up with this simple recipe, which turned out to be a great hit. It is essential that the Perrier water be truly cold.

6 large eggs	2 tablespoons chopped fresh
Salt	tarragon or watercress
2 cups heavy cream	Freshly ground pepper
Thoroughly chilled Perrier water	

Put the eggs in a saucepan of boiling water with 2 tablespoons of salt. Boil for 6 minutes. Drain and cool under cold running water.

Peel and halve the eggs. Set aside on a serving platter.

Beat the cream. Just before it turns into whipped cream, slowly add 1½ tablespoons of Perrier water. Beat for a few minutes, then add salt and a generous amount of pepper. Fold 1½ tablespoons tarragon or watercress into the thick cream.

Cover each egg with the cream and sprinkle the remaining tarragon on top. Serve with a tomato salad.

6 servings

Baked Eggs with Sorrel

PREPARATION: 20 MINUTES   COOKING: 25 MINUTES

Sorrel is a small green leaf that is sometimes called bitter grass by Americans. This dish is very colorful—the yellow of the yolk makes a lovely contrast to the deep green of the sorrel.

1 pound sorrel	12 eggs
6 tablespoons butter	2 tablespoons chopped chives
Salt and pepper	1 loaf Italian or French bread
1¼ cups heavy cream	2 tablespoons chopped parsley

Preheat the oven to 375°.

Wash the sorrel and cut off the stems. Drain and pat dry with paper towels. In a saucepan, melt 2 tablespoons butter; when the butter is hot, add the sorrel. Add salt and pepper to taste, cover the saucepan and cook over medium heat for 1 minute. Uncover and cook, stirring all the while, until all the water evaporates. Remove from heat.

In a small saucepan, bring the heavy cream to a boil. Add the boiling cream to the sorrel, mix well with a wooden spoon and simmer for 2 or 3 minutes more. Turn off the heat and set aside.

Butter 6 ramekins generously. Break two eggs into each, being careful not to break the yolks. Place the ramekins in a baking dish and fill the baking dish half full with boiling water. Sprinkle the eggs with salt and pepper and a little of the chopped chives.

Bake in the oven for about 5 minutes, or until the whites of the eggs are opaque—the yolks should still be liquid.

While the eggs are baking, cut the Italian bread lengthwise. Butter each side, then cut it in two again. Cut each piece into 6-inch strips (these are called mouillettes). Sprinkle each strip with parsley and the remaining chives, and place on a cookie sheet. Heat in the oven for 3 to 4 minutes.

Remove the ramekins from the oven, pour 1 tablespoon sorrel in each, and serve right away with the mouillettes.

6 servings

Eggs with Yogurt

PREPARATION: 5 MINUTES   COOKING: 15 MINUTES

2 cups plain yogurt
1 clove garlic, crushed
1 teaspoon paprika
Salt to taste

4 eggs
½ teaspoon vinegar
1 tablespoon butter, melted
Pinch of cayenne

In a bowl, beat the yogurt, garlic, paprika and salt with a whisk until light. Place the bowl in a pan of hot water, stirring occasionally until the yogurt is warm.

Meanwhile, poach eggs in a saucepan of simmering water to which vinegar has been added; drain. Pour the warm yogurt on a platter and arrange the eggs on top. Pour the melted butter on the eggs and sprinkle cayenne on top. Serve as the main course for luncheon or as an appetizer.

2 servings

Eggplant in Oil

PREPARATION: 15 MINUTES   COOKING: 30 MINUTES

2 large eggplants
2 cups oil
2 pounds tomatoes
1 pound small white onions

Salt and freshly ground pepper
3 large cloves garlic, chopped
½ cup wine vinegar

Peel the eggplants. Cut in two lengthwise and slice. In a large skillet, heat half the oil. When the oil is hot, fry the eggplant slices until browned on each side. Drain on paper towels. Peel and seed the tomatoes by squeezing over a strainer set on top of a bowl. Quarter them. Peel the onions, leaving them whole.

In an ovenproof casserole, place half the onions, then half the tomatoes, then all the eggplant. Sprinkle with salt, pepper and garlic. Cover the eggplant with the remaining onions and tomatoes. Pour the vinegar over them. Bring to a boil, then simmer covered for 15 minutes. Uncover and cook for another 15 minutes.

Serve at room temperature as an hors d'oeuvre.

The eggplant can be refrigerated for a few days and served cold.

8 to 10 servings

Jerusalem Artichokes with Mozzarella

PREPARATION: 30 MINUTES   COOKING: 12 MINUTES

I live on an Italian street. At the corner, facing the Church of St. Anthony, is probably the best mozzarella store in the city. I have bought my cheese there from the day we moved into our house. For ten years the only thing I heard from the owners was "Good morning" and "Good-bye," until I ran for county committeewoman. Suddenly everyone on my street became very friendly, especially the owner of the cheese store. We exchanged recipes, she bought my book, I bought her cheese. She gave me the recipe for this refreshing dish. Serve it as an appetizer with a green salad.

2 pounds Jerusalem artichokes*   2 tablespoons milk
18 slices Italian bread   1 cup fresh bread crumbs
1 pound mozzarella   Oil for deep frying
2 eggs   Parsley for garnish

Peel the Jerusalem artichokes and cut into slices ¼ inch thick. Trim the crust off the bread. Cut the mozzarella into twelve ½-inch thick slices the same width as the bread. Put the eggs and milk in a bowl and beat.

Thread a small skewer with a slice of bread, a slice of artichoke and a slice of mozzarella, and then another slice of bread, cheese and artichoke. Thread the remaining skewers the same way.

Dip each skewer in the egg mixture and then in the bread crumbs. Heat the oil in a large skillet to 360°. Fry the prepared skewers until golden brown, or about 2 minutes. Drain on paper towels.

Serve garnished with parsley.

6 servings

*The Jerusalem artichoke originated in North America and was imported around the seventeenth century to France, where it is widely used. This brown-skinned tuber has a taste vaguely resembling that of the more familiar globe artichoke and is delicious raw in salads.

Mushroom Flan

PREPARATION: 40 MINUTES   COOKING: 30 MINUTES

½ pound mushrooms   1 teaspoon paprika
2½ tablespoons butter   Salt and pepper
2 egg yolks   Pinch of nutmeg
1 egg   4 tablespoons grated Parmesan
1 cup heavy cream

Preheat the oven to 400°.

Clean and quickly wash the mushrooms. Pat dry with paper towels and thinly slice. In a skillet, melt 2 tablespoons butter and sauté the mushrooms for 5 minutes. Remove from heat.

In a bowl, beat the egg and yolks with the cream. Add the spices, 2 tablespoons Parmesan, salt and pepper.

Butter a soufflé dish. Pour the mushrooms in and sprinkle with half the Parmesan. Pour in the egg-and-cream mixture and sprinkle the top with the remaining Parmesan. Bake in the oven for 25 to 30 minutes.

Serve hot as an appetizer.

4 servings

Mushrooms with Mussels and Clams

PREPARATION: 30 MINUTES   COOKING: 20 MINUTES

1 pint mussels
2 dozen cherrystone clams
1½ pounds mushrooms
5 tablespoons butter
1 cup dry white wine
4 small onions, chopped

1 clove garlic, chopped
2 tablespoons Crème Fraîche
  (see p. xvi)
3 tablespoons chopped parsley
Salt and freshly ground pepper

Wash and scrape the mussels. Soak in cold water for 10 minutes. Wash the clams and soak in water for 10 minutes. Wash the mushrooms and chop coarsely.

In a skillet, melt 3½ tablespoons butter. When the butter is hot, add the mushrooms, salt and pepper. Simmer for 15 minutes.

Meanwhile, place the mussels and the clams in a large saucepan. Add the white wine. Bring to a boil and cook until the clams and mussels open.

Remove the mussels and the clams to a bowl, and when cool to the touch, remove the mussels and clams from their shells.

In a skillet, melt the remaining butter. Sauté the onions and garlic. Add the mussels and clams; sprinkle with pepper, add the crème fraîche, and mix well. Heat through, but do not boil.

Put the mushrooms on a serving platter, cover with the mussels and clams, sprinkle with parsley, and serve.

4 servings

Mustard Pie

PREPARATION: 15 MINUTES   COOKING: 40 MINUTES

Pâte Brisée I (see below)   3 tablespoons Crème Fraîche
2 full tablespoons strong   (see p. xvi)
  Dijon-style mustard   Salt and pepper
4 large tomatoes   Freshly chopped parsley

Preheat the oven to 400°.
  Make the pâte brisée and let it stand for 15 minutes.
  Butter a 9-inch pie pan. Roll out the dough on a floured board and
line the pan. Prick the dough with a fork and spread the mustard on it.
  Wash and pat dry the tomatoes and cut into thick slices. Spread the
crème fraîche on top of the mustard. Place the sliced tomatoes on top
of the crème. Sprinkle with salt and pepper. Bake for 40 minutes.
  Remove from the oven and sprinkle with parsley. Serve at room
temperature.
  6 servings

Pâte Brisée I (for appetizers or meats)
PREPARATION: 10 minutes

1¾ cups flour   1 egg
1 stick (¼ pound) butter, chilled   2 tablespoons oil
  and cut into 1-inch pieces   ½ cup ice water
1 teaspoon salt

Place the flour, butter and salt in a food processor. Run the machine
until these ingredients are well mixed; then add the egg and the oil. Run
the machine for 30 seconds, then slowly add the ice water.
  Stop the machine. Form a ball with the dough. Wrap it in waxed paper
and chill it in the refrigerator for 30 minutes.
  This dough can keep for several days in the refrigerator or it can be
frozen.
  Makes 2 9-inch pie shells

Asparagus Omelette

PREPARATION: 5 MINUTES   COOKING: 15 MINUTES

Asparagus, which is a vegetable fit for a king (it was in fact Louis XIV's favorite vegetable), is delicious served in an omelette with a spicy vinaigrette. This dish can be served as an hors d'oeuvre or as a main course for lunch.

2 pounds asparagus	8 eggs
1 tablespoon wine vinegar	3½ tablespoons butter
3 tablespoons oil	Salt and pepper
2 tablespoons mixture of chopped fresh parsley, chives and basil	

Wash and trim the asparagus, removing any tough stems. Steam the asparagus over ½ cup boiling water for 8 minutes, or until tender but still firm. Remove to a platter and set aside.

Mix together the vinegar, oil, salt and pepper. Add the herbs.

In a bowl, beat the eggs. Cut 1½ tablespoons butter in very small pieces and add to the beaten eggs.

Heat a large skillet and add the remaining butter. When the butter is hot enough to sizzle, add the eggs. Shake the pan while pushing back the cooked edges of the eggs with a fork to allow the uncooked part in the middle to run to the sides. Place the asparagus on one half of the

omelette* and add half of the vinegar-oil mixture. Using a spatula, fold the omelette and slide it onto a platter. Serve with the remaining vinegar-oil mixture. The omelette can also be served cold.
4 servings

*As a special touch, before folding the omelette, line up the asparagus spears on one half of the omelette with the thick ends clustered in the center and the tips spaced, thus creating a fan like effect (see illustration on p. 11). The tips should extend an inch or so beyond the edges of the omelette, so that bits of green will show after the omelette has been folded.

Omelette with Goat Cheese and Mint

PREPARATION: 10 MINUTES   COOKING: 15 MINUTES

10 fresh mint leaves   ½ pound fresh goat cheese
10 eggs   5 tablespoons butter
Salt and pepper   Parsley for garnish

Wash and dry the mint leaves, and chop fine. Break the eggs in a large bowl. Add the mint, salt and pepper and beat the eggs with a fork. In a plate, mash the cheese with a fork.
Heat a large skillet and add the butter. When the butter is hot enough to sizzle, add the eggs. Cook the omelette over medium heat for 5 minutes, shaking the pan while pushing back the cooked edges of the eggs with a fork to allow the uncooked part to run to the sides. Spread the cheese on top and cook for another five minutes. With a spatula, fold the omelette and cook for a few minutes more. Slide the omelette onto a hot serving platter and garnish with parsley. Serve right away.
6 servings

Omelette with Red Lumpfish Caviar

PREPARATION: 10 MINUTES   COOKING: 15 MINUTES

Michel Warren, a French artist, served me this omelette late one night in Paris. Since then I have served it many times for lunch or as an hors d'oeuvre.

8 eggs
Salt and pepper
¼ cup Madeira
Half of 8-ounce container plain
   yogurt
6 fresh mint leaves, chopped

1 teaspoon lemon juice
3 tablespoons red lumpfish
   caviar
2 tablespoons butter
Small Italian olives for garnish

In a large bowl, break the eggs and beat with a fork until they are fluffy. Add salt and pepper and the Madeira.

In a bowl, beat the yogurt, add the mint and lemon juice and mix well. Add some freshly ground pepper and the caviar.

In a large skillet, melt the butter. When the butter is hot and foamy, pour in the eggs. Cook over medium heat, shaking the pan while pushing back the cooked edges of the eggs with a fork to allow the uncooked part to run to the sides.

Spoon the caviar-yogurt mixture across the center of the omelette and fold gently with a spatula so as not to break the tiny balls of the caviar. Slide the omelette onto a warm serving platter. Garnish with olives and serve.

6 servings

Pâtés de Romarin

PREPARATION: 30 MINUTES   COOKING: 20 MINUTES

When I was fourteen years old my father decided to educate my palate. Every Sunday he carefully chose a good restaurant and *made* me try new dishes every time. The first few weeks I felt quite miserable, but one Sunday he took me to a small country restaurant that served these pâtés, which I loved. I very quickly learned how to make them.

½ pound black Italian olives
½ pound sweet Italian sausage
1 clove
¼ teaspoon freshly ground
   pepper

¼ teaspoon salt
¼ cup melted butter
1 pound phyllo*
1 tablespoon dried rosemary
6 Boston lettuce leaves

Preheat the oven to 400°. Pit the olives and chop coarsely. Set aside. With a sharp knife, slit the sausage's casing and remove the sausage

*See headnote on p. 18 for description and availability.

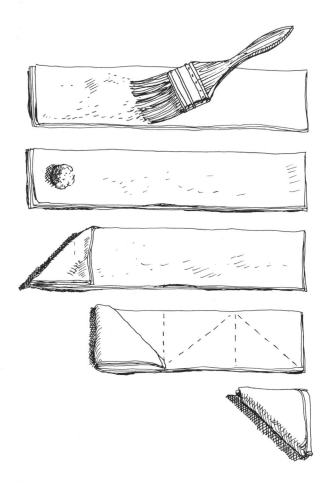

meat. Put the sausage meat, the olives and all the spices in a bowl; mix well with your hands or with a fork.

In a saucepan, melt the butter and clarify* it. Divide the phyllo in half. Cut each half in 3- to 4-inch-wide strips. With a pastry brush, brush some butter on each sheet of phyllo. Place some sausage meat at the end of each strip. Fold the end to form a triangle, and fold again, until all the strips are used. Brush some butter on the top layer of each triangle and press some rosemary on top.

Place the pâtés on a floured cookie sheet and bake for 20 minutes, or until golden brown. Serve hot on a bed of lettuce leaves.

6 servings

*To clarify butter: Melt the butter and then strain it slowly, leaving the whitish deposit at the bottom of the pan. Your butter should be completely clear.

Parmesan Puffs

PREPARATION: 15 MINUTES   COOKING: 10 MINUTES

3 egg whites
3½ ounces grated fresh
  Parmesan
1½ cups bread crumbs

Oil for deep frying
Salt and pepper
Parsley for garnish

In a bowl, beat the egg whites until stiff, and slowly add the grated Parmesan. Place the bread crumbs in a large bowl. Using a teaspoon, form balls of the egg-white mixture and roll in the bread crumbs.

In a deep skillet, heat the oil to 360°. Drop the balls in the sizzling oil and cook for a few seconds, or until golden brown. Drain on paper towels and keep warm until you have used up all the mixture. Sprinkle with salt and freshly ground pepper. Serve garnished with parsley.

6 servings

Fried Samosas

PREPARATION: 30 MINUTES   COOKING: 45 MINUTES

Last summer I spent three months in a small town in Tanzania called Dodoma. There was a shortage of bread and flour, so every afternoon I would walk to town to pick up a loaf of bread from an old Greek gentleman called Mr. Fotis, the owner of the Fotis Hotel, the only place in town that still had some flour. Mr. Fotis would always ask me in for a cup of Greek coffee. (He liked Frenchwomen.) With the coffee he served me a samosa, a small fried turnover filled with spicy beef. It was the highlight of my day. It took me six weeks of patient courtship to get the recipe for these delicious samosas.

PASTRY
1 cup flour
½ teaspoon salt

¼ cup oil

FILLING
8 ounces chopped beef
1 clove garlic, crushed
½ teaspoon chopped fresh
  ginger
2 tablespoons chopped Chinese
  parsley

2 green chilies, seeded and
  chopped
1 onion, chopped
2 tablespoons water
Oil for deep frying
3 limes
Salt and pepper

In the container of a food processor or blender, place the flour and salt. Add 1 cup water and run the machine until the dough forms a ball.

On a floured board, make walnut-sized balls. Roll each ball in a circle about 3 inches in diameter. Brush some oil on each circle and sprinkle with flour. Put one circle on top of another, enclosing the oiled surface; then roll each double circle into a circle 8 inches in diameter.

Heat a large cast-iron skillet and fry each circle for 1 minute on each side. Set aside and prepare the filling.

In the container of a food processor, place the meat, garlic, ginger, parsley, chili and onion. Run the machine until the mixture is thoroughly blended.

Remove to a bowl and add salt and pepper to taste.

Fill each circle with 1 tablespoon of the meat. Fold the circle to form a turnover and seal the edges with water.

In a deep fryer, heat the oil to 360° and fry the samosas until golden brown. Drain on paper towels and serve piping hot with lime wedges.
6 servings

Talmousses

PREPARATION: 25 MINUTES   COOKING: 45 MINUTES

Puff pastry mixed with cheese is an old recipe found in most cookbooks. In the South of France the puff pastry is rolled in dough and shaped like Napoleon's hat. Served with a vegetable pâté instead of bread, these light golden puffs become an elegant hors d'oeuvre.

Pâte Brisée I (see p. 10)   1 cup grated Swiss cheese
1 stick (¼ pound) butter   ½ cup grated Parmesan
1 cup flour   ¼ teaspoon nutmeg
4 eggs   Salt and freshly ground pepper

Preheat the oven to 400°. Make the pâte brisée before making the puff pastry.

In a saucepan, bring 1 cup water to a boil and add the butter; when the butter is melted, add the flour all at once. Mix with a wooden spoon over medium heat until the dough detaches itself from the sides of the pan. Transfer this puff-pastry dough to the container of a food processor. Turn the machine on and add 3 eggs, one at a time. Add the Swiss cheese and the Parmesan, the nutmeg, salt and pepper. Mix well and remove to a bowl.

Roll the pâte brisée dough very thin, and with a 5-inch round pastry cutter, cut 16 circles. Place 1 tablespoon of puff pastry in the center of each circle, and using some ice water to seal the edges, pinch the dough on three sides, so that it looks like a three-cornered hat.

Beat the remaining egg with ½ tablespoon of water and brush the pieces of dough with the egg. Bake for 35 minutes, or until the talmousses are golden brown. Serve right away with a vegetable pâté.

The talmousses can keep for a day or two wrapped in foil. To reheat: Place in a 300° oven for 10 minutes.

16 talmousses

Four-and-Twenty Asparagus Quiche

PREPARATION: 15 MINUTES   COOKING: 40 MINUTES

When my son was quite young, his favorite song was "Sing a Song of Six Pence." He wanted me to bake him a pie with four and twenty blackbirds, so I came up with this recipe and told him that the blackbirds turned green when cooked.

Pâte Brisée I (see p. 10)   ¾ cup heavy cream
2 pounds asparagus   Salt and pepper
4 eggs   Nutmeg

Preheat oven to 375°. Butter a 9-inch pie pan.

On a floured board, roll out the dough for the pâte brisée. Line the pan with the dough, cutting off any excess dough. Line the pan with waxed paper and fill with raw rice. Bake for 15 minutes.

Meanwhile cut the asparagus tips 3 inches from the top (save the remainder for making a soup). Steam the asparagus for 5 minutes over 1½ cups water. Remove to a plate and keep warm.

In a bowl, beat the eggs and cream. Add salt, pepper and nutmeg. Pour the mixture in the baked pie shell and bake for 30 minutes. Remove the quiche from the oven and stick in the asparagus tips upright. Bake for another 5 minutes and serve right away.

6 servings

Broiled Mussels with Ham and Bacon

PREPARATION: 45 MINUTES   COOKING: 10 MINUTES

1½ quarts fresh mussels
2 shallots, chopped
1 cup dry white wine
2 ¼-inch-thick slices boiled ham
8 slices smoked bacon
1 egg

1 cup fresh bread crumbs
4 tablespoons butter
1 lemon, cut in wedges
Pepper to taste
Parsley for garnish

Preheat the oven to 450°. Wash and scrub the mussels (see footnote on p. 154 for instructions on how to do this). Chop the shallots. Put the mussels and shallots in a heavy saucepan and add the white wine. Cover and, shaking the pan from time to time, cook over medium heat until the mussels open. Drain the mussels, reserving the liquid. When the mussels are cool, remove them from their shells and set them aside.

Cut the ham and the bacon into 1-inch pieces. String alternately on each skewer one mussel, one piece of ham and one piece of bacon.

Beat the egg with 1 tablespoon water and pour onto a large platter roughly as wide as the length of the skewer. Spread the fresh bread crumbs on another plate. Roll the skewers in the egg and then in the bread crumbs. Broil for 3 minutes on each side, or until the bacon is crisp.

Strain the mussel juice. Melt the butter in a saucepan and add the juice. Heat through. Season with pepper (don't add salt because the mussels are already salty).

Serve the mussels on a platter, garnished with lemon wedges and parsley, with the sauce on the side.

6 servings

Phyllo Stuffed with Bay Scallops and Spinach

PREPARATION: 25 MINUTES   COOKING: 50 MINUTES

Phyllo, the paper-thin dough from the Middle East, makes feather-light flaky pastry. Sold in sheets rolled and kept in plastic wrap, it is found in specialty stores and even in some supermarkets. It can keep for weeks refrigerated in sealed plastic bags.

1 package phyllo
1 pound bay scallops
1 pound spinach
1 stick (¼ pound) butter
Salt and pepper

¼ teaspoon paprika
3 tablespoons Crème Fraîche
  (see p. xvi) or sour cream
1 egg
3 tablespoons chopped chives

Preheat the oven to 375°. Cut the phyllo in 4-inch-wide strips. Wash and pat dry the scallops with paper towels.

Wash and trim the spinach. In a large saucepan, add salt to 4 cups water and bring to a boil. Add the spinach, bring to a boil again, cover and turn off the heat. Let the spinach stand for 5 minutes, then drain and cool under cold running water. Squeeze the spinach to remove all the water. Chop coarsely with a knife and set aside.

In a skillet, melt 4 tablespoons butter. When the butter is hot, add the scallops. Sauté for 4 minutes over high heat. Sprinkle with salt, pepper and paprika. Add the spinach, mix well and remove from the heat.

In a small saucepan, melt the remaining butter. With a pastry brush, brush melted butter on each phyllo strip.

Add the crème fraîche to the spinach and scallops. Mix well and correct the seasoning. Place some spinach and scallops at one end of each phyllo strip; fold the dough in a triangle and continue to fold until the stuffing is firmly enclosed (see illustration, p. 14).

Beat the egg with 1 tablespoon water. Brush some egg on each phyllo triangle. Sprinkle some chives on top and bake for 20 to 25 minutes, or until the phyllo is golden brown.

Serve piping hot with a chilled dry white wine.

6 large or 8 medium-size pastries

Snail Stew with Walnuts

PREPARATION: 10 MINUTES   COOKING: 25 MINUTES

2 cans snails
4 cups dry white wine
2 cups chicken bouillon or stock
4 tablespoons butter
2 tablespoons chopped parsley

2 pints heavy cream
1 cup coarsely chopped shelled
  walnuts
Salt and pepper

In a large saucepan, bring to a boil the wine and bouillon or stock.

Drain the snails. When the bouillon comes to a boil, add the snails. Bring to a boil again and turn off the heat. Let the snails stand in the bouillon for 15 minutes. Drain, reserving the liquid.

In a skillet, melt the butter. When the butter is hot, add the snails. Sprinkle with 1 tablespoon parsley and sauté for 5 minutes. Remove the snails with a slotted spoon. Discard the butter in the skillet and add the reserved bouillon. Boil the bouillon until it is reduced by half. Add the cream and continue to boil until the cream has been reduced by half. Add the walnuts and snails, and heat through without boiling. Add salt and pepper to taste.

Pour into a serving bowl and sprinkle with parsley. Serve right away with French garlic bread.

6 servings

Boudin Blanc with Hazelnuts

PREPARATION: 5 MINUTES   COOKING: 35 MINUTES

Boudin blanc is a pork or chicken sausage traditionally served in France at Christmas or New Year's. If you live in a town that has a French butcher or a specialty store, try this recipe. Serve it as an hors d'oeuvre with a beet salad or as a main course with a carrot purée.

1 cup shelled hazelnuts	Salt and pepper
6½ tablespoons butter	Parsley for garnish
6 boudins blancs	

Place the hazelnuts in a saucepan and cover with cold water. Bring to a boil and cook over medium heat for 30 minutes.

Meanwhile, in a skillet, melt 3½ tablespoons butter. Add the boudins and cook for 5 minutes. Turn and cook for another 5 minutes, then remove to a plate.

Drain the hazelnuts. Add the remaining butter to the skillet. When the butter is hot, add the nuts and brown on all sides. Sprinkle with salt and pepper. Heat the broiler and broil the boudins for a few minutes on each side.

Put the boudins on a platter and surround with the hazelnuts. Garnish with parsley.

6 servings

Chicken Livers with Port

PREPARATION: 5 MINUTES   COOKING: 20 MINUTES

This is a quick appetizer to serve in individual ramekins with buttered white toast. It goes particularly well with a pasta dish as the main course of a dinner that also includes a green salad and a chilled white wine.

6 tablespoons butter
12 chicken livers
Salt and pepper
Pinch of four-spices (see p. xv)
4 ounces brown raisins

1 cup tiny frozen onions
½ cup port
6 slices white bread
Watercress for garnish

In a large skillet, melt 4 tablespoons butter. When the butter is hot, add the chicken livers, salt, pepper and four-spices. Simmer over medium heat for 10 minutes. Then add the raisins, onions and port. Cook for 10 more minutes.

Meanwhile, toast the slices of bread and butter them. Place 2 chicken livers in each ramekin, garnish with watercress, and surround with the white toast. Pour the sauce over the chicken livers and serve.

6 servings

Hot Prosciutto with Fresh Tarragon and Shallots

PREPARATION: 10 MINUTES   COOKING: 15 MINUTES

Every spring I take to Paris about thirty students on an exchange program. On our way back, in the confusion caused by thirty excited teen-agers, I often manage to go through customs with some fresh goodies from Paris. The last time I brought back a large bunch of fresh tarragon. If you grow tarragon in your garden or on your windowsill, try this recipe. The sauce is also good on steak. You can substitute dried tarragon for the fresh, but the aroma will not be quite the same.

⅓ cup wine vinegar
2 shallots, finely chopped
½ tablespoon chopped chervil
10 leaves fresh tarragon or 2
   teaspoons dried tarragon,
   chopped
3 sprigs parsley, chopped

3 egg yolks, beaten
¾ cup heavy cream
Salt and pepper
2 tablespoons butter
12 slices prosciutto
4 tablespoons brandy
Watercress

In an enamel saucepan, place the vinegar, shallots and herbs; boil over high heat until reduced by half. Lower the heat and add the egg yolks, beating with a wire whisk. Slowly add the cream and simmer for 2 minutes (don't let it boil). Add salt and pepper to taste. Strain the sauce through a fine sieve and keep warm over a saucepan of simmering water.

In a skillet, melt the butter. Sauté the prosciutto for 1 minute on each side. Pour on the brandy and ignite. Fold each slice of prosciutto and place two slices on each plate. Cover with the sauce and garnish with watercress.

6 servings

Sweetbread Mousse

PREPARATION: 15 MINUTES   COOKING: 30 MINUTES

1 sweetbread
Salt
2 shallots
½ pound mushrooms
5 tablespoons butter
Freshly ground pepper
1 tablespoon flour

2 generous tablespoons Crème
   Fraîche (see p. xvi)
3 egg yolks
3 egg whites
2 large mushrooms, sliced, for
   garnish

Preheat the oven to 375°. Wash the sweetbread under running water and drain.

Place the sweetbread in a saucepan and cover with boiling water. Add ½ teaspoon salt, bring to a boil and simmer for 10 minutes.

Meanwhile peel the shallots. Wash the mushrooms and drain.

Put the mushrooms and shallots in the container of a food processor or a blender and process until finely chopped.

In a skillet, melt 1½ tablespoons butter. When the butter is hot, add the shallots and mushrooms, sprinkle with salt and pepper, and simmer for 10 minutes. Remove them with a slotted spoon and set aside. In the same skillet, melt the remaining butter. When the butter is hot, add the flour and mix well with a wooden spoon. Cook for a few minutes, then add the crème fraîche. Mix well until the dough detaches itself from the spoon. Let it cool.

With a knife, remove the thin membrane that covers the sweetbread. Place the sweetbread, the egg yolks and the dough in the container of the food processor and run the machine for 1 minute, then add the mushrooms and run it again until all the ingredients are puréed. Transfer the mixture to a bowl. Beat the egg whites until they form peaks and gently fold them into the sweetbread.

Butter the ramekins. Pour the purée into them and bake for 10 minutes.

Garnish with the sliced raw mushrooms.

4 servings

Grenouillettes de Veau

PREPARATION: 6 MINUTES   COOKING: 10 MINUTES

Grenouille—such a difficult French word to pronounce! It means frog, and that is what my son Thomas calls me when I don't understand his favorite sport, baseball! He gnawed these grenouillettes—"frogs" of yet another kind—the first time I served them, as they do look like little frog's legs.

4 veal scallops   Salt and pepper
6 tablespoons flour   1 bunch parsley, chopped
Oil for frying   1 head lettuce

Cut the veal into 3½-inch sticks and roll them in flour. Heat the oil in a deep skillet until very hot and fry the veal for 2 minutes. Drain on paper towels and sprinkle with salt, pepper and parsley. Serve piping hot on a bed of lettuce.

6 servings

Cold Hors d'Oeuvre

Avocado with Red Caviar

PREPARATION: 20 MINUTES

6 ounces Crème Fraîche (see
   p. xvi) or heavy cream
1 teaspoon Dijon-style mustard
3 avocados
Salt and pepper

2 lemons
1 ice cube
1 jar salmon caviar
1 head of Boston lettuce

Mix the crème fraîche with the mustard and put in the freezer. Cut the
avocados in half and remove the pits. Sprinkle with salt and pepper.
Squeeze the juice of 1 lemon and pour it over the avocado halves.

Remove the crème from the freezer; add an ice cube and beat with an
electric beater until the crème is frothy. Fill the avocados with the crème
and garnish with the red caviar.

Wash the Boston lettuce and line a large platter. Put the avocados on
the lettuce and decorate with lemon wedges.

6 servings

Cold Chicken Balls

PREPARATION: 20 MINUTES   COOKING: 20 MINUTES

4 dried Chinese mushrooms
1 large carrot
3 cups chicken stock
1 chicken breast, boned and
   skinned
1 egg, beaten

1 teaspoon soy sauce
¼ teaspoon sesame oil
1 tablespoon dry sherry
Lettuce leaves
Ginger Sauce (see below)

Soak the Chinese mushrooms in 1 cup hot water for 20 minutes. Scrape and wash the carrot, then julienne in the food processor. Set aside.

In a saucepan, bring the chicken stock to a boil. When the stock is boiling, add the chicken breast and poach for 10 minutes. Remove with a slotted spoon and cool.

Cut the chicken in several pieces and chop in the food processor. Drain the mushrooms, remove their stems and cut into thin strips.

In a bowl, mix together the chicken, carrots, mushrooms, egg, soy sauce and sesame oil. Shape the mixture into balls the size of walnuts and flatten a little so that the carrots stick out. Poach in the chicken stock with the sherry for 8 minutes. Remove carefully with a slotted spoon onto a platter. Refrigerate until ready to serve.

To serve, line each small individual plate with a lettuce leaf and place a cold chicken ball on top.

Serve with soy sauce or ginger sauce.

4 servings

Ginger Sauce
PREPARATION: 5 to 8 MINUTES

4 scallions, cut into 1-inch
 pieces
½ teaspoon sesame oil*
2-inch piece fresh ginger, peeled
 and sliced

¼ cup peanut oil
Salt and pepper

Finely chop all the ingredients in a food processor or blender. Remove to a bowl. Add salt and pepper to taste. This sauce can be stored in the refrigerator for 1 week or more.

*Sesame oil can be found in large supermarkets, health-food stores or Chinese grocery stores.

Crème de Foies de Volaille au Calvados
(Creamed Chicken Livers with Calvados)

PREPARATION: 15 MINUTES   COOKING: 10 MINUTES

My eldest daughter, Marianne, decided one summer to start a catering business. She made pâtés, which she sold to some neighborhood restaurants. One restaurant asked her if she could make them a crème de foies.

She said, "Of course," having no idea how to make it. She pored over cookbooks but found nothing. She called Tanzania, where I was at the time, to no avail—I was not in Dodoma. Finally she came up with this very light crème de foies. Her special touch was the Calvados, the last bottle my stepfather had sent me from Normandy the year before, that I had hidden away for some special occasion. Since she gave me the recipe, I forgave her for breaking into it.

8 ounces chicken livers	½ cup heavy cream plus
6 tablespoons butter	2 tablespoons
½ clove garlic, mashed	4½ tablespoons Calvados
1 teaspoon four-spices (see	Salt and pepper
p. xv)	Parsley for garnish

Trim the chicken livers. In a large skillet, melt the butter. When the butter is hot, add the chicken livers, lower the heat and simmer them for 8 minutes, stirring from time to time. Sprinkle with salt and pepper. With a slotted spoon, remove the livers to the container of a food processor. Add 2 tablespoons of the butter in the skillet, four-spices and garlic and run the machine until the livers are puréed.

Discard the remaining butter from the skillet but do not wash the skillet. Add to the skillet ½ cup cream and 3½ tablespoons Calvados. Stir with a wooden spoon, scraping the sides of the skillet. Heat the cream gently—do not let it boil.

Remove the cream from the heat and add to the liver purée. Run the machine for 30 seconds. Remove to a bowl and refrigerate. Just before serving, add 2 tablespoons cream, the remaining Calvados and freshly ground pepper. Mix well and divide into 6 small bowls. Garnish with parsley.

Serve with toasted white-bread points and an arugola salad.

6 servings

Basket of Crudités with Sauces

Nothing enriches a warm summer evening more than a still life of a heaping basket of fresh, crisp, raw vegetables with an array of different sauces. Here are some vegetables to use:

Cauliflower: Remove the center core and separate the florets, leaving stems 1½ to 2 inches long.
Radishes: Wash carefully and remove some of the green leaves. Cut off the strings on top. Keep in ice water until ready to serve.

Cherry tomatoes: Wash and dry.
Cucumber: Wash and cut into 4-inch sticks. Keep in ice water until ready
   to serve.
Scallions: Clean and wash.
Baby carrots: Scrape and wash.
Artichokes: Boil for 20 minutes, drain and cool.
Fennel: Wash, trim and quarter.
Celery: Wash, trim and cut into wide strips.
Turnips: Peel and slice.

Arrange all the vegetables to form a beautiful palette of colors and
serve surrounded with the following sauces in separate bowls:

Pink Sauce
PREPARATION: 15 MINUTES

1 egg yolk
1 tablespoon Dijon-style
   mustard
1 cup vegetable oil
Salt and pepper

1 tablespoon vinegar
1 teaspoon tomato paste
1 tablespoon Scotch
Pinch of cayenne

Place the egg yolk and mustard in the container of a food processor or
blender. Run the machine until the egg is frothy. With the machine
running slowly, add the oil. Transfer the sauce to a bowl. Add salt,
pepper and vinegar and stir with a wooden spoon. Add the tomato paste
and Scotch. Mix well. Add the cayenne and mix again. Refrigerate until
ready to serve.
   2 cups

Rouille
PREPARATION: 15 MINUTES

3 slices white bread
2 large cloves garlic
1 egg yolk
1 cup vegetable or olive oil

1 teaspoon tomato paste
1 tablespoon vinegar
Salt and pepper

Soak the bread in ½ cup of water. Squeeze the bread to remove the water.
   In the container of a food processor or blender, place the garlic and
the bread. Run the machine until the garlic and the bread form a paste.
Add the egg yolk, mix well, then slowly add the oil. Then add the

tomato paste, vinegar, salt and pepper. Run the machine for 30 seconds. Correct the seasoning.

Refrigerate until ready to serve.

2 cups

Basil and Cream Sauce

PREPARATION: 15 MINUTES

½ cup heavy cream
½ cup plain yogurt
½ tablespoon mustard

Juice of half a lemon
½ cup fresh basil leaves
Salt and pepper

Place all the ingredients in the container of a food processor or blender. Run the machine until all the basil is finely chopped. Add salt and pepper to taste. Refrigerate until ready to serve.

2 cups

Avocado Cream with Olives

PREPARATION: 15 MINUTES

1 ripe avocado
Juice of 1 lemon
3 drops Tabasco

6 black Greek olives
Salt and pepper

Peel the avocado. Place it in the container of a food processor with the lemon juice and Tabasco. Run the machine until the avocado is puréed.

Reserving one whole olive, remove the pits from the olives. Add them to the avocado and run the machine for 30 seconds. Correct the seasoning with salt and pepper. Refrigerate until ready to serve. Use the unpitted olive as a garnish on top.

1 cup

Tapenade for Crudités

PREPARATION: 5 MINUTES

Tapenade is a specialty of the South of France. Serve this savory purée with radishes, sliced raw turnips and cucumber, julienne of carrots and celery, and cauliflower and broccoli florets.

8 ounces black Greek olives
2 tablespoons capers
3½ ounces anchovy filets

½ cup olive oil
Pepper

Pit the olives, using the point of a small sharp knife. Put the olives, capers and anchovy filets in the container of a food processor or blender and run the machine until these ingredients are puréed. Slowly add the olive oil—drop by drop in the beginning. Add some freshly ground pepper to taste.

The tapenade can keep for a week refrigerated in a sealed container.

About 1 cup

Mousse de Caviar

PREPARATION: 30 MINUTES   REFRIGERATION: 30 MINUTES

½ cup Mayonnaise (see below)
1 envelope unflavored gelatin
3 hard-boiled eggs
1 tablespoon chopped onion
1 tablespoon chopped ginger
½ teaspoon tomato paste

2 tablespoons lemon juice
2 ounces red lumpfish caviar
1 head Boston lettuce
Parsley for garnish
Salt and pepper

Make the mayonnaise and refrigerate. In a bowl, dissolve the gelatin in 3 tablespoons of cold water. Set the bowl over a saucepan of simmering water and stir until the gelatin is dissolved.

In the container of a food processor, place the eggs, onion, ginger, tomato paste and lemon juice. Run the machine until all the ingredients are puréed. Transfer to a bowl. Add the gelatin and the mayonnaise and mix well. Fold in the caviar. Correct the seasoning.

Pour the mousse into a mold and place in the freezer for 30 minutes. Unmold by dipping in hot water for a second. Unmold on a bed of lettuce. Garnish with parsley.

Serve with sesame crackers or buttered white toast.

6 servings

Mayonnaise
PREPARATION: 4 MINUTES

2 egg yolks
2 cups olive or vegetable oil

Juice of 1 lemon
Salt and pepper

Place the egg yolks in the container of a food processor. Run the machine until the eggs are creamy, then slowly add the oil in a steady stream. After using the first cup of oil, check the consistency of the sauce—if it is smooth, start the machine again and slowly add half the second cup. When the mayonnaise is thick, add the lemon juice and salt and pepper to taste. Run the machine for 4 seconds, then add the remaining oil and run the machine for a few seconds more.

The mayonnaise will keep for over a week in a tightly sealed jar.

2½ cups

Mousse de Roquefort

PREPARATION: 20 MINUTES

¾ cup heavy cream
2 tablespoons ice water
4 ounces Roquefort or blue
   cheese

6 tablespoons butter
¾ cup walnuts

Put the cream with 2 tablespoons ice water in a cool bowl. Beat until the cream is thick enough to form peaks.

Place the cheese and the butter cut into small pieces in the container of a food processor. Run the machine until the ingredients have the consistency of cream. Transfer to a bowl.

Set aside 2 tablespoons of walnuts for garnish. Without washing the food processor, add the remaining walnuts and run the machine until they are coarsely chopped. Add to the cheese mixture and mix well. Fold in the whipped cream and garnish with the whole walnuts. Refrigerate until ready to serve.

Serve with a tomato salad and whole-wheat Italian bread.

6 to 8 servings

Cold Fish Pâté with Peppercorns

PREPARATION: 25 MINUTES   COOKING: 40 MINUTES

1 quart water
2 cups dry white wine
1 tablespoon vinegar
1 onion stuck with 1 clove
Salt and pepper
½ teaspoon thyme
1 bay leaf
3 pounds skinless, boneless
   whitefish

3 eggs
1½ teaspoons dried tarragon
½ teaspoon cumin
1½ cups fresh bread crumbs
¼ cup crushed peppercorns*
Green Sauce (see below)

In a large saucepan, bring the water, wine and vinegar to a boil. Add the onion, salt, pepper, thyme and bay leaf. Simmer for 20 minutes.

Meanwhile, prepare the fish. In the container of a food processor or a blender, place the fish, eggs, tarragon and cumin. Run the machine until all the ingredients are finely chopped. Transfer to a bowl. Add ½ cup of the bread crumbs and mix well. (If the mixture is too liquid, add more bread crumbs.) Shape the fish mixture like a loaf of bread, roll in a piece of cheesecloth and tie both ends. Carefully place the roll in the court bouillon and simmer for 15 minutes.

Remove the roll from the court bouillon. Carefully remove the cheesecloth and cool the pâté at room temperature.

Mix together the remaining bread crumbs with the peppercorns. Roll the pâté in the mixture and place on a serving platter. Serve cold with green sauce.

6 servings   .

*To crush peppercorns, place them between two sheets of brown wrapping paper and pound them with a heavy mallet. If you don't have a mallet, the flat bottom of a cast-iron skillet will do the trick.

Green Sauce
PREPARATION: 10 MINUTES

Green sauce is especially delicious with cooked tomatoes, pasta, cold chicken, fish and artichokes.

1 cup washed fresh basil or
   spinach
½ cup chopped fresh parsley
½ cup chopped watercress

¾ cup oil
Salt and pepper
Lemon juice (optional)

Wash all the greens and pat dry with paper towels. Blend all the ingredients in a food processor. Remove to a bowl and add salt and pepper. If you are serving the sauce with a vegetable, either cold or hot, add some lemon juice to taste.

2 cups

Pâté with Herbs

PREPARATION: 30 MINUTES   COOKING: 45 MINUTES

2 pounds fresh spinach
1 pound Swiss chard
2 tablespoons oil
4 tablespoons butter
3 onions, chopped
4 cloves garlic, chopped
¼ teaspoon nutmeg
2 teaspoons dried thyme
2 teaspoons four-spices
   (see p. xv)
½ pound sweet Italian sausage

1 bunch parsley, chopped
2 tablespoons chopped fresh
   basil
3 slices white bread
¼ cup milk
3 eggs
Tiny onions in vinegar for
   garnish
Salt and pepper

Preheat the oven to 400°. Remove the stems, then wash and drain the spinach and Swiss chard. (Reserve the Swiss chard stems to make a vegetable soup.) Place them in a large saucepan, add 4 cups boiling water and boil for 5 minutes. Drain and cool under cold running water. Squeeze all the water out and chop finely.

In a large skillet, heat the oil and 3 tablespoons butter. Add the chopped vegetables, the onion, garlic, nutmeg, thyme and four-spices. Sauté and cook, uncovered, for 15 minutes, stirring from time to time.

Remove the sausage meat from its casing and crumble. Add to the sautéed mixture, along with the parsley and basil. Soak the bread in milk and squeeze out the milk. Mix well. Add to the sautéed mixture and correct the seasoning. Beat the eggs and add to the mixture.

Butter a 1-quart pâté mold. Pour in the mixture and bake for 45 minutes.

Unmold and garnish with the tiny onions. Serve hot or cold with a beef or chicken stew.

6 servings

Rabbit Pâté

PREPARATION: 40 MINUTES   COOKING: 2 HOURS   REFRIGERATION: 2 HOURS

Frozen rabbit from Canada is easily found in the freezer department of most large supermarkets. This easy-to-make pâté is coarse in texture but delicate in taste. Serve it on a bed of lettuce with Dijon mustard and a loaf of French or Italian bread.

1 frozen rabbit
Salt and pepper
6 ounces fatback,* sliced
4 medium-size carrots, sliced
2 large onions, sliced
1 teaspoon thyme

1 bay leaf
1 quart chicken bouillon
3 envelopes clear gelatin
4 tablespoons mirabelle (plum
    brandy) or other brandy
1 head Boston lettuce

Defrost the rabbit in the refrigerator the night before. Cut the meat off the bone with a paring knife, then cut into small cubes. Place the meat in a large bowl and sprinkle with salt and pepper. Mix well.

Line the inside of a pâté mold with the fatback. Place a layer of rabbit in the bottom; cover with a layer of sliced carrots, then a layer of sliced onions. Sprinkle with thyme. Repeat the procedure until all the rabbit is used. Finish with a layer of sliced carrots and onions. Place a bay leaf on top of the pâté and spoon the brandy over it.

Seal the pâté with foil. Make a small hole in the center to let the steam escape while the pâté is cooking. Place mold in a pan filled with boiling water, which should come halfway up the outside of the mold. Bake for 2 hours.

Meanwhile, bring the bouillon to a boil. Melt the gelatin with 3 tablespoons water and add to the hot bouillon. Stir well and simmer for 5 minutes.

Remove the pâté from the oven. Pour the bouillon into the pâté and refrigerate for about 2 hours, or until it becomes firm. Unmold and serve on a bed of lettuce.

6 servings

*Fatback is fat taken from the back of the hog. It is sold fresh in pork stores or salted in supermarkets. If you buy the salted kind, blanch it by dipping it in boiling water for 5 minutes. Drain, wipe dry and use as you would fresh pork fat.

Vegetable Pâté in Aspic

PREPARATION: 40 MINUTES   COOKING: 25 MINUTES

Dinner parties become a challenge when your friends are vegetarians. I have many such friends. One of them, Anna N., is both a vegetarian and a long-distance runner. The night before a race I served her this vegetable pâté. She won!

3 cups vegetable, beef or chicken
  stock
3 envelopes unflavored gelatin
1 teaspoon soy sauce
2 tablespoons port

Salt and pepper to taste
2 cups each of carrots, turnips,
  leeks, string beans
2 teaspoons sugar
Parsley for garnish

Heat the stock in a saucepan until it boils. Meanwhile, in a bowl, dissolve the gelatin in 2 tablespoons cold water. Add the gelatin to the hot stock and boil for 1 minute, stirring constantly. Add the soy sauce (for color), then the port. Add salt and pepper to taste. Pour into a bowl and refrigerate for 10 minutes.

Pour ¼ cup of the cooled stock into a 1½-quart loaf pan and put it in the freezer while preparing the vegetables.

Scrape and wash the carrots and cut into ¼-inch strips. Peel and wash the turnips and cut into ¼-inch strips. Wash and cut the leeks into 2-inch pieces, discarding the green part. Wash and string the string beans.

Cook each vegetable separately in boiling salted water until barely tender. When cooking the carrots, add sugar to the water. Drain the vegetables, cool them under cold running water, and drain them again.

Remove the loaf pan from the freezer and lay strips of carrot lengthwise at the bottom, on top of the gelled stock. Sprinkle with salt and pepper. Put a layer of leeks and then of turnips, finishing with the string beans. Sprinkle each time with salt and pepper. Slowly pour in the remaining stock.

Cover the pan with foil and refrigerate until ready to serve. If the pâté is to be served the same night, put it in the freezer for 20 minutes. When ready to serve, unmold the pâté onto a platter. Garnish with parsley. Serve with mayonnaise to which chopped basil and parsley have been added or with a purée of uncooked fresh tomatoes.

8 servings

Pears and Kiwis with Prosciutto

PREPARATION: 5 MINUTES

6 ripe Bosc pears
3 tablespoons sherry
3 kiwis*

2 lemons
12 slices prosciutto

Peel the pears, leaving the stem on. Place them in a bowl and spoon the sherry over them. Refrigerate until ready to serve. Peel and slice the kiwis. Cut the lemons in wedges.

Just before serving, put 2 slices of prosciutto on a plate, place a pear on top of the prosciutto and surround with 2 slices of kiwi and a lemon wedge.

6 servings

*Kiwi is an Australian fruit with a brown skin. When peeled, it is light green with tiny black seeds in the center. It is now grown in the United States and is available almost everywhere.

Prosciutto Stuffed with Watercress

PREPARATION: 20 MINUTES

1 bunch watercress
Juice of 2 lemons
2 envelopes unflavored gelatin
6 tablespoons port

Salt and pepper
12 slices prosciutto
¾ cup sour cream
Pinch of nutmeg

Wash and pat the watercress dry with paper towels. Take half the watercress and season with salt and pepper and lemon juice.

In a bowl, mix the gelatin with 3 tablespoons cold water. Add 2 cups boiling water and stir until the gelatin is dissolved. Add the port, salt and pepper and keep in the freezer while preparing the prosciutto.

Spread on each slice of prosciutto some sour cream, a few sprigs of the seasoned watercress, and nutmeg. Roll tightly and arrange the prosciutto rolls side by side on a serving platter, leaving some space in between them. Place sprigs of the unseasoned watercress between the prosciutto rolls and pour the gelatin liquid over the prosciutto. Place the platter in the freezer for 8 minutes, then refrigerate until ready to serve.

Serve as an appetizer or with drinks.

6 servings

Ricotta with Fines Herbes

PREPARATION: 15 MINUTES

This mixture of ricotta and herbs is excellent for stuffing cherry tomatoes, mushrooms or celery or to serve as is with hot Italian or French bread.

2 pounds ricotta	2 tablespoons chopped chives
5 shallots, chopped	Salt and pepper
2 tablespoons chopped parsley	1 tablespoon olive oil

In a bowl, mix together the ricotta, the shallots, parsley and 1 tablespoon chives. Add salt and pepper to taste. Mix well.

Smooth the surface of the ricotta with a fork. Sprinkle with the remaining chives and spoon the olive oil over the top. Refrigerate until ready to serve.

6 to 8 servings

Marinated Salmon

PREPARATION: 15 MINUTES   REFRIGERATION: 2 DAYS

Anita, a Swedish friend, consistently refused to invite me to dinner on the grounds that I am a better cook. One day I flatly said that I wanted to have dinner at her house and that I would be happy to be served fresh bread, garlic, salami or a hamburger as long as I did not have to cook. She surprised me with this delicious salmon served on a bed of lettuce, a capon cooked to perfection and a delicious salad. I quickly asked for the recipe for the salmon. I have since made it several times and have always found it the best way to eat salmon.

Prepare two days ahead of time and serve with a fennel salad. Ask the fishmonger to remove the center bone and the small bones on the side.

2 pounds salmon taken from the center	2½ tablespoons chopped fresh dill
2 tablespoons coarse salt	1 head Boston lettuce
2 tablespoons sugar	2 lemons, cut into wedges
1½ tablespoons freshly ground white pepper	

Wipe the salmon—do not wash it. Mix together the salt, sugar, pepper and dill. Spread open the salmon and smear half the mixture on one side and half on the other side. Press together the two sides of the salmon and refrigerate for 2 days.

When the fish is ready to be used, wipe off the spices and cut into thin slices about ¼ inch thick. Arrange on a bed of lettuce surrounded with lemon wedges.

6 servings

Salmon Rillettes

PREPARATION: 30 MINUTES   COOKING: 15 MINUTES

¼ pound fresh salmon, skinned   2 tablespoons brandy
  and boned   1 stick (¼ pound) butter
¾ cup dry white wine   Parsley for garnish
¼ pound smoked salmon   Salt and pepper
2 tablespoons olive oil

Dice the fresh salmon and put in a skillet. Cover with the wine and bring to a boil, then simmer for 5 minutes and drain.

Cut the smoked salmon into 1-inch pieces. In another skillet, heat the olive oil until it is hot and add the diced fresh salmon. Brown it for a few minutes and add the brandy and salt and pepper. Mix well. Remove from heat and set aside to cool.

In the same skillet, melt 3½ tablespoons butter. When the butter is hot, add the smoked salmon and cook for a few minutes, stirring with a wooden spoon. Remove from heat. Place the smoked salmon and the remaining butter in the container of a food processor or blender and run the machine until the mixture looks like a smooth cream.

Mix the smoked-salmon paste with the pieces of fresh salmon and put in a serving bowl. Garnish with parsley, cover and refrigerate until ready to serve. Serve with a green salad as an hors d'oeuvre.

6 servings

Smoked Salmon with Asparagus and Celery Root

PREPARATION: 20 MINUTES   COOKING: 8 MINUTES

1 pound fresh asparagus
1 celery root* *(see illustration, p. 185)*
2 tablespoons vinegar
6 tablespoons oil

8 slices smoked salmon
Watercress
Salt and pepper
1 lemon, sliced

Steam the asparagus over 1 cup of water until barely done. Cool.

Peel the celery root and cut into thin strips in a food processor. Prepare the vinaigrette by mixing the vinegar and oil. Cut the asparagus into 1-inch pieces and add to the celery root. Pour on the vinaigrette and toss lightly.

Place 2 slices of smoked salmon surrounded with the salad on each individual plate and garnish with watercress. Place a slice of lemon on top of the salmon.

Serve with a chilled dry white wine.

4 servings

*Also known as celeriac or celery knob, celery root is a variety of celery. It is a large root used in salads or braised as a hot vegetable, and is found in most vegetable stores and supermarkets.

Marinated Sole Filets

PREPARATION: 10 MINUTES   REFRIGERATION: 2 HOURS

Marinated raw filet of fish, served as an appetizer, is a delicious beginning to a summer dinner. The filets have to be thinly sliced and marinated for at least 2 hours.

4 lemon-sole filets
6 tablespoons olive oil
Juice of 2 lemons
1 tablespoon chopped chives

1 tablespoon chopped Chinese parsley*
Salt and pepper
Parsley for garnish

*Also known as coriander or cilantro.

Cut the lemon-sole filets into 1-inch slices. Mix together the olive oil, lemon juice, chives and Chinese parsley to make the sauce. Add salt and pepper to taste.

Put one layer of fish in an oval bowl, cover with the oil and lemon sauce, add another layer of fish, then cover with the sauce. Refrigerate for 2 hours.

Serve garnished with parsley and thin white toast.

Sweetbread Salad with Raw Mushrooms and Fennel

PREPARATION: 10 MINUTES   COOKING: 10 MINUTES

1 whole sweetbread	6 tablespoons oil
5 tablespoons butter	2 tablespoons vinegar
Salt and pepper	3 shallots, thinly chopped
1 pound large white mushrooms	1 tablespoon chopped fresh
1 large bulb fennel	tarragon

Wash the sweetbread. Remove the thin membrane and cut the sweetbread into small pieces.

In a skillet, melt the butter; when the butter is hot, add the sweetbread and sauté it for 10 minutes. Sprinkle with salt and pepper. Set aside to cool.

Wash the mushrooms and pat dry with paper towels. Cut them into thin slices. Wash and cut up the fennel with the julienne blade of a food processor.

Make the vinaigrette by mixing together the oil, vinegar, shallots, tarragon, salt and pepper.

In a salad bowl, place the sweetbread (it should be slightly warm), mushrooms and fennel. Pour the vinaigrette over them, toss lightly and serve with hot French or Italian bread.

6 servings

Terrine of Turkey

PREPARATION: 45 MINUTES   COOKING: 10 MINUTES   REFRIGERATION: 2 HOURS

For the day after Thanksgiving when you are left with enough turkey to feed an army . . .

3 tablespoons butter
2 large carrots, sliced
2 stalks celery, sliced
15 tiny frozen onions
Salt and pepper
6 ounces smoked bacon, diced
½ cup tiny frozen peas

3 tablespoons brandy
2 cups apple cider
3 envelopes unflavored gelatin
2 cups diced, cooked turkey
1 tablespoon sage
1 head Boston lettuce

In a large skillet, melt the butter. When it becomes hot, add the carrots, celery, onions and salt and pepper to taste. Cook over medium heat for 10 minutes, stirring from time to time. Add the bacon and cook 10 more minutes on a higher flame. Add the peas and heat through. Add the brandy and ignite. Remove the skillet from the heat and let it cool.

Meanwhile, heat the cider in a saucepan. Dissolve the gelatin in 2 tablespoons water. Add to the cider and cook for 3 minutes, then pour the cider in a bowl and place in the freezer.

When the cider is nearly jelled, pour ¼ cup in a pâté pan and freeze for 5 minutes. Drain the vegetable-bacon mixture. Make a layer of vegetables, then a layer of turkey sprinkled with sage, then another layer of vegetables. Pour the remaining cider over the pâté. Cover with foil and refrigerate for 2 hours. Serve sliced on a bed of lettuce.

10 slices

Pickled Summer Vegetables

In summer when vegetables are at their best, take the smallest and firmest vegetables, steam them until they are cooked but still crisp, and marinate them with hot vinegar and spices—you will have delicious pickles in a day or two. Serve with cold meats and chicken.

Pickled Beets
PREPARATION: 5 MINUTES   PICKLING: 2 DAYS

Beets take nearly 2 hours to cook unless cooked in a pressure cooker. Canned beets are excellent and can be used instead of the fresh.

1-pound can small whole beets
2 cups white vinegar
1 teaspoon salt

1 tablespoon sugar
5 peppercorns
½ teaspoon allspice

Drain and slice the beets in two. Boil the vinegar with the salt, sugar, peppercorns and allspice for 5 minutes, then cool.

Put the beets in a glass jar and pour the vinegar over them. Cover the jar and set aside in a cool place for 2 days before serving.

Pickled Eggplant
PREPARATION: 10 MINUTES   PICKLING: 2 DAYS

6 small eggplants
10 very small onions, peeled
1 green chili, chopped
2 cloves

4 peppercorns
1 bay leaf
⅛ teaspoon salt
2 cups white vinegar

Wash and dry the eggplants. Cut into 1-inch pieces. Place in a steamer and steam over 1 cup boiling water for 10 minutes. Squeeze out the water. Set aside to cool.

Pack the eggplants, onions, chili, cloves, peppercorns and bay leaf into a jar. Add salt and pour the vinegar over them. Seal the jar tightly and set aside in a cool place for 2 days.

Cauliflower with Brussels Sprouts
PREPARATION: 10 MINUTES   PICKLING: 2 DAYS

1 pound Brussels sprouts
10 small cauliflower florets
2 cups white vinegar
2-inch piece fresh ginger

4 peppercorns
2 cloves garlic, crushed
⅛ teaspoon salt

Steam the Brussels sprouts and cauliflower in a steamer over 1 cup water for 10 minutes.

Boil the vinegar with the ginger and peppercorns. Add salt and cool.

Pack the Brussels sprouts, cauliflower and garlic into a glass jar and add the vinegar. Seal tightly and store for 2 days.

Eggplant with Peppers

PREPARATION: 10 MINUTES   COOKING: 15 MINUTES

1 large eggplant
2 medium-size green peppers
1 red bell pepper
4 cloves garlic
4 tablespoons plain yogurt
1 tablespoon cumin

1 tablespoon lemon juice
2 tablespoons olive oil
Salt and pepper
Pinch of cayenne
Black Greek olives for garnish

Wash the eggplant and pat dry. Place the eggplant directly over a high flame on a gas stove (or in a 450° oven for 30 minutes). Roast for 8 minutes on one side, then turn over and roast for another 8 minutes. Remove to a plate.

Roast the green peppers and the red pepper the same way. With a spoon, remove the pulp of the eggplant, discarding the skin. Peel the peppers.

Place in a food processor the eggplant, peppers, garlic, yogurt, cumin, lemon juice, oil, salt, pepper and cayenne. Run the machine for 1 minute, or until all the ingredients are puréed. Remove to a bowl, garnish with olives and refrigerate until ready to serve.

Serve with crackers or toasted pita bread. This eggplant is also excellent with barbecued lamb.

4 servings or 2 cups

Soups

Cold Avocado Soup

PREPARATION: 10 MINUTES   COOKING: 35 MINUTES

4 leeks
½ pound potatoes
1 avocado

Salt and pepper
1-inch piece fresh ginger
Chopped parsley

Trim and wash the leeks. Cut off the green part and slice it. Also slice the white part. Peel and wash the potatoes and cut into small dice.

Put the green part of the leeks in a saucepan, add 1 quart water and bring to a boil, then strain the water over a saucepan so that the green part (which is quite tough and often bitter) can be discarded. Bring the water to a boil again and add the white part of the leeks and the diced potatoes. Add salt and pepper and simmer for 30 minutes.

Peel the avocado and add to the soup. Peel and chop the ginger and add to the soup. Cook for another 5 minutes. Correct the seasoning.

Pour the soup into the container of a food processor and purée all the vegetables. Transfer to a large bowl and refrigerate until ready to serve.

Sprinkle with chopped parsley and serve with fresh French or Italian bread.

6 servings

Cold Beet and Tomato Soup

PREPARATION: 15 MINUTES

2 scallions
6 large tomatoes*
1-pound can whole beets**
2 cups chicken stock or bouillon

1 tablespoon sugar
¼ teaspoon cumin
Salt and pepper
8 ounces sour cream

*You can use canned whole tomatoes and follow the same procedure for preparing fresh tomatoes.

**You can use fresh beets but beets take at least 45 minutes to cook. If you use fresh beets, use the beets' cooking liquid for the soup.

Trim and thinly slice the scallions. Cut in half crosswise and seed the tomatoes by squeezing over a strainer set over a bowl. Drain the beets (reserve the juice) and cut them in half.

In a food processor or blender, purée the tomatoes with the stock. Add the beets and their juice and run the machine for 1 minute.

Pour the soup into a large bowl. Add the sugar, cumin and salt and pepper to taste. Mix well and refrigerate for 30 minutes, or until ready to serve.

Pour the soup into individual soup bowls. Add 1 tablespoon of sour cream to each bowl and sprinkle the soup with the sliced scallions.

6 servings

Chilled Peanut Soup

PREPARATION: 20 MINUTES

When we lived in Dodoma, John, a young architect working with my husband, would stop at the market square every afternoon and buy some raw peanuts. He would mix them with oil and salt and roast them over charcoal. The results were magnificent. We ate peanuts by the pound. John was our great mentor and expert on the subject. One night, tired of roasting peanuts, he made this delicious soup, which he served us with some roasted baby goat. The dinner was a great success, and in exchange for a loaf of freshly baked bread (bread was quite rare there), he gave me the recipe.

1 cup roasted peanuts
4 cups beef broth
1 teaspoon curry
¾ cup milk
Salt and pepper

1 large Chinese radish or 3
    medium-size turnips
4 tablespoons heavy cream
Chinese parsley* for garnish

Skin the peanuts by rubbing them between your palms and purée them in a food processor. Slowly add 2 cups of the beef broth, then the curry, milk, salt and pepper to taste. Run the machine until the ingredients are thoroughly mixed. Transfer to a bowl and refrigerate.

Using the fine grating blade of a food processor, peel and grate the radish. Just before serving, pour the soup into individual bowls. Add 1

---

*Also known as coriander or cilantro. If you can't find it, you can substitute the common variety of parsley.

tablespoon of heavy cream and 1 teaspoon of grated radish to each bowl, and garnish with a sprig of Chinese parsley. Serve with a chilled white wine.

6 servings

Cold Tomato Soup with Cucumber

PREPARATION: 20 MINUTES

4 large very ripe tomatoes
1 large cucumber
Juice of half a lime
Pinch of cayenne
Salt

6 cups cold chicken stock or bouillon
2 tablespoons Crème Fraîche (see p. xvi)
6 basil leaves

Soak the tomatoes in a bowl of boiling water for a couple of seconds. Cool under running cold water. Peel, cut in half crosswise and seed the tomatoes by squeezing over a strainer set over a bowl. Peel the cucumber, cut it in half and remove the seeds, then cut it into small pieces.

In a food processor or a blender, purée the tomatoes, cucumber, lime juice, cayenne and salt. While the machine is still running, add 2 cups of the stock. Pour the soup into a tureen and add the remaining stock. Correct the seasoning and refrigerate until ready to serve.

Pour the soup into individual bowls. Drop a teaspoon of crème fraîche in each bowl, place a basil leaf on top of the crème fraîche and serve.

6 servings

Tomato Soup with Fennel (Cold or Hot)

PREPARATION: 20 MINUTES   COOKING: 50 MINUTES

3 ripe tomatoes
1 fennel
5 tablespoons olive oil
1 teaspoon thyme
1 bay leaf
4 cloves garlic, chopped

4 cups chicken stock or bouillon
¼ cup rice
Salt and pepper
¼ cup fresh basil leaves
1 egg yolk

Soak the tomatoes in boiling water for a couple of minutes. Cool under cold running water. Peel and quarter them.

Julienne the fennel in a food processor. In a large saucepan, heat 3 tablespoons oil. Add the tomatoes and fennel and sauté for 5 minutes over medium heat. Add the thyme and bay leaf and *half* the garlic. Mix well and simmer, covered, for 10 minutes. Add the stock and rice. Add salt and pepper to taste. Bring to a boil, lower the heat and simmer for 15 minutes.

Meanwhile, put the basil and the remaining garlic in a food processor and run the machine until the basil is finely chopped. Add the egg yolk, and with the processor still running, slowly add the remaining oil. Add salt and pepper to taste. Transfer the mixture to a bowl.

Pour the soup into the container of the food processor and purée the vegetables. Put the soup in a bowl.

If the soup is to be served *cold,* refrigerate for 30 minutes. Add the mixture of basil and egg yolk to the soup, mix well and correct the seasoning. Refrigerate until ready to serve.

If the soup is to be served *hot,* mix a couple of tablespoons of the soup into the bowl containing the mixture of basil and egg yolk, then slowly pour the contents into the soup, stirring with a wooden spoon. Pour the soup into a saucepan and heat very slowly. Do not boil or the egg will curdle. Correct the seasoning and serve.

4 servings

Tapioca and Asparagus Soup

PREPARATION: 10 MINUTES   COOKING: 20 MINUTES

My grandmother, a fearsome paragon of frugality and a great cook, never wasted anything. Whenever she served asparagus for dinner, the next night we would be sure to have asparagus soup, for she always said that nothing in the kitchen should be wasted. When you make an asparagus dish, save the cooking liquid and two or three spears for garnish so that you can make this soup.

1½ tablespoons butter
1 tablespoon flour
1 cup of water in which asparagus was cooked
1 quart chicken broth

½ cup quick-cooking tapioca
¾ cup fresh peas or ½ cup tiny frozen peas
Salt and pepper
4 asparagus spears for garnish

In a large saucepan, melt 1 tablespoon butter. When it is hot, add the flour and cook over medium heat for 3 minutes. Add the asparagus water, little by little, to the saucepan. Simmer for 5 minutes, or until it becomes hot, then add the chicken broth. Add the tapioca and the peas and cook for 5 minutes, or until they are cooked. Add the remaining butter and salt and pepper to taste.

Just before serving, cut the asparagus into 1-inch pieces and add to the soup.

4 servings

Beef Soup with Marrow

PREPARATION: 40 MINUTES   COOKING: 20 MINUTES

6 or 8 marrow bones
3 tablespoons bread crumbs
2 tablespoons finely chopped
    parsley
1½ teaspoons grated lemon rind
Salt and pepper

Pinch of nutmeg
1 egg white
6 cups beef stock or broth
1 tablespoon sherry
3 slices white bread, cut into
    triangles and toasted

Wash the bones and pat them dry with paper towels. With a sharp knife, remove the marrow from the bones (there should be about 2 tablespoons). In a bowl, combine the bread crumbs, the marrow, parsley, lemon rind, salt and pepper and the nutmeg. Mix well with a fork. Add the egg white and mix again until the mixture is the consistency of thick paste. Shape into small balls. Refrigerate for 30 minutes.

Heat the stock to the boiling point. Add the sherry and drop the marrow balls into the soup. Lower the heat and simmer for 15 minutes. Serve in a tureen with toast.

6 servings

Brussels Sprouts Soup

PREPARATION: 15 MINUTES   COOKING: 40 MINUTES

2 tablespoons butter
1 large onion, chopped
2 leeks, the white part only,
    chopped
1 clove garlic, chopped
2 quarts chicken stock or water

Pinch of thyme
1 bay leaf
2 cups Brussels sprouts
Pinch of nutmeg
Salt and pepper
1 tablespoon chopped parsley

In a large saucepan, melt the butter. When it becomes hot, add the onion, leeks and garlic and sauté over medium heat for 5 minutes. Add the chicken stock, thyme and bay leaf and simmer for 20 minutes.

Meanwhile, trim and wash the Brussels sprouts. Steam over 1 cup of water for 5 minutes.* Setting aside 3 Brussels sprouts, coarsely chop the rest and add to the soup. Add nutmeg and salt and pepper to taste. Remove the bay leaf.

Serve in individual bowls, with half a Brussels sprout added to each bowl and sprinkled with chopped parsley.

6 servings

*If you don't have a steamer, cook the Brussels sprouts in 1 quart of salted boiling water until tender but not soft.

Cabbage Soup with Blue Cheese

PREPARATION: 20 MINUTES   COOKING: 45 MINUTES

1 small head cabbage	1 onion
½ pound bacon in one piece	Salt and pepper
2 carrots	¼ pound blue cheese
2 turnips	6 slices toasted French bread
2 potatoes	

Cut the bacon into 1-inch pieces. In a large saucepan, place the bacon and cover with 2½ quarts water. Bring to a boil and skim off the froth with a slotted spoon. Lower the flame and simmer for 20 minutes. (If you do not want to eat the bacon, remove it with a slotted spoon just before adding the vegetables.)

Meanwhile, peel the carrots, turnips, potatoes and onion. Wash and pat dry with paper towels. In a food processor, slice all the vegetables, including the cabbage.

Add the vegetables to the soup. Add freshly ground pepper and correct the seasoning, adding salt if necessary. Cook for 20 minutes. Just before serving, add the blue cheese and stir with a wooden spoon until the cheese has melted.

Place a piece of toast in each serving bowl, pour the soup over it and serve.

6 servings

Carrot Soup

PREPARATION: 20 MINUTES   COOKING: 30 MINUTES

In the spring the carrots are at their best. The aroma of this soup will enhance your appetite.

2 tablespoons oil
1 pound young carrots, thinly sliced
2 large onions, chopped
2 quarts beef stock
Salt and pepper

1 tablespoon chopped parsley
2 tablespoons tapioca
1 egg yolk
3 tablespoons heavy cream
3 tablespoons butter
3 slices white toast

In a large saucepan, heat the oil and add the carrots and onions. Cook, covered, over medium heat, for 10 minutes. Add the beef stock, salt and pepper, parsley and tapioca. Cook, covered, for 15 minutes more.

Pour the soup into the container of a food processor and purée the carrots and onions. Pour the soup back into the saucepan. In a small bowl, mix the egg yolk with the cream and slowly add to the soup, stirring all the while. Garnish with parsley and serve with buttered toast.

6 servings

Cream of Fennel Soup

PREPARATION: 20 MINUTES   COOKING: 45 MINUTES

Fennel is a marvelous vegetable often ignored in the United States. It is excellent eaten raw—sliced with drinks or in a salad—braised or used to make a light, tasty soup. Adding the crème fraîche makes this soup more velvety.

3 bulbs fennels
4 tablespoons butter
2 medium-size onions, sliced
2 cloves garlic, chopped
2 tomatoes

Salt and pepper
2 tablespoons Crème Fraîche (see p. xvi) or heavy cream
Parsley for garnish

Bring 4 cups water to a boil. Trim, wash and quarter the fennel bulbs, and with the slicing blade of a food processor, slice them. Put the fennel in a bowl and cover with boiling water for 5 minutes to blanch it. Dip the tomatoes in boiling water for a few seconds and peel them. Cut them in half crosswise and squeeze to seed them.

Drain the fennel. In a large saucepan, melt the butter, and when it is hot, add the onion and sauté over a low flame until transparent. Add the fennel and sauté for a few minutes. Add 6 cups water, the garlic and tomatoes. Bring to a boil, stirring all the while. Add salt and freshly ground pepper. Cover and simmer for 20 minutes.

Pour the soup through a colander into a bowl. Put the vegetables and ½ cup of the soup into the container of a blender or food processor, and run the machine until the vegetables are puréed. Pour the soup back into the saucepan, add the puréed vegetables and bring slowly to a boil. Stirring constantly with a wooden spoon, slowly add the crème fraîche or cream to the soup. Do not let it boil. Correct the seasoning. Garnish the soup with chopped parsley and serve.

6 servings

Yogurt Soup

PREPARATION: 10 MINUTES

4 8-ounce containers plain yogurt	Salt and pepper
Juice of 2 lemons	3 tablespoons red lumpfish caviar or salmon caviar
3 cups chicken stock or bouillon	1 tablespoon chopped fresh mint

Mix together the yogurt and lemon juice and slowly add the chicken stock; mix well. Correct the seasoning with salt and freshly ground pepper. Pour into a bowl and refrigerate.

Just before serving, divide the soup into 6 bowls. Put ½ tablespoon caviar on top of the yogurt, garnish with chopped mint and serve.

6 servings

Dried Lima Bean Soup

PREPARATION: BEANS SOAKED OVERNIGHT   COOKING: 45 MINUTES TO 1 HOUR

Winter is the time to make hearty soups with dried beans. Serve this delicious soup with croutons and a good hearty burgundy.

½ pound dried lima beans,
  soaked overnight
1 onion
1 clove garlic
1 bay leaf
3 tablespoons butter
4 stalks celery, chopped

2 leeks, the white part only,
  chopped
4 large tomatoes, cut into small
  pieces
Salt and pepper
2 eggs

In a large saucepan, place the lima beans and cover with 2½ quarts water. Add the onion, garlic and bay leaf. Bring to a boil, reduce the heat and cook over medium heat for about 45 minutes, or until the beans are tender.

Meanwhile, melt the butter in a skillet. Add the celery and leek, and when they are cooked, but not browned, add the tomatoes. Simmer until the beans are done.

Remove the bay leaf and onion from the soup. In a food processor, add, in two batches, the beans and the tomato-celery mixture. Add half the liquid to the food processor. Run the machine until the ingredients are puréed. Pour the purée back into the rest of the soup in the saucepan and add salt and pepper to taste.

Just before serving, bring to a boil, reduce the heat and beat the eggs in a bowl. Stirring with a wooden spoon, slowly add 2 tablespoons of the hot soup, then pour into the soup. Turn the heat off immediately and serve.

6 servings

Lentil Soup

PREPARATION: 10 MINUTES   COOKING: 1 HOUR

1 pound lentils
1 medium-size onion
1 smoked pork hock or 1 ham
  bone with some meat

Salt and pepper
3 slices bacon
3 cloves garlic, chopped
5 frankfurters, sliced thin

Put the lentils in a saucepan and cover them with 8 cups cold water. Add the onion. Wash the pork hock and add it (or the ham bone). Add salt and pepper, and bring the soup to a boil. Skim off the froth. Lower the heat and cook, covered, for 1 hour.

Meanwhile, fry the bacon in a skillet and drain it on paper towels. Add the garlic to the bacon fat and sauté until light brown. Add the garlic and 3 tablespoons of bacon fat to the lentils. Correct the seasoning.

Slice the frankfurters very thin and add them to the soup; bring slowly to a boil. Just before serving, crumble the bacon and add it to the soup. This soup can be made a day ahead and reheated.

6 servings

Mushroom Consommé

PREPARATION: 20 MINUTES   COOKING: 20 MINUTES

2 tablespoons dried mushrooms*   6 cups beef stock or broth
½ pound fresh mushrooms plus   Salt and pepper
  6 mushrooms for garnish   4 tablespoons dry sherry

Place the dried mushrooms in a bowl, pour ½ cup boiling water over them and let soak for 20 minutes. Wash and trim the fresh mushrooms and chop in a blender or food processor.

In a saucepan, place the mushrooms, stock and the liquid from the dried mushrooms (save the dried mushrooms for future use in another dish) and simmer for 15 minutes. Meanwhile, slice the raw mushrooms to be used for garnish. Strain the consommé through a very fine sieve placed over a saucepan. Add salt, pepper and sherry and bring to a boil. Pour the soup into 6 cups, add the sliced raw mushrooms and serve.

6 servings

*Polish and Italian dried mushrooms can be found in all supermarkets or Italian pasta stores. They come in either sealed cellophane envelopes or small white plastic jars.

Mussel Soup

PREPARATION: MUSSELS SOAKED 1 HOUR; 45 MINUTES   COOKING: 50 MINUTES

This soup is a meal in itself. Serve the soup with a chilled dry wine, French or Italian bread, a green salad and some cheese.

1 fish head
1 onion stuck with 1 clove
3 carrots, cut into 1-inch slices
1 celery stalk, cut into 1-inch
  slices
Salt and pepper
2 quarts mussels
3 tomatoes
3 cloves garlic

3 onions, quartered
1 leek, cut into 1-inch pieces
3 tablespoons olive oil
½ teaspoon saffron
3 shallots, chopped
1 cup dry white wine
3 sprigs parsley, chopped, for
  garnish

In a large saucepan, put the fish head, the onion stuck with a clove, the celery and one-third of the carrot slices. Cover with 4 cups cold water. Bring to a boil, skim off the froth on top, and add salt and pepper to taste. Cook, covered, over low heat for 20 minutes.

Clean the mussels by scrubbing them with a stiff brush under cold running water and cut off the "beards" on the shells. Discard mussels that are not shut tight or feel too light or too heavy. Soak the mussels for at least 1 hour.

Peel the tomatoes and seed them by cutting in half crosswise and squeezing over a bowl with a strainer placed on top of it. In a blender or food processor, finely chop the garlic, onions, leek, tomatoes and the remaining carrots.

Pour the fish stock through a strainer set on a bowl. Set aside.

Heat the olive oil in a large skillet. When the oil is hot, add the vegetables and sauté for a few seconds. Add the saffron. Slowly add the fish stock and simmer covered for 25 minutes.

Meanwhile, put the mussels in a large saucepan and add the shallots and white wine. Cook over very low heat, shaking the saucepan from time to time. The mussels are done when they are all open. Drain them through a colander placed over a bowl and remove them from their shells. Strain the mussel broth through a very fine sieve and add the mussels and the broth to the skillet. Correct the seasoning. Serve piping hot sprinkled with parsley.

4 servings

Oyster Stew

2 cups chicken stock
1 bottle clam juice (1 cup)
1 pound freshly shucked oysters
   with their juice
½ head cabbage, julienned

½ pound snow peas
6 large mushrooms, sliced
Parsley for garnish
Freshly ground pepper

Put the chicken stock in a large saucepan and add the clam juice and oyster juice. Bring to a boil. Reduce the heat and add the cabbage. Cook for 6 minutes, add the snow peas and cook for 5 minutes. Add the mushrooms and oysters and cook for 2 minutes. Add pepper and garnish with parsley. Serve in individual bowls.

    6 servings

Soupe de Poissons de Décembre

This soup is more like a stew. The fish is served with the soup and the vegetables on the side. Have on the table coarse salt, freshly ground pepper. With a chilled dry white wine you will have a splendid dinner.

2 large sweet potatoes
2 large potatoes
2 carrots
½ pound pumpkin (if available)
1 cup oil
3 pounds fish (you can use sole,
   flounder, halibut, pollack, cod
   or sea bass), cut into 1½-inch
   slices

3 onions, chopped
3 cloves garlic, chopped
1 small can tomato paste
3 small turnips
3 stalks celery
1 bay leaf
1 teaspoon thyme
1 small chili pepper
Salt and pepper

Peel both kinds of potatoes. Scrape the carrots and peel the pumpkin. Cut all the vegetables into large dice.

    In a large casserole, heat 3 tablespoons oil and add the potatoes. Sauté until they are golden brown and, with a slotted spoon, remove to a plate.

    Add the fish and sauté until golden brown. Transfer to a plate.

    Add a bit more oil to the casserole and sauté the onions and garlic.

Add the tomato paste, mix well, then put back the potatoes. Add the carrots, turnips, celery, pumpkin, bay leaf, thyme and pimiento. Add salt and pepper to taste. Cover with 2 quarts of boiling water. Add the fish and cook over medium heat, covered, for 15 minutes. Remove the fish and keep warm in a turned-off oven. Cook the soup for 15 minutes, or until all the vegetables are tender. Put the fish back in for a couple of minutes to warm.

Transfer the fish with a slotted spoon to a tureen. Arrange the vegetables on a round serving platter. Pour the soup over the fish. Serve with the vegetables, steamed rice and fresh Italian or French bread.

6 servings

Codfish Soup from Cardiff

PREPARATION: 25 MINUTES   COOKING: 45 MINUTES

My mother-in-law, a Welshwoman born and raised in Cardiff, used to make this soup when we would come and visit her. Her great secret was fifteen drops of Tabasco—"Not twelve or sixteen, Colette," she used to say, "but fifteen!" After dinner she would sing Welsh songs to my young children. They never forgot the songs, nor the soup.

1 pound fresh cod filets
2 onions
Half a lemon, sliced
1 bay leaf
2 tablespoons vinegar
Salt
3½ tablespoons butter
2 potatoes, cut into cubes

1 leek, cut into thick slices
2 carrots, cut into thick slices
1 green pepper, diced
1 clove garlic, crushed
1 cup dry white wine
1 tablespoon chopped parsley
15 drops Tabasco

Wash and pat dry the filets of fish with paper towels and cut into dice. Chop 1 onion. Place the fish in a large saucepan and cover with the lemon slices, chopped onion and bay leaf. Cover with 2 cups water and the vinegar. Add salt and bring to a boil; reduce the heat and simmer for 15 minutes.

Meanwhile, quarter the remaining onion. Heat the butter in a skillet and add the onion, potatoes, leek, carrots, green pepper and garlic. Sauté for a few minutes, then add 2 cups water. Bring to a boil, reduce the heat and simmer for 15 minutes.

Remove the fish from the saucepan with a slotted spoon and strain the cooking liquid through a fine sieve.

Transfer the vegetables and their cooking juices from the skillet to the saucepan. Add the wine, fish broth, parsley and Tabasco. Correct the seasoning and cook for 10 minutes. Add the fish and heat through to serve piping hot.

6 servings

Soupe de Petits Pois (Pea Soup)

PREPARATION: 10 MINUTES   COOKING: 20 MINUTES

4 cups chicken stock or bouillon
1 package tiny frozen peas
5 tablespoons butter
6 thin slices French bread
Salt and freshly ground pepper

2 tablespoons dried chives
1 egg yolk
¼ cup heavy cream
4 slices Virginia ham, diced

In a saucepan, bring the chicken stock to a boil; add the peas and boil for 5 minutes.

Melt the butter in a skillet. When the butter is hot, add the slices of bread and sauté until they are golden brown. Remove with a slotted spoon and keep warm.

Put the soup in the container of a food processor or a blender jar and purée the peas. Pour the soup back into the saucepan, correct the seasoning with salt and pepper, and add the chives.

In a tureen, mix together the egg yolk and the cream.

Bring the soup to a boil, and slowly pour it into the tureen while stirring the tureen with a wooden spoon. Add the ham and place the sautéed slices of bread on top. Serve immediately.

4 servings

Portuguese Soup

PREPARATION: 20 MINUTES   COOKING: 40 MINUTES

I once did research on the Portuguese living in Soho for a New York magazine. My son's best friend John was Portuguese. His mother, Maria, and I started talking about Portuguese food. Finding that I knew very little about it, she and my son's Portuguese friends all got together and cooked a delicious meal for our entire family. The best thing was this Portuguese soup made by Maria.

4 large potatoes, peeled and
   quartered
2 quarts chicken stock or
   bouillon

1½ pounds Swiss chard
¾ pound paprika sausage
2 tablespoons olive oil
Salt and pepper

Put the potatoes in a large saucepan and cover them with 2 quarts of chicken stock. Bring the stock to a boil and simmer for 20 minutes, or until the potatoes are done.

Remove the potatoes from the soup and mash them in a blender or food processor. Return them to the soup and mix well.

Wash the Swiss chard and pat it dry with paper towels. Push it through the shredding blade of a food processor or cut in very thin slices with a sharp knife. Slice the paprika sausage into ¼-inch slices. Add the Swiss chard and the sausage to the soup. Mix well and simmer for 10 minutes.

Just before serving, add the olive oil and correct the seasoning, adding salt and pepper if needed. Serve piping hot with Portuguese or Italian bread.

6 servings

Potage à la Viande (Beef Soup)

PREPARATION: 10 MINUTES   COOKING: 1 HOUR

2 tomatoes
1 tablespoon oil
3 tablespoons butter
½ pound London broil, cut into
   small dice
3 leeks, chopped

1 onion, chopped
1 tablespoon flour
1½ quarts beef stock or bouillon
Salt and pepper
4 tablespoons heavy cream
2 tablespoons chopped parsley

Cut the tomatoes in half crosswise and seed them by squeezing over a strainer set on top of a bowl.

In a large saucepan, heat the oil and butter. Add the beef, leeks and onion and sauté for 5 minutes while stirring. Add the flour and mix well. Add the beef stock, salt and pepper to taste. Bring to a boil, reduce the heat and simmer for 40 minutes. Add the tomatoes and cook for 15 minutes.

Just before serving, stir in the cream and parsley. Serve with hot French or Italian bread.

4 servings

Shrimp Soup

PREPARATION: 20 MINUTES   COOKING: 6 MINUTES

This quick, simple shrimp soup was made for me one night by the Japanese painter Arakawa, who taught me numerous Japanese dishes. To make this soup, you must have the freshest ingredients.

6 large shrimp	6 cups chicken stock
6 large fresh mushrooms	1 tablespoon soy sauce
6 spinach leaves	Salt and pepper

Shell and devein the shrimp. Cut each shrimp crosswise in two pieces. Wash the mushrooms, pat dry with paper towels and remove the stems. Wash the spinach and dry on paper towels.

In a saucepan, bring the stock to a boil, then add the shrimp and mushrooms. Cook for 6 minutes.

Add the soy sauce to the soup. Correct the seasoning with salt and pepper.

Put a spinach leaf in each individual bowl and pour the hot soup over it. Serve right away.

6 servings

Sorrel Soup

PREPARATION: 15 MINUTES   COOKING: 20 MINUTES

2 pounds sorrel	6 cups chicken stock
4 tablespoons butter	Salt and pepper
1 large onion, coarsely chopped	1 cup heavy cream
1 tablespoon flour	6 tablespoons sour cream

Wash and trim the sorrel. In a saucepan, melt the butter and sauté the onion until lightly browned. Add the flour and mix well; slowly add the chicken stock, stirring all the while with a wooden spoon. Add the sorrel and cook for 15 minutes over medium heat.

Purée the soup in a food processor. Pour it back into the saucepan and add salt, pepper and heavy cream. Heat through but do not boil.

Pour the soup into individual bowls and top with 1 tablespoon sour cream. Serve immediately.

This soup is also delicious cold.

6 servings

Tomato Soup

PREPARATION: 20 MINUTES   COOKING: 20 MINUTES

3 tablespoons olive oil
5 large onions, finely chopped
8 cups chicken stock or bouillon
2 sprigs parsley
1 bay leaf
6 cloves garlic

6 tomatoes, quartered
Salt and pepper
2 egg yolks
2 tablespoons wine vinegar
French bread, 1 day old
¼ cup grated Swiss cheese

Preheat the oven to 425°. In a skillet, heat the oil and add the onions. Cook over low heat for 5 minutes, stirring from time to time to prevent them from browning.

In a large saucepan, bring the chicken stock to a boil. Add parsley, bay leaf, garlic cloves and tomatoes and cook over medium heat until the tomatoes are tender. Add the onions, mix well and correct the seasoning. Strain the soup over a bowl, pushing the vegetables through a fine-mesh strainer.

In a tureen, beat together the egg yolks and vinegar.

Slice the French bread. Sprinkle grated cheese on each slice and bake for 5 minutes.

Heat the soup and slowly pour it into the tureen while stirring the tureen with a wooden spoon. Serve with the toast.

6 servings

Green Soup

PREPARATION: 15 MINUTES   COOKING: 12 MINUTES

This soup can be made with any leftover greens, such as celery, salad greens, string beans, spinach, Swiss chard. It is a warming and appetizing soup for a cold winter night.

1 small head Boston lettuce
2 leeks, cut into 1-inch pieces
2 stalks celery, cut into 1-inch pieces
1 bunch parsley (reserve 2 sprigs for garnish)

1 quart chicken stock or broth
Salt and pepper
1 egg yolk
1 cup milk

Wash the lettuce and cut the leaves into three or four pieces. Drain and set aside.

In a blender or food processor, finely chop the lettuce, leeks, celery and parsley. In a saucepan, bring the stock to a boil and add the chopped greens. Lower the heat and simmer for 10 minutes. Correct the seasoning with salt and pepper.

Beat the egg yolk with the milk, and just before serving, add the mixture to the soup, stirring all the while. Cook for 1 more minute.

Garnish with parsley and serve in a tureen with fresh Italian bread.

4 servings

Potage Emeraude (Split-Pea Soup)

PREPARATION: PEAS SOAKED OVERNIGHT; 15 MINUTES   COOKING: 2 HOURS

As children we would go and spend part of our winter vacation at my grandmother's. Throughout the whole house there would often be the delicious aroma of split-pea soup simmering on the stove, and after playing in the snow, we would sit in front of a steaming bowl of soup.

½ pound split peas, soaked
   overnight
Bouquet garni (1 bay leaf,
   1 teaspoon dried thyme and
   2 sprigs parsley tied
   together in a piece of
   cheesecloth)
2 cloves garlic
2 onions
2 carrots, scraped

2 stalks celery, cut into 1-inch
   pieces
2 leeks, the white part only, cut
   into 1-inch pieces
2 tablespoons oil
Salt and pepper
3 tablespoons Crème Fraîche (see
   p. xvi)
A bowl of croutons sautéed in 2
   tablespoons oil

In a large saucepan, cover the peas with 2 quarts of cold water and add the bouquet garni, garlic and salt and pepper. Bring to a boil and simmer for 1 hour, stirring from time to time.

Chop coarsely the onions, carrots, celery and leeks in a food processor. In a large skillet, heat the oil and add the vegetables. Sauté for 10 minutes over medium heat, stirring with a wooden spoon to prevent browning. Sprinkle with salt and pepper. Add to the split peas and simmer the soup for another hour.

Remove the bouquet garni. Remove from heat and add the crème fraîche. Mix well and correct the seasoning. Serve very hot with a bowl of croutons.

6 servings

Spring Soup

PREPARATION: 20 MINUTES   COOKING: 30 MINUTES

This soup should be made with the freshest vegetables that you find at the greengrocer in the spring. Be sure not to overcook so that the fresh taste of the vegetables remains intact.

4 tablespoons butter
½ pound fresh peas, shelled
1 leek, thinly sliced
2 spring onions,* chopped
2 carrots
2 new potatoes, diced
2 quarts chicken stock or
    bouillon

Salt and pepper
A handful of spinach, coarsely
    chopped
4 or 5 Boston lettuce leaves,
    coarsely chopped
2 tablespoons chopped fresh
    chervil or any other fresh herb
6 buttered slices of toast

In a large saucepan, melt 2 tablespoons butter. Add the peas, leek, spring onions, carrots and potatoes; sauté for 3 minutes, stirring with a wooden spoon. Add the chicken stock, season with salt and pepper and simmer for about 20 minutes, or until the potatoes are done. Add the spinach, lettuce and herbs and cook for 2 minutes.

Place the remaining butter in a tureen and pour the soup over it. Serve with toast.

6 servings

*Spring onions look like overgrown scallions. Their bulbs are firm and crunchy and not as strong in flavor as regular onions.

Watercress Soup

PREPARATION: 10 MINUTES   COOKING: 10 MINUTES

2 tablespoons butter
4 scallions, chopped
2 bunches watercress
6 cups chicken stock or broth

2 egg yolks
½ cup heavy cream
2 large mushrooms, sliced
Salt and pepper

In a saucepan, melt the butter, add the scallions and sauté for 3 to 4 minutes. Remove from heat and set aside.

Wash and trim the watercress and dry well with paper towels. Set aside 3 watercress sprigs for garnish.

Put the watercress in a blender or a food processor; add the scallions and 2 cups of chicken stock. Run the machine until the watercress is puréed.

Pour the watercress purée and the remaining chicken stock into a large saucepan and bring the soup to a boil, stirring constantly. Add salt and pepper. Keep warm over very low heat until ready to serve.

Just before serving, beat the egg yolks and cream in a bowl. Stirring all the while, add the mixture to the soup. Correct the seasoning. Heat through, but do not let the soup come to a boil.

When setting the table, place in each soup bowl 2 slices of raw mushroom and a watercress leaf.

6 servings

Beef

Rib Steak with Vinegar and Herbs

PREPARATION: 5 MINUTES   COOKING: 20 MINUTES

Always hanging in my mother's kitchen was a calico bag filled with herbes de Provence. My mother could not cook without them. Every year she went south and came back with her winter supply of dried herbs. Herbes de Provence is a mixture of chives *(ciboulette)*, thyme, marjoram, tarragon and sage. Today I grow these herbs in my garden in New York, use them fresh in the spring, then dry them in the summer for winter use. Herbes de Provence are found in most food specialty stores; they are wonderful used with beef, lamb or fish.

2½ tablespoons butter　　　　　1 teaspoon herbes de Provence
2 rib steaks　　　　　　　　　　3½ ounces wine vinegar
Salt and pepper　　　　　　　　Watercress for garnish
4 cloves garlic, chopped

In a large skillet, heat 1½ tablespoons butter. Add the rib steaks, brown them and cook to desired doneness. Sprinkle with salt and pepper. Transfer to a warm serving platter and keep warm while making the sauce.

Melt the remaining butter in the same skillet. Add the garlic, herbs and vinegar. Stirring all the while, cook for 4 minutes. Pour the sauce on the steaks.

Garnish with watercress and serve with French fries.

2 servings

Broiled Marinated Steak

PREPARATION: 10 MINUTES   COOKING: 25 MINUTES

3 tablespoons oil
Juice of 3 lemons
1 onion, chopped
3 cloves garlic, chopped
2 shallots, chopped

1 sprig thyme, finely chopped
1 bay leaf, crushed
3 pounds London broil
Salt and pepper

In a wide bowl, mix the oil and the lemon juice and add the onion, garlic, shallots, thyme and bay leaf. Mix well. Add the meat and let it marinate, turning it over once in a while, while preparing the rest of the dinner.

Heat the broiler and broil the meat for about 10 minutes on each side, or until it is cooked to desired doneness. Transfer the meat to a warm platter and let it stand for 5 minutes. Pour the juice from the meat into a saucepan and add 6 tablespoons of the marinade. Heat the juice, correct the seasoning and pour over the steak.

Serve with French fries and a salad.

4 servings

Broiled Steak with Black Olive Sauce

PREPARATION: 15 MINUTES   COOKING: 20 MINUTES

2 cloves garlic
4 tablespoons butter
12 pitted black Greek olives

Salt and pepper
1 cup basil leaves
3½-pound London broil

Put all the ingredients except the steak in the container of a food processor or in a blender jar and run the machine until they are thinly chopped and thoroughly mixed. Set aside.

Heat the broiler. Broil the steak on one side for about 10 minutes, then turn it over, spread half the olive butter and broil for another 10 minutes, or until cooked to the desired doneness.

Place the steak on a heated platter and spread with the remaining butter. Serve with Purée of Watercress with Bean Curd Sauce.

4 servings

Pan-Broiled Steak with Onion Sauce

PREPARATION: 10 MINUTES   COOKING: 15 MINUTES

4½ tablespoons butter
6 onions, thinly sliced
2 tablespoons prepared mustard,
   such as the Dijon type
4½ ounces heavy cream

2 to 2½ pounds steak (sirloin,
   London broil or other tender
   cuts), ¾ to 1 inch thick
Salt and pepper

In a skillet, melt 3 tablespoons butter over a low heat; when the butter is hot (but not brown), add the onions. Sauté over medium heat, stirring from time to time, until they are golden. As soon as the onions are cooked, add the mustard and mix well. Add the cream and mix well. Add salt and pepper and simmer the sauce while cooking the steak.

Dry the steaks with paper towels. Melt the remaining butter in a large skillet. When the butter sizzles, add the steak. Sauté the steak on one side for 3 to 4 minutes. Turn the steak and cook for another 5 minutes or longer if you do not like medium-rare meat. Season with salt and pepper.

Transfer the steak to a platter. Scrape the juices from the pan and pour over the steak. Serve the steak with the onion sauce* on the side.

4 servings

*If there is any leftover sauce, it can be refrigerated for several days and used for a pork roast or for hamburgers.

Filets Mignons with Artichoke Hearts

PREPARATION: 30 MINUTES   COOKING: 30 MINUTES

4 marrow bones
4 tablespoons butter
4 filets mignons about 2 inches
   thick
Salt and pepper
2 tablespoons brandy

4 slices white bread
4 canned artichoke hearts
1 cup Béarnaise Sauce (see
   below)
2 tablespoons Crème Fraîche (see
   p. xvi), optional

Wash the bones under cold water and put them in a saucepan. Cover with boiling water and boil for 5 minutes. Drain and remove the marrow by tapping the bone on the side of a plate. Set aside and keep warm by putting it on a heatproof plate over a saucepan partly filled with simmering water.

In a large skillet, melt the butter. When the butter is hot, add the filets. Sauté on one side for about 5 minutes, then turn over and cook for another 5 minutes or longer, depending on your taste. Sprinkle with salt and pepper.

Transfer the filets onto a hot serving platter. Pour the brandy into the skillet and ignite. When the flame has died down, add the artichoke hearts and sauté for a couple of minutes.

Toast the bread. Put a slice of toast next to each filet and an artichoke heart on top of the toast. Fill the hearts with Béarnaise sauce and top with sliced marrow.

If you want to add the crème fraîche, put it in the skillet, mix well and pour the sauce over the filets. Serve right away.

4 servings

Béarnaise Sauce

PREPARATION: 10 MINUTES   COOKING: 5 MINUTES

1 stick (¼ pound) butter	1 tablespoon tarragon vinegar
3 egg yolks	2 tablespoons white wine
2 tablespoons lemon juice	3 shallots, minced
Salt and pepper	1 teaspoon dried tarragon

Melt the butter in a small saucepan.

Blend the egg yolks and lemon juice in a blender or food processor. While the machine is still running, slowly pour the hot butter in. Season with salt and pepper. Remove the sauce to a bowl and keep warm over a saucepan of simmering water.

Put the vinegar, wine, shallots and tarragon in a saucepan and cook over high heat until the liquid has boiled down to 1 teaspoon. Add this slowly to the sauce and mix well. Correct the seasoning and serve.

1 cup

Steak with Coffee Sauce

PREPARATION: 5 MINUTES   COOKING: 15 MINUTES

I was served this strange but tasty dish by Andrea Brants, a Dutch friend, who has spent most of her life in Indonesia. The bitter taste of the coffee mixed with sugar and cayenne has an unusual flavor. You will find this recipe worth trying.

4 beef steaks (any tender cut)
1 tablespoon butter
1 medium-size onion, chopped
  (about 3 tablespoons)
3 tablespoons very finely ground
  coffee

3 tablespoons very fine sugar
1 teaspoon cayenne
3 tablespoons brandy
Parsley for garnish

Broil the steaks to desired doneness.

In a skillet, heat the butter and add the onion. When the onion is transparent, add the coffee, then the sugar. Stir over high heat with a wooden spoon. When the sugar starts to caramelize, add the cayenne and mix well. Add the brandy and ignite. While the sauce is still aflame, spoon a tablespoon of it (it should look like black tar) over each steak. Garnish with parsley and serve.

4 servings

Roast Beef with Cranberries

PREPARATION: 10 MINUTES   COOKING: 1 HOUR AND 10 MINUTES

Cranberries are traditionally associated with turkey or goose. Here is a recipe where the cranberries transform an ordinary roast beef into something unusual.

3 pounds top round roast
5 tablespoons butter
Salt and pepper
2 onions, quartered
15-ounce package whole
  cranberries

¾ cup sugar
½ cup red vermouth
Chopped parsley for garnish

Preheat the oven to 375°. Spread the beef with the butter, sprinkle salt and pepper on it and surround with the onions. Roast for 1 hour, basting from time to time with the drippings.

Meanwhile, wash the cranberries and place in a saucepan. Add ½ cup water and the sugar. Bring to a boil, then lower the heat and cook the cranberries until they pop.

Half an hour before the roast is ready, pour the cranberries a-round it.

When ready to serve, put the roast on a cutting board and slice it. Arrange the slices on a serving platter. Add the juices on the cutting board to the cranberries and spoon some cranberries on top of the sliced roast. Garnish with parsley.

Purée the remaining cranberries in a food processor. Add the vermouth, correct the seasoning and serve the sauce separately.

6 servings

Roast Beef with Fresh Herbs

PREPARATION: 5 MINUTES   COOKING: 1 HOUR AND 10 MINUTES

This is a new way to give a roast beef a taste of spring by using fresh herbs.

4 pounds beef for roasting (eye round, sirloin or any other tender cut)
1 tablespoon chopped marjoram
3 tablespoons chopped parsley

2 tablespoons chopped chives
4 tablespoons butter
2 tablespoons Dijon-style mustard
Salt and pepper

Preheat the oven to 375°. Place the beef in a roasting pan. In a food processor, blend the marjoram, parsley, chives, butter and mustard.

Spread the mixture on the beef and roast to the desired doneness. Transfer to a warm platter. Add ½ cup water to the roasting pan and scrape the brown bits clinging to the pan. Add salt and pepper to taste and bring to a boil. Boil for 5 minutes and serve the sauce in a sauceboat with the roast.

6 servings

Braised Roast with Shallots

PREPARATION: 10 MINUTES   COOKING: 1 HOUR (ABOUT 15 MINUTES PER POUND)

3½ pounds round roast (top or bottom)
6 slices bacon
4 shallots, chopped
1 bay leaf

2 sprigs parsley
¼ teaspoon thyme
Salt and pepper
1 tablespoon butter
Parsley for garnish

Wrap the roast with bacon and tie with string. Heat a fireproof casserole without adding any fat. Brown the roast on one side for 15 minutes over low heat. Add the the shallots, bay leaf, parsley, thyme and 2 table-spoons water; sprinkle with salt and pepper. Turn over the roast, and sprinkle with salt and pepper and cook for 15 minutes. Turn over again, raise the heat to medium and cook for another 15 minutes. Turn off the heat and let the roast stand for 10 minutes (less if you want it rarer).

Transfer the roast to a carving board and slice it. Arrange the slices on a warm platter. Add the juice on the carving board to the sauce in the casserole, then add the butter. Heat through. Strain the juice and correct the seasoning. Garnish with parsley and serve with the sauce on the side. Accompany the roast with a Swiss Chard Pie (see p. 208).

6 servings

Filet of Beef with Stuffed Prunes

PREPARATION: 40 MINUTES   COOKING: 30 MINUTES

16 large pitted prunes	½ cup Madeira
2 cups strong hot tea	½ cup beef stock or bouillon
4 tablespoons butter	6-ounce can liver pâté
2-pound filet of beef	4 kiwis, peeled and sliced
Salt and freshly ground pepper	Chopped parsley for garnish

Preheat the oven to 400°. Place the prunes in a bowl, cover with hot tea and soak for 25 minutes.

Meanwhile, heat the butter in a large skillet and add the filet. Brown on all sides and sprinkle with salt and pepper. Pour the Madeira over the filet, then add the beef bouillon. Cook over medium heat for 30 minutes.

Drain the prunes and fill with the liver pâté. Place in a shallow baking dish and bake for 5 minutes.

Place the filet on a warm platter and slice into 8 pieces. Surround the filet with the kiwi slices and put a prune on top of each slice of kiwi. Pour the cooking juices over the filet, sprinkle with chopped parsley and serve immediately.

8 servings

Beef with Lingonberries

PREPARATION: 10 MINUTES   COOKING: 45 MINUTES

This delicious dish requires good-quality beef because it should be cooked medium rare or rare. The combination of the tart lingonberries and the currants makes the taste resemble that of a sweet-and-sour Chinese beef or pork dish.

6 tablespoons butter
6 shallots chopped
1 tablespoon brandy
1 cup burgundy
1 cup beef stock or bouillon
2 tablespoons dried or chopped
   fresh chives
Salt and pepper

2 ounces dried currants
8 ounces lingonberry preserves
10-ounce can cèpes or straw
   mushrooms*
2 pounds sirloin, cut into 1-inch
   cubes
1 bunch watercress for garnish

In a large skillet, heat 2 tablespoons butter; add the shallots and sauté for 2 to 3 minutes, or until they are transparent. Add the brandy and ignite. Stir well, then add the wine and bouillon. Add 1 tablespoon chives, salt and pepper to taste and simmer for 10 minutes.

Meanwhile, melt 2 tablespoons butter in another skillet. When the butter is hot, add the currants, sauté for 2 minutes, then add the lingonberries. Lower the heat and simmer for 5 minutes.

Drain the cèpes and add them to the currants. Stir with a wooden spoon and simmer for 5 minutes, or until the cèpes are heated through. Add the currant-cèpe mixture to the wine sauce. Correct the seasoning and keep warm on the side of the stove while cooking the beef.

In a large skillet, heat the remaining butter and add the beef cubes. Sauté over very high heat for 5 minutes, stirring all the while. Sprinkle with salt and pepper and add 1 tablespoon chives. Cook for 3 minutes more.

Place the beef on a heated platter and surround with the watercress. Serve the sauce in a sauceboat alongside. Serve with sautéed sliced zucchini and a beet and endive salad.

6 servings

*Long, thin mushrooms available at Chinese grocery shops.

Rolled Beef with Bacon

PREPARATION: 20 MINUTES   COOKING: 10 MINUTES

6 very thin slices beef round
3 cloves garlic, cut into slivers
6 tablespoons chopped parsley

6 tablespoons butter, very cold
Salt and pepper
6 slices bacon

Cut each slice of beef into three equal parts. In the center of each piece, put a sliver of garlic, ½ tablespoon parsley and 1 teaspoon butter; sprinkle with salt and pepper.

Roll each slice very tightly and wrap with half a slice of bacon. Secure the bacon with toothpicks.

Broil the beef rolls for 5 minutes on each side. (They can also be broiled over charcoal.)

Serve with boiled new potatoes.

6 servings

Rolled Beef with Carrots

PREPARATION: 20 MINUTES   COOKING: 1 HOUR AND 15 MINUTES

As a young bride I lived in Udine in the north of Italy between Trieste and Venice. We rented the attic of an old house near the marketplace. I soon became quite famous in my neighborhood, especially with the butcher, because I was the only one who bought steak, real steak, at least once or twice a week. All the other women bought thinly sliced beef. The beef was sliced not with a knife but by machine. One day I asked the butcher what these women did with these thin slices. He gave me his wife's recipe. When I make it in New York, I ask my butcher to slice the meat as thin as possible, about ⅛ inch thick.

6 thin slices beef cut from the
  sirloin
2 pounds carrots
½ pound sweet Italian sausage
3 tablespoons fresh bread
  crumbs
2 tablespoons chopped parsley
3 tablespoons milk

Pinch of nutmeg
Pinch of paprika
Salt and pepper
3 tablespoons oil
4 slices bacon
1 cup white wine
2 tablespoons tomato paste
Parsley for garnish

Scrape and wash the carrots. Slice with the slicing blade of a food processor.

Remove the casing from the sausage and put the sausage meat in a bowl. Add the bread crumbs, parsley, milk, nutmeg, paprika, salt and pepper. Spread the sausage mixture on each beef slice. Roll tightly and tie a piece of string around it.

Heat the oil in a large saucepan. Line the bottom of the saucepan with the bacon; place on top the sliced carrots, then the beef rolls. Cook for 15 minutes over high heat. Add the wine and the tomato paste, diluted with ½ cup water. Cover and reduce the heat. Simmer for 1 hour, basting from time to time.

Transfer the rolls to a warm serving platter and remove the string. Remove the carrots with a slotted spoon and surround the meat with them. Strain the sauce through a fine sieve and pour over the meat. Garnish with parsley and serve with steamed new potatoes.

6 servings

Beef Bracioli Stuffed with Swiss Chard

PREPARATION: 20 MINUTES   COOKING: 45 MINUTES

2 pounds Swiss chard
1 stick (¼ pound) butter
2 cloves garlic, chopped
¼ teaspoon nutmeg
Salt and pepper

6 thin slices beef bracioli
¼ pound sliced Swiss cheese
½ cup Madeira
½ cup beef stock or bouillon
Parsley for garnish

Wash and trim the Swiss chard. Put it in a large saucepan of boiling water to which 1 teaspoon salt has been added and cook for 8 minutes. Drain, press the water out with a fork and chop it.

In a skillet, heat 2 tablespoons butter and add the garlic. Sauté for a few minutes, then add the Swiss chard, nutmeg, salt and pepper to taste. Cook for 5 minutes and set aside.

Sprinkle the bracioli with salt and pepper. Put some Swiss chard in the center of each slice, cover with a slice of Swiss cheese, roll and tie with a piece of string.

In a large skillet, heat the remaining butter and add the bracioli. Brown on all sides, then add the Madeira and beef stock. Bring to a boil and simmer for 20 minutes.

Arrange the slices of beef on a serving platter. Pour the sauce over them, garnish with parsley, and serve with buttered steamed potatoes.

6 servings

Hamburgers with Anchovy Potatoes

PREPARATION: 20 MINUTES   COOKING: 25 MINUTES

12 small potatoes	2 pounds ground round
3 anchovy filets	1 clove garlic, chopped
1 stick (¼ pound) butter	4 tablespoons chopped fresh
Freshly ground pepper	parsley
Oil for deep frying	Salt

Peel and wash the potatoes. Pat dry with paper towels. With a melon-ball cutter, scoop as much flesh out of the center as possible and set aside the scooped-out balls. Cut a slice off the bottom so that each potato shell stands upright. Set the potatoes aside, wrapped in a damp paper towel, until ready to use. Blend the anchovies, butter and a pinch of freshly ground pepper in a blender or food processor for 30 seconds, or until the butter is creamy. Place the butter-anchovy mixture in a bowl and refrigerate until ready to use.

In a deep fryer, heat the oil to 360°.

Meanwhile, prepare the beef patties: Add garlic, 2 tablespoons parsley and salt and pepper to the ground beef. Mix well, but lightly, and shape into 4 patties 2½ inches thick.

Put both the potato shells and balls in the deep fryer.

While the potatoes are cooking, heat a frying pan sprinkled with 1 tablespoon salt and cook the beef patties to the desired doneness, turning them once, and remove to a warm platter.

When the potatoes are golden brown, remove them with a slotted spoon onto paper towels to drain.

Place the potato balls around the hamburgers and fill each potato shell with a teaspoon of anchovy butter. Sprinkle with the remaining parsley and serve immediately.

4 servings

Hamburger Tartare

PREPARATION: 15 MINUTES   COOKING: 15 MINUTES

One night I was preparing steak tartare for dinner with capers, mustard and all the other traditional ingredients. Charles Simons, the sculptor, was to have dinner with us. As he entered the kitchen he took one look at the mound of raw beef and said "Not for me!" Crestfallen, I abandoned the kitchen to Charles, who proceeded to cook our dinner. He called the results "hamburger tartare."

2 egg yolks	1 teaspoon capers
1 tablespoon mustard	2 pounds chopped round
2 tablespoons oil	¼ cup Scotch
¼ teaspoon Tabasco	Salt and freshly ground pepper
1 onion, chopped	Parsley for garnish
½ cup chopped green olives	

In a bowl, mix together the egg yolks, mustard, oil, Tabasco, onion, olives and capers.

Mix together the chopped steak and the Scotch and add the egg-yolk mixture, salt and pepper. Mix well and form 6 patties.

Broil to the desired doneness, turning once, and serve garnished with parsley.

6 servings

Hamburger with Crème Fraîche

PREPARATION: 5 MINUTES   COOKING: 20 MINUTES OR LESS

This is a slightly different version of an American's idea of a hamburger.

1 egg	1 tablespoon chopped parsley
1 tablespoon Crème Fraîche (see	¾ pound freshly ground beef
p. xvi)	Salt and pepper
1 tablespoon Dijon mustard	2 tablespoons butter
Juice of half a lemon	3 sprigs parsley

In a bowl, beat the egg with the crème fraîche and the mustard; add the lemon juice, parsley, beef, and salt and pepper. Mix well with a fork and form three hamburgers.

In a skillet, melt the butter and cook the hamburgers to the desired doneness. Garnish with a sprig of parsley and serve with buttered string beans.

3 servings

Cold Roast Beef with Mushroom Sauce

PREPARATION: 15 MINUTES

Cold roast beef, sliced
1 tablespoon prepared mustard
2 tablespoons wine vinegar
2 small pickled onions
1 tablespoon dried tarragon or 2
sprigs fresh tarragon

1 kosher pickle, cut into ½-inch
pieces
5 tablespoons olive oil
Salt and freshly ground pepper
6 large mushrooms, sliced

Blend the mustard, vinegar, onions, tarragon and pickle in a food processor or a blender. With the machine still running, add the oil. Remove the sauce to a bowl and add salt and pepper.

Add the mushrooms to the sauce; mix well and serve with the roast beef.

1½ cups

Stuffed Lemons

PREPARATION: 20 MINUTES   COOKING: 30 MINUTES

This is an old recipe that my grandmother used to make with leftover pot roast or veal. The lemons look like golden eggs and taste slightly sour.

8 lemons
1 slice white bread
1 tablespoon heavy cream
¾ pound leftover veal or pot
roast, cut into dice
1 egg yolk

2 tablespoons oil
Rind of 1 lemon
Salt and pepper
2 tablespoons butter
½ cup beer
Parsley for garnish

Choose lemons of equal size and with smooth skin. In a saucepan of boiling water, boil the lemons for 10 minutes. Drain and cool.

Cut 1 inch off the top of the lemons and set aside. With a grapefruit knife, remove all the inside flesh, being careful not to break the skin. Set aside.

Soak the bread in the cream. Finely chop the meat, egg yolk, 1 tablespoon oil, bread and lemon rind in a food processor or a blender. Remove to a bowl, add salt and pepper to taste.

Stuff the lemons with this mixture. Cover the lemons with their tops and secure with toothpicks.

In a casserole, melt 1 tablespoon oil and butter. Place the lemons, side by side, in the casserole; add the beer and cook for 30 minutes. Check from time to time during cooking to make sure that the lemons do not caramelize too much—add some beer if necessary.

Serve in a round deep serving bowl with a light potato purée.

4 servings

Potée

PREPARATION: 30 MINUTES   COOKING: 2¾ HOURS

Potée is a soup served all over France in the winter. The recipe varies according to the particular province or town—or even the housewife. The soup is served very hot along with vegetables, meat, chicken and sausage. Aïoli (see p. 171), prepared French mustard, horseradish and a fresh loaf of French or Italian bread are essential accompaniments for this delicious dish.

3 pounds short ribs of beef
1 onion stuck with 2 cloves
5 or 6 peppercorns
1 tablespoon coarse salt
2 bay leaves
2 cloves garlic, crushed
3 sprigs parsley
1 medium smoked ham butt
3½-pound chicken
1 kielbasa (Polish sausage)

6 turnips, peeled and quartered
6 carrots, scraped and cut in two
6 parsnips, peeled and quartered
6 leeks, washed, trimmed and
   tied together with string
6 medium-size potatoes, peeled
   and quartered
1 head cabbage, cut in
   wedges

In a large soup kettle, place the ribs of beef and the onion stuck with cloves in 5 quarts of water. Bring to a boil and skim the froth off the top. Add the peppercorns, salt, bay leaf, parsley and garlic. Simmer, covered, for 1 hour.

Meanwhile, prepare the vegetables. Wipe and truss the chicken.

Add the ham to the soup kettle and cook for 30 minutes. Add the chicken and cook for 30 minutes. Add the kielbasa and cook for 15 minutes.

Remove the chicken, ham and sausage to a large platter, pour some hot broth over them and cover with foil. Keep them warm in a 200° oven.

Add all the vegetables except the cabbage to the soup and cook for 30 minutes. Cook the cabbage separately for 30 minutes in a saucepan filled with 3 cups of broth.

Remove the vegetables carefully with a slotted spoon, arrange them on a heated platter and pour 1 cup of broth over them.

Remove the short ribs from the soup kettle. Carve the chicken and slice the ham and sausage. Arrange all the meats on a hot platter and pour 1 cup of broth over them.

Heat the broth and correct the seasoning. Serve with the meats and the vegetables, accompanied by the aïoli, French mustard and horseradish. Remember to also have a small dish of coarse salt and a pepper mill on the table.

10 servings

Lamb, Veal and Pork

Baby Lamb Chops with Lemon

PREPARATION: 5 MINUTES   COOKING: 10 TO 12 MINUTES

In the spring, when lamb is at its most succulent, quickly pan-broiled chops are the best. Serve on a bed of watercress with steamed broccoli. Allow two lamb chops per person (personally, I can eat at least three of them).

8 lamb chops
1 tablespoon kosher salt
Watercress

Freshly ground pepper
2 tablespoons chopped parsley
1 lemon, sliced

Trim the fat from the lamb chops.
   Heat a large skillet with salt sprinkled on it. Quickly pan-broil the chops over very high heat, 5 to 6 minutes on each side.
   Put the chops on a bed of watercress on a warm platter. Sprinkle them with pepper and parsley and place a slice of lemon on each chop.
   4 servings

Charcoal-Broiled Lamb Chops with Sauce Piquante

PREPARATION: 20 MINUTES   COOKING: 20 MINUTES

4 double-rib lamb chops
1 red sweet pepper
4 small tomatoes
4 cloves garlic, peeled
1 cup oil
2 slices French bread (a day old
   if possible)

2 tablespoons blanched almonds
3 tablespoons pine nuts
2 tablespoons chopped parsley
1 tablespoon wine vinegar
Salt
½ teaspoon paprika
Cayenne

Trim the lamb of any excess fat. Set aside until ready to broil.

When the charcoal fire is ready, broil the pepper and tomatoes. As soon as the skin turns black, remove and cool under running water. Pat dry with paper towels and peel. Cut the pepper in two and remove the seeds. Cut the tomatoes in two and remove the seeds by squeezing over a strainer set over a bowl.

Heat 2 tablespoons oil in a skillet; add the sliced bread and fry on both sides. Drain on paper towels and cut into small pieces.

Purée the garlic, tomatoes, pepper, bread, almonds and pine nuts in a food processor or blender. With the machine still running, add the parsley, vinegar and the remaining oil. Remove to a bowl. Add salt, paprika and enough cayenne to make the sauce quite hot.

Broil the chops to the desired doneness, turning once, and serve with the sauce.

4 servings

Broiled Lamb Steaks with Garlic Butter

PREPARATION: 10 MINUTES   COOKING: 10 MINUTES

6 lamb steaks cut from the leg
2 tablespoons olive oil
1 stick (¼ pound) butter, cut
   into small pieces

4 cloves garlic, peeled
Salt and pepper
Parsley for garnish

Rub some oil on the steaks. Heat the broiler and broil the steaks to the desired doneness. Place the butter and garlic in the container of a food processor and run the machine for 30 seconds. Add salt and pepper and process until the ingredients are well mixed. Refrigerate for 10 minutes.

Place the lamb steaks on a heated platter. Put 1 teaspoon of the garlic butter on top of each steak. Garnish with parsley and serve.

6 servings

Stuffed Saddle of Lamb

PREPARATION: 30 MINUTES   COOKING: 50 MINUTES

In the spring when lamb is young and tender, the best cut is the saddle (the part of the back that includes both loins). Make friends with your butcher, choose a time when he is not too busy and ask him to bone the saddle. Then stuff and roast the saddle, and you will have a fabulous dinner.

1 pound spinach
3 cloves garlic
¾ pound boiled ham
½ cup chopped parsley
Salt and pepper
1¼ cups fresh bread crumbs
2 eggs, beaten
4-pound saddle of lamb, boned

5 tablespoons butter
3 tablespoons olive oil
¼ teaspoon paprika
3 shallots, chopped
¼ teaspoon dried thyme
1 bay leaf
Salt and pepper

Preheat the oven to 475°.

Wash the spinach and cut off the stems. Put the spinach in a large saucepan and add 3 cups of boiling water. Bring to a boil and cook for 2 minutes. Drain and cool. Squeeze the water out, put between two layers of paper towels and squeeze again to remove all moisture.

Chop the spinach together with the garlic and ham. Add parsley, salt, pepper, bread crumbs and eggs. Mix well and let stand for 10 minutes.

Spread the saddle open. Sprinkle with salt and pepper and spread the stuffing. Put the two sides together and tie with string.

Place the saddle in a roasting pan and spread butter on top. Mix olive oil with paprika and pour over the saddle. Sprinkle the shallots, thyme and bay leaf around it and season with salt and pepper.

Bake for 45 minutes, basting from time to time. Remove the saddle to a warm serving platter and pour the juice over it.

6 to 8 servings

Spring Leg of Lamb with Tarragon

PREPARATION: 10 MINUTES   COOKING: 1¼ HOURS

6½-pound leg of lamb
4 cloves garlic, quartered
1 stick (¼ pound) butter
2 cups beef stock

2 tablespoons dried tarragon
1 tablespoon soy sauce
Salt and pepper

Preheat the oven to 375°. Remove excess fat from the leg of lamb. With the point of a knife, make holes in the leg of lamb and insert a piece of garlic in each hole. Sprinkle with salt and pepper and smear the leg with butter.

Place the leg in a roasting pan and bake, basting occasionally with the beef stock, for 1 hour and 10 minutes (the meat will be medium rare). Remove the lamb to a carving board.

Add the tarragon and the soy sauce to the cooking juices and scrape the sides and bottom of the pan with a wooden spoon. Bring the sauce to a boil and correct the seasoning.

Carve the leg and serve with the sauce in a sauceboat. Serve with French fries and a watercress salad.

6 to 8 servings

Hot Lamb Pâté

PREPARATION: 40 MINUTES   COOKING: 1 ¼ HOURS

2 pounds lamb for stewing	Salt and pepper
4 pounds spinach	8 eggs
1 onion	1 cup grated Swiss cheese
4 cloves garlic	Pinch of nutmeg
4 slices white bread	1 stick (¼ pound) butter
4 tablespoons olive oil	3 cups Tomato Sauce (see
1 tablespoon tomato paste	below)

Preheat the oven to 425°. Cut the meat into small dice. Wash and trim the spinach. Put it in a large saucepan with 2 cups water, bring to a boil and cook 5 minutes. Drain, put in a bowl and set aside.

Peel and chop the onion and garlic. Cut the bread into small pieces. In a large saucepan, heat the olive oil and add the lamb. Stir for a few minutes, then add the onions, garlic and tomato paste. Season with salt and pepper and add 1 cup water. Mix well, lower the heat and simmer, covered, for 30 minutes.

Beat the eggs and add the cheese, bread and nutmeg. Add the mixture to the spinach and mix well.

Remove the saucepan from heat and add the egg-spinach mixture to the lamb. Stir with a wooden spoon.

Butter a loaf pan and fill it with the egg-spinach-lamb mixture. Bake for 15 minutes in a 425° oven. Melt the butter and pour it over the pâté. Lower the heat to 325° and bake for 20 minutes. Meanwhile, make the tomato sauce.

Unmold the pâté on a serving platter and serve with tomato sauce on the side.

6 servings

Tomato Sauce

PREPARATION: 15 MINUTES   COOKING: 20 MINUTES

2 tablespoons butter   1 teaspoon parsley
1 tablespoon olive oil   1 teaspoon thyme
¼ cup chopped onion   1 bay leaf
1 clove garlic, crushed   Salt and pepper
4 tomatoes   1 teaspoon sugar

In a skillet, heat the butter and oil and add the onion and garlic. Sauté until golden brown.

Peel, halve and seed the tomatoes by squeezing over a strainer set on top of a bowl. Add the tomatoes to the onion along with the thyme, parsley, bay leaf, salt and pepper. Cover and cook over low heat for 20 minutes, stirring from time to time. Add the sugar and mix well.

1 cup

Sautéed Lamb with Yogurt Sauce

PREPARATION: 15 MINUTES   COOKING: 1 HOUR

This is an Oriental recipe. In Egypt the lamb is often boiled before being sautéed. This is to remove the fat as well as any strong taste the meat may have.

2 cups lamb cut from the leg   5 cups Yogurt Sauce (see below)
    and into 1½-inch cubes   2 teaspoons dried mint
4 cups chicken broth   Salt and pepper
12 small onions   3 cloves garlic, sliced
6 tablespoons butter   ½ teaspoon coriander seeds

Place the lamb in a large saucepan and cover with the chicken broth. Bring to a boil and simmer, uncovered, for 30 minutes, or until the lamb is cooked. Remove with a slotted spoon to a plate. Save 1 cup of the broth.

Place the onions in a saucepan of boiling water and boil for 5 minutes. Drain.

In a large skillet, heat 4 tablespoons butter and add the lamb and onions. Stir to brown on all sides.

Add the yogurt sauce, mint, salt and pepper to taste and simmer for

25 minutes, or until the onions are done. If the sauce thickens too much, add some of the reserved broth.

Just before serving, heat the remaining butter in a small skillet and add the garlic and coriander seeds. Fry lightly for about a minute and pour over the lamb. Serve piping hot with saffron-flavored rice.

4 servings

Yogurt Sauce
PREPARATION: 10 MINUTES

This excellent sauce is a very good substitute for sour cream if you are watching your calories. It can be stored in the refrigerator for as long as a week in a tightly sealed jar.

1 quart plain yogurt
1 tablespoon cornstarch

1 egg white
1 teaspoon salt

In a food processor or a blender, mix all the ingredients for 1 minute. Pour into a saucepan, bring to a boil over medium heat and simmer for 10 minutes, or until the sauce thickens, stirring all the while with a wooden spoon. Serve right away with meat or vegetables or refrigerate when cool.

Spring Lamb with Sorrel

PREPARATION: 10 MINUTES   COOKING: 1 HOUR

½ pound sorrel
6 tablespoons butter
⅓ cup oil
3 pounds lamb for stewing (shoulder and breast), cut into cubes

Salt and pepper
2 onions, chopped
2 tablespoons flour
1 cup chicken stock or bouillon
⅓ cup heavy cream

Wash and drain the sorrel. In a large saucepan, heat 3 tablespoons butter with the oil. Add the lamb and sauté until browned on all sides. Add salt and pepper and set aside.

In a skillet, melt the remaining butter. Add the onions and sauté until translucent. Sprinkle with the flour, mix well and add the chicken stock, salt and pepper. Pour the sauce over the lamb and add the sorrel. Simmer, covered, for 45 minutes.

Remove the lamb to a serving platter. Bring the sauce to a boil and correct the seasoning. Add the cream, mix well and pour over the lamb. Serve with steamed new potatoes.

6 servings

Sautéed Spring Lamb with Salsify (Oyster Plant)

PREPARATION: 15 MINUTES   COOKING: 1 HOUR

Salsify is a root that looks like a long stick, and is black on the outside and white inside. It is not often found fresh in American markets, but they do appear in some health-food stores and vegetable stores. They can be found canned. If you find any, try this recipe; it is a good substitute for potatoes.

2 pounds lamb, cut from the leg and into large cubes
2 pounds salsify
½ cup vinegar
4 tablespoons butter
5 onions
2 cloves
Salt and pepper

1 carrot, scraped and cut in 1-inch pieces
1 bay leaf
2 tablespoons chopped fresh basil
2 cups chicken stock or bouillon
Chopped parsley for garnish

Peel and cut the salsify into 3-inch pieces and drop in a bowl of water with the vinegar so that they don't blacken. Steam over 2 cups of water for 30 minutes.

Meanwhile, in a saucepan, heat the butter and add the lamb. Turn to brown on all sides, then add 4 onions. Stick the remaining onion with the cloves and add to the lamb. Add salt and pepper and sauté for 5 minutes. Add the carrots, bay leaf and basil. Add some of the chicken stock and mix well. Simmer for 45 minutes. Add the salsify, correct the seasoning and cook for 10 minutes more.

Place the lamb and vegetables on a serving platter and pour the sauce over them. Sprinkle with parsley and serve.

4 servings

French Winter Lamb Stew

PREPARATION: 15 MINUTES   COOKING: 1¾ HOURS

2 tablespoons goose fat (or	2 cloves garlic, crushed
2 tablespoons butter plus	2 tablespoons flour
1 tablespoon oil)	4 cups chicken stock or bouillon
2 pounds lamb for stewing,	1 cup white wine
bones in, cut into chunks	½ teaspoon salt
2 pounds lamb neck, cut into	10 peppercorns
chunks	1 bay leaf
1 onion, chopped	

In a large casserole, heat the goose fat and add the lamb. Brown on all sides, then add the onion and garlic and mix well. Sprinkle the lamb with the flour and cook for 5 minutes. Add the chicken stock and wine. Mix well. Add salt, peppercorns and bay leaf. Reduce the heat and simmer, covered, for 1½ hours, stirring from time to time.

Serve with steamed potatoes.

6 servings

Charcoal-Broiled Lamb with Fresh Laurel

PREPARATION: 25 MINUTES   COOKING: 20 MINUTES

Sometimes in the summer I can find fresh laurel at some vegetable stand in the country. Fresh laurel gives broiled lamb a delicious aroma. If you cannot find fresh laurel, use dried Jamaican laurel: Soak the leaves for a couple of minutes in hot water to soften them so they won't break when you put them on a skewer.

1 pound lamb, preferably cut
   from the leg
Salt and pepper
Juice of 2 limes
2 tablespoons olive oil
¼ pound thickly sliced bacon

12 fresh laurel leaves
8 small onions
4 firm tomatoes, halved
½ teaspoon thyme
8-ounce container plain yogurt

Cut the lamb into cubes and put in a bowl. Sprinkle with salt and pepper, lime juice and oil. Mix well and set aside. Cut the bacon into 8 ½-inch cubes.

You will need 4 long skewers. Put on each skewer a cube of lamb, then a laurel leaf, an onion, another cube of lamb, tomato and bacon. Repeat this procedure and finish with a laurel leaf and a cube of lamb. (Use three laurel leaves per skewer.) Sprinkle each skewer with thyme.

Charcoal-broil on a grill for 20 minutes, or until the lamb is done. It should be medium rare.

Serve with a bowl of yogurt and steamed rice.

4 servings

Veal Roast in Milk

PREPARATION: 5 MINUTES   COOKING: 3 HOURS

This is an old Norman recipe I learned from my stepfather, Almire Ducreux. I almost left this recipe out, for the veal has to cook for 3 hours, but it would be worth your while to take the afternoon off or to serve dinner quite late; your guests will certainly forgive you, for when the milk has nearly evaporated, they will be rewarded with a thick delicious sauce.

4-pound veal roast
1 cup slivered almonds
5 tablespoons butter
1 quart milk
2 cloves

1 large clove garlic
2 onions, quartered
Salt and freshly ground pepper
1 tablespoon chopped fresh
   tarragon or 1½ tablespoons
   dried tarragon

Have the butcher tie the veal roast with string.

With the point of a knife, make holes in the veal and insert the slivered almonds.

In a large saucepan, heat the butter and brown the roast over medium heat on all sides. Do not let the butter burn.

When the roast is browned on all sides, remove to a platter and discard the butter. Put the roast back in the saucepan and cover with milk. Add the cloves, garlic, onions, salt and pepper.

Simmer the roast for 2½ hours, or until the meat can be easily pierced with a fork and the milk has nearly disappeared.

Remove the meat and cut into thin slices. Arrange the slices on a serving platter and pour the sauce over them. Sprinkle with tarragon. Serve with sautéed carrots.

8 servings

Baked Veal Chops with Ham

PREPARATION: 30 MINUTES   COOKING: 45 MINUTES

6 tablespoons butter
6 veal chops
Salt and pepper
½ pound mushrooms
3 shallots
¼ cup Madeira
4 teaspoons tomato paste

1 tablespoon chopped parsley
¾ cup chicken stock or bouillon
3 thick slices ham
3 tablespoons Crème Fraîche (see p. xvi) or heavy cream
Parsley for garnish

Preheat the oven to 350°. In a large skillet, heat 4 tablespoons butter and add the veal chops. Sauté on one side for 5 minutes, then on the other side for another 5 minutes. Butter a roasting pan large enough to hold all the chops side by side. Put the chops in the roasting pan and sprinkle with salt and pepper.

Chop the mushrooms and shallots in a food processor. Add the remaining butter to the skillet in which the chops were sautéed. When the butter is hot, add the mushrooms and shallots. Sauté for a few minutes, then add the Madeira, tomato paste, parsley and chicken stock. Stir with a wooden spoon. Add salt and pepper and simmer for 20 minutes, stirring from time to time.

Spread the mushroom mixture on each chop. Cover each chop with half a slice of ham. Cover the roasting pan with foil and bake for 25 minutes.

Remove the chops to a serving platter. Put the crème fraîche in the roasting pan and stir, scraping the bottom of the pan with a spoon. Pour the sauce over the chops, garnish with parsley and serve.

6 servings

Veal Scaloppine with Clams

PREPARATION: 20 MINUTES   COOKING: 25 MINUTES

24 clams	1 tablespoon oil
1 cup white wine	12 veal scaloppine
Pepper to taste	1 tablespoon cornstarch
2 shallots, chopped	1 tablespoon chopped parsley
2 tablespoons butter	1 tablespoon fresh bread crumbs

Wash and scrub the clams under cold running water. Put them in a large saucepan; cover with the wine and add pepper and the shallots. Bring to a boil. When the clams open, turn off the heat. Remove the clams with a slotted spoon and set aside. Reserve the liquid.

In a large skillet, heat the butter and oil. When the butter becomes foamy, add the veal. Sauté on one side for 5 minutes, then turn over and sauté for another 5 minutes. Strain the clam liquid through a very fine sieve to remove any sand. Remove the clams from their shells and add to the veal. Sprinkle the clams and veal with cornstarch and add the reserved liquid to make a sauce. Cook for 5 minutes.

Put the veal and clams on a serving platter and pour the sauce over them. Mix the parsley with the bread crumbs and sprinkle over the veal.

Serve with a light potato purée.

4 servings

Veal Scaloppine with Grapefruit

PREPARATION: 15 MINUTES   COOKING: 20 MINUTES

I love this dish because the grapefruit gives it a bittersweet taste that reminds me of a sweet-and-sour Chinese dish. It is unusual but truly delicious.

2 tablespoons oil	1 large grapefruit
3 tablespoons butter	1 teaspoon sugar
6 veal scaloppine	1 egg yolk
2 tablespoons flour	½ cup grapefruit juice
Salt and pepper	2 tablespoons chopped parsley

In a skillet, heat the butter and the oil. Dredge the veal with flour and sauté, browning on both sides. Sprinkle with salt and pepper and remove to a serving platter. Keep warm in a turned-off oven while preparing the grapefruit.

Peel and slice the grapefruit. Sauté the grapefruit slices in the same skillet in which the veal was sautéed. Sprinkle with sugar and cook over medium heat for 5 minutes. Surround the veal with the grapefruit. Beat the egg yolk with ½ cup grapefruit juice. Add to the sauce and cook over low heat for 5 minutes—do not let it boil. Pour over the veal and sprinkle with the chopped parsley.

3 servings

Veal Scaloppine with Lemon and Avocado Purée

PREPARATION: 15 MINUTES   COOKING: 20 MINUTES

1½ pounds veal scaloppine
½ cup flour
4 tablespoons butter
¼ cup oil

1 avocado
2 lemons
Parsley for garnish

Dredge the veal with flour. In a large skillet, heat the butter and oil. When the butter becomes foamy, add the veal and sauté on one side for 5 minutes, then turn and sauté for another 5 minutes. Reduce the heat and cook gently while preparing the avocado.

Peel the avocado and purée in a food processor or blender. Add the juice of 1 lemon, salt and pepper.

Spread the avocado purée over the veal and simmer for 2 minutes. Correct the seasoning and arrange on a serving platter. Slice the remaining lemon and place around the veal. Garnish with parsley and serve.

6 servings

Veal Scaloppine with Marinated Italian Artichoke Hearts

PREPARATION: 10 MINUTES   COOKING: 16 MINUTES

8 veal scaloppine
3 tablespoons flour
3 tablespoons butter
1 jar marinated Italian artichoke
  hearts

Salt and pepper
3 tablespoons chopped parsley
1 lemon, sliced, for garnish

Dust the veal lightly with flour.

In a large skillet, heat the butter and sauté the scaloppine for 5 minutes on each side. Add the artichoke hearts with their oil and stir gently with a wooden spoon. Lower the flame and cook for 6 minutes more. Sprinkle with freshly ground pepper and very lightly with salt.

Arrange the scaloppine on a hot platter. Sprinkle with parsley and garnish with lemon slices.

4 servings

Sautéed Veal with Small White Onions

PREPARATION: 15 MINUTES   COOKING: 1½ HOURS

Calvin Trillin, the *New Yorker* writer, once wrote that he didn't think I even kept ice cubes in my refrigerator because I disliked frozen foods so much. This is not quite accurate. I do prefer fresh ingredients to frozen ones, but there are two vegetables that I think lose little or no taste when frozen. They are peas and small white onions (sometimes called pearl onions). Peeling close to 2 pounds of these onions for a dish such as this one would take so much time that it would discourage even me. Most supermarkets carry these small onions ready to use.

½ pound bacon, cut into 1-inch
   pieces
1 pound fresh white mushrooms
6 tablespoons olive oil
2½ pounds veal, cut from the
   leg and into 1-inch pieces
Salt and pepper

1 tablespoon flour
3½ ounces chicken stock or
   bouillon
¾ cup Madeira
40 frozen small white onions
6 slices French bread, toasted
6 basil leaves for garnish

Blanch the bacon in a saucepan of boiling water for 5 minutes and drain. Wash and pat dry the mushrooms with paper towels. In a large saucepan, heat 3 tablespoons olive oil, add the veal and brown on all sides for 7 to 8 minutes. Sprinkle with salt and pepper, reduce the heat and sprinkle with the flour. Mix well and add the chicken stock and Madeira. Mix well again and add the bacon and onions. Cover and cook over medium heat for 1¼ hours, or until the veal is tender. Stir from time to time.

Meanwhile, fry the slices of bread in the remaining oil. Drain on paper towels.

Correct the seasoning of the veal. Place a slice of bread on each plate and cover with the veal, vegetables and sauce. Garnish with a basil leaf and serve.

6 servings

Veal Loaf

PREPARATION: 15 MINUTES   COOKING: 50 MINUTES

3 slices white bread
½ cup milk
4 tablespoons butter
3 shallots, chopped
½ pound mushrooms, sliced
3 tablespoons dry sherry

1 pound veal, chopped
¾ pound pork, chopped
3 eggs
½ teaspoon thyme
Salt and pepper

Preheat the oven to 350°. Soak the bread in milk. In a skillet, heat the butter, add the shallots and sauté until transparent. Add the mushrooms and sauté for 2 minutes. Add the sherry, cook for 3 minutes and remove from heat.

In a bowl, mix together the veal and pork. Squeeze out the milk from the bread and add to the meat along with the eggs, thyme, salt and pepper. Mix well. Add the shallots and mushrooms and mix well.

Form the mixture into a loaf. Place in a baking pan and bake for 50 minutes, basting from time to time. Serve with cauliflower and Green Peppercorn Sauce (see below).

6 servings

Green Peppercorn Sauce
PREPARATION: 20 MINUTES

Green peppercorns are fresh peppercorns preserved in water. Available at any specialty store, they come in 4-ounce cans or in larger cans. They can be stored in their liquid in plastic containers in the refrigerator for several weeks. This sauce is excellent with such dishes as roast veal, pork chops and stuffed onions.

¾ cup Mayonnaise (see p. 29)
3 tablespoons chopped scallions
3 tablespoons chopped shallots
1 tablespoon chopped parsley
1 tablespoon capers, coarsely
chopped

1 tablespoon green peppercorns,
drained and chopped
1 cup plain yogurt
3 tablespoons white vinegar

Mix together all the ingredients.
About 3 cups

Veal Hamburgers

PREPARATION: 30 MINUTES   COOKING: 20 MINUTES

This is a pleasant change from regular hamburgers. Serve with sautéed potatoes, peas and asparagus and a fresh tomato salad for a light dinner in the spring.

4 slices white bread
3½ ounces milk
1½ pounds chopped veal
¾ cup grated Parmesan
2 eggs, beaten
1 shallot, chopped

Pinch of nutmeg
3½ ounces bread crumbs
2½ tablespoons butter
6 salad-green leaves
Freshly ground pepper

Soak the bread in the milk. Squeeze out the milk and mash the bread with a fork. Add to the veal; add the Parmesan and mix well. Add the eggs, shallot and nutmeg. Mix well and form 6 patties. Roll them in the bread crumbs.

In a skillet, heat the butter and add the patties. Cook over medium heat for 10 minutes on each side.

Place each patty on a salad-green leaf and sprinkle with pepper.
6 servings

Roast Pork

PREPARATION: 1 HOUR   COOKING: 2 HOURS

5-pound boneless loin of pork*	1 teaspoon thyme
3 cloves garlic, cut into thin slivers	Salt and pepper
	12 pitted prunes
2 carrots, chopped	6 ounces shelled walnuts
2 onions, chopped	1½ cups port

Preheat the oven to 325°. With the point of a knife, make small holes in the roast and insert the slivers of garlic.

Place the carrots and onions in the bottom of a large roasting pan. Place the roast on top of the carrots and onions and insert a meat thermometer in the thickest part. Sprinkle with thyme, salt and pepper. Add ½ cup water to the pan and bake for 2 hours, or until the thermometer registers 160°.

Meanwhile, stuff the prunes with the walnuts. In a saucepan, bring the port to a boil, add the prunes and turn off the heat. Let the prunes stand in the port for 1 hour.

Drain the prunes over a bowl and set aside. Baste the roast with the port.

When the roast is done, remove to a platter and let it stand for 5 minutes before carving.

Pour the sauce into a saucepan and spoon off some of the fat. Add the prunes to the sauce and heat through.

Slice the roast. Arrange the slices on a platter and surround them with the prunes. Serve the sauce in a sauceboat.

8 servings

*A crown roast of pork, made of 16 chops, is a very elegant dish. The preparation is the same as above, but before serving, fill the center of the crown roast with the prunes and garnish with parsley.

Roast Pork with Cherries

PREPARATION: 25 MINUTES   COOKING: 2 HOURS

We had a house in the Vesinet outside of Paris with a cherry orchard. Early every summer all the grandchildren would gather in the country to pick the cherries. We would eat as many cherries as we put in our baskets. The great reward for the work (it was a lot of work) was a marvelous roast pork baked with dozens of cherries—my grandmother's masterpiece.

15 cloves
10 peppercorns
½ teaspoon cinnamon
4 tablespoons butter
3-pound loin of pork, boned
2 pounds cherries (preferably the red kind)

2 cups red wine
1 teaspoon kosher salt
Beurre Manié (see below)
Salt and pepper

Preheat the oven to 350°. Put 3 cloves, peppercorns, cinnamon and butter in the container of a food processor. Run the machine until the ingredients form a paste. Spread this all over the roast and stud it with the remaining cloves.

Bake the roast for 1½ hours.

Meanwhile, wash and pit the cherries (there is a gadget sold in department stores for pitting cherries). Set aside 1 cup cherries.

Pour the wine into a saucepan and bring to a boil. Add the cherries and simmer for 20 minutes.

Remove the roast from the oven and keep warm on a platter. Skim off the fat from the juice in the pan.

In a food processor, purée the reserved cup of cherries together with the pan juice and kosher salt. Transfer to a saucepan and bring to a boil. Add the beurre manié and cook the sauce for 8 minutes. Correct the seasoning with salt and pepper.

Pour the cherries and the sauce around the roast. Serve right away.

6 servings

Beurre Manié

Heavy cream and especially Crème Fraîche (see p. xvi) help thicken a sauce, but if you are calorie-conscious, use beurre manié instead.

1 tablespoon butter   1 tablespoon flour

Mix both ingredients with the tips of your fingers until the butter has absorbed all the flour. Add to your sauce, stirring until the butter has melted.

Roast Pork with Black Peppercorns

PREPARATION: 10 MINUTES   COOKING: 2 HOURS

5 black peppercorns
2 medium-size onions, quartered
Half a carrot
3 juniper berries
1 bay leaf
¼ teaspoon thyme

½ teaspoon sage
3½-pound loin of pork,
    backbone removed
1 bunch watercress for garnish
Salt

Preheat the oven to 375°. Put 6 cups water in a large ovenproof casserole and add the peppercorns, onions, carrot, juniper berries, bay leaf, thyme and sage. Boil for 5 minutes, then add the pork. Cover the casserole and bake for 1½ hours.

Remove the pork to a warm platter. In a food processor or blender, blend the sauce in which the pork was cooked. Pour the sauce into a saucepan, correct the seasoning and heat through.

Carve the pork. Pour the sauce over it, garnish with the watercress and serve.

6 servings

Roast Pork with Pommes de Terre Boulangère

PREPARATION: 15 MINUTES   COOKING: 1¾ HOURS

2 pounds potatoes
3-pound loin pork roast, boned
    but with bones saved
4 cloves garlic
1½ tablespoons thyme

¼ teaspoon nutmeg
2 bay leaves, crushed
2 tablespoons chicken or goose
    fat
Salt and pepper

Preheat the oven to 400°. Peel the potatoes, wash and pat dry with paper towels.

In a large saucepan, place the pork and the bones and cover with boiling water. Bring to a boil, lower the heat and simmer for 30 minutes.

Meanwhile, thinly slice the potatoes. Peel the garlic and chop. Rub a large baking dish with a piece of garlic. Cover the bottom of the dish with a layer of sliced potatoes and sprinkle with thyme, nutmeg, bay leaves, chicken or goose fat, some of the chopped garlic, salt and pepper. Add a second layer of the same ingredients. Cover the potatoes with the water in which the pork was cooked.

Bake the pork for 15 minutes, then place it on top of the potatoes and cook for 1 hour, or until the potatoes have absorbed all the liquid and are golden brown.

Slice the pork and put it back on top of the potatoes.

6 servings

Roulades de Porc   (Pork Rolls)

PREPARATION: 15 MINUTES   COOKING: 1¼ HOURS

3 bulbs fennel
9 shallots
4 tablespoons chopped parsley
1 stick (¼ pound) butter
6 thin, wide pork slices cut from
  the leg

6 thin slices Virginia ham
2 pounds carrots, sliced
1 pound small white onions
1 cup white wine
1½ cups beef stock or bouillon
Salt and pepper

Wash and pat dry the fennel with paper towels and chop finely in a food processor along with the shallots and parsley.

In a skillet, heat 4 tablespoons butter and add the fennel mixture, salt and pepper. Cook gently for 30 minutes and remove the vegetables with a slotted spoon.

Cover each pork slice with a slice of ham and some of the fennel mixture. Roll and tie with string.

In a casserole, heat the remaining butter and add the carrots and onions. Sauté over high heat until the onions are browned. Remove with a slotted spoon and set aside. Add the pork rolls and brown on all sides. Add the carrots and onions, the wine and beef stock, salt and pepper. Cover and simmer for 30 minutes.

Arrange the pork rolls on a serving platter and surround with the vegetables. Pour the sauce over them and serve.

6 servings

Pork Filet with Prunes

PREPARATION: 20 MINUTES   COOKING: 50 MINUTES

12 prunes
3 tablespoons brandy
8 slices pork filet, 1½ inches
    thick
1 cup beer
2 tablespoons oil
4 onions, quartered
2 cloves garlic, crushed

2 cloves
½ teaspoon thyme
1 bay leaf
1 tablespoon Dijon-style
    mustard
6 slices bacon, cubed
¼ cup Crème Fraîche
    (see p. xvi)

Preheat the oven to 350°. Soak the prunes in ¼ cup hot water mixed with the brandy.

Place the pork filets in a Pyrex or earthenware roasting pan and pour the beer and oil over them. Add the onions, garlic, cloves, thyme, bay leaf, prunes and mustard. Mix well.

In a skillet, sauté the bacon until half cooked. Drain on paper towels and add to the pork filets.

Put the casserole in the oven and bake for 40 minutes.

Remove from the oven. Add the crème fraîche and mix well. Return to the oven for 5 minutes.

Serve right away from the baking pan.

4 servings

Pork Cubes with Cherrystone Clams

PREPARATION: 10 MINUTES   COOKING: 45 MINUTES

This is one of my friend Maria's Portuguese recipes. It was given to her by her grandmother, who is still alive and well in Portugal.

3 dozen cherrystone clams
4 tablespoons olive oil
5 cloves garlic, crushed

2 pounds lean pork, cubed
1 bay leaf
Salt and pepper

Scrub the clams under running water. Discard those with open or cracked shells. To make sure that the clams are free of sand, soak them in water for about 30 minutes.

Heat the olive oil in a skillet, add the garlic and brown rapidly.

Remove the garlic with a spatula and add the pork to the hot oil. Then add the bay leaf, ¼ cup water, salt and pepper to taste, and cook, uncovered, for 15 minutes over medium heat. Add ¼ cup water (the pork should always be kept moist) and continue cooking for another 15 minutes. Add the clams and stir thoroughly. Cover and cook for 15 minutes more, or until all the clams are open. Serve with steamed rice covered with the sauce.

6 servings

Pork Liver en Croûte

PREPARATION: 20 MINUTES   COOKING: 40 MINUTES

Pork liver is seldom eaten in the United States, which is a pity. Baked wrapped in bacon, it is a great treat.

1¾-pound pork liver in one
   piece
8 slices bacon
½ cup slivered almonds
1 loaf Italian crusty bread, about
   8 inches long and 4 inches
   wide

4 tablespoons butter
Pepper

Preheat the oven to 375°. Wrap the pork liver completely with the slices of bacon. Tie with string in several places. With the point of a knife, make holes in the liver and insert the slivered almonds halfway through. The liver should look like a porcupine.

Place the liver in a roasting pan, sprinkle with pepper and bake for 20 minutes.

Meanwhile, cut the top off the bread and remove the soft inside. You should have just a crusty box (see illustration). In a small saucepan, melt the butter and spread it all over the crust, inside and out. Bake for 20 minutes in the oven.

Remove the liver from the oven. Remove the string and put the liver inside the crust. Put the top back on and carve at the table. The liver will be slightly pink inside.

Serve with braised endives and a salad.

6 servings

Ham Steaks with Shallots

PREPARATION: 15 MINUTES   COOKING: 25 MINUTES

6 ham steaks
4 tablespoons butter
4 tablespoons chopped shallots
1 cup dry white wine
2 tablespoons vinegar

1 cup heavy cream
1 tablespoon tomato paste
Salt and pepper
¼ teaspoon nutmeg
1 egg yolk

Preheat the oven to 325°. Arrange the ham steaks in a gratin dish.

In a skillet, heat the butter and sauté the shallots until they are lightly browned. Add the wine and vinegar and boil until the liquid has been reduced to 3 tablespoons. Add the cream and tomato paste, reduce the heat and simmer. Add salt, pepper and nutmeg. Mix well and remove from heat.

Put the egg yolk in a bowl, and stirring all the while, slowly add the cream sauce. Pour the sauce over the ham and bake for 20 minutes.

6 servings

Calf's Liver with Bacon

PREPARATION: 5 MINUTES   COOKING: 20 MINUTES

This simple but expensive dish depends on the quality of the calf's liver. Ideally, calf's liver should be served brown on the outside and pink inside.

1 stick (¼ pound) butter
6 slices calf's liver, ⅜ inches
    thick
Salt and pepper

12 thick slices bacon
Half a lemon
1 lemon, sliced, for garnish

Remove all membrane from the liver. In a large skillet, heat 6 table-spoons butter and add the liver. Cook over medium heat for 3 to 4 minutes on each side. Add salt and pepper. Remove the liver to a warm platter and place over a saucepan of boiling water to keep it warm.

Add to the skillet the slices of bacon and cook over medium heat until they are crisp. Put the bacon slices between the slices of liver. Add the remaining butter to the skillet and cook over high heat. Add to it the juice of half a lemon. Pour the butter over the liver and surround the liver with slices of lemon. Serve with steamed potatoes.

6 servings

Whole Calf's Liver in White Wine

PREPARATION: 15 MINUTES   COOKING: 50 MINUTES

When I was a child, I had a Swiss governess, a paragon of rectitude. She believed that raw calf's liver would make me grow tall and strong. The end result was that today I am five two, and for years I would not touch liver, until one day I was served this marvelous braised liver at a friend's house. It had been simmered in white wine. It was tender and unusual. If you can gather around you some friends who all like liver, try this recipe. The liver should be as light in color as possible. Ask the butcher to remove the thin membrane that covers it.

3-pound whole calf's liver
3½ ounces prosciutto, thinly
  sliced
Salt and pepper
Fatback
6 tablespoons butter

3½ ounces white wine
1 cup chicken stock or bouillon
12 small white onions
¼ pound bacon
12 small mushrooms

Wrap the liver with the slices of prosciutto and sprinkle with salt and pepper. Slice the fatback very thin and wrap the liver. Tie with string in several places.

In a saucepan, heat 4 tablespoons butter, add the liver and brown on all sides. Pour the wine and the chicken stock over the liver and simmer, covered, for 40 minutes.

Meanwhile, heat 2 tablespoons butter in a skillet, add the onions and sauté over medium heat.

Dice the bacon and blanch in boiling water. Drain, add to the onions and cook until the bacon is crisp.

Add the onions, bacon and mushrooms to the liver 5 minutes before it is done. Transfer the liver to a platter. Remove the prosciutto and fat. Slice the liver and surround it with the onions, mushrooms and the sauce.

Poached Calf's Liver

PREPARATION: 5 MINUTES   COOKING: 5 MINUTES

This dish takes only 5 minutes to cook. The secret is to have the butcher cut the liver into paper-thin slices, which are then cut into squares. Serve on top of a String Bean Purée (see p. 207) surrounded with sautéed julienne carrots and you will have a meal with both color and flavor.

6 slices calf's liver, sliced
  paper-thin
Salt and pepper

1 tablespoon butter
Juice of 2 lemons

Cut the calf's liver into 2-inch squares and set aside on a plate.
In a large saucepan, bring 4 cups water to a boil. Add 1 tablespoon salt and freshly ground pepper. Add the butter and the lemon juice. When the water boils, add the liver and turn off the heat. Cover and let the liver stand in the water for 4 minutes.
Remove the liver with a slotted spoon. Serve immediately.
4 servings

Calf's Liver with Oranges

PREPARATION: 10 MINUTES   COOKING: 20 MINUTES

3 teaspoons Dijon mustard
4 slices calf's liver, ⅜ inches
  thick
5 tablespoons flour

5 tablespoons oil
2 large oranges
Chopped parsley for garnish
Salt and pepper

Spread the mustard on the slices of calf's liver, then roll them in flour and shake off the excess flour.

In a skillet, heat the oil and add the liver. Cook for 7 minutes on each side. Remove to a warm platter.

Add 2 tablespoons water to the skillet and scrape it with a wooden spoon. Add the juice of one orange and stir well. Correct the seasoning with salt and pepper and pour the sauce over the liver. Slice the other orange and surround the liver with the orange slices. Sprinkle with chopped parsley and serve immediately.

4 servings

Veal Kidneys en Bateau

PREPARATION: 20 MINUTES   COOKING: 40 MINUTES

4 veal kidneys	1 tablespoon oil
4 very large baking potatoes	4 teaspoons Crème Fraîche (see
2 shallots, chopped	p. xvi)
3 tablespoons chopped parsley	4 tablespoons butter, melted
1 egg yolk	Salt and pepper

Preheat the oven to 425°. Wash the kidneys in cold running water. Dry with paper towels and remove the fat.

Wash the potatoes and wrap in foil. Bake for 20 minutes.

Mix the shallots and parsley together. Beat the egg yolk on a plate. Roll the kidneys in the egg yolk, then in the shallot-parsley mixture. Sprinkle with salt and pepper.

Remove the potatoes from the oven. Reduce the oven temperature to 375°. Remove the foil from the potatoes and make a slit the length of each potato. With a fork, remove all the potato flesh, leaving just the skin. Set the potato flesh aside.

Place a kidney inside each potao shell and tie with string in several places. Place the filled potato shells on an oiled baking pan and bake for 20 minutes.

Meanwhile, put the potato flesh in a bowl, and add the crème fraîche and melted butter. Using a fork, mash it to make a purée. Add salt and pepper to taste. Keep the purée hot over a saucepan of boiling water.

To serve, surround the kidneys in the potato shells with the purée.

4 servings

Sautéed Sweetbreads

PREPARATION: 20 MINUTES   COOKING: 25 MINUTES

2 pairs sweetbreads
1 tablespoon salt
4 ounces dried Chinese
  mushrooms*
4 tablespoons butter

½ cup dry white wine
1 tablespoon soy sauce
1 tablespoon dried tarragon
Salt and pepper

Wash the sweetbreads. In a saucepan, bring 4 cups water to a boil and add salt. Add the sweetbreads and mushrooms and simmer for 20 minutes. Drain and rinse in cold water. Remove the filament enclosing the sweetbreads and cut into bite-sized pieces. Trim the mushrooms, removing their stems.

In a large skillet, heat the butter and add the sweetbreads and mushrooms. Sauté for 5 minutes. Add the wine, soy sauce and tarragon. Sprinkle with salt and pepper and cook over medium heat for 15 minutes. Correct the seasoning and serve over steamed rice with a green salad.

4 servings

*These range in color from dark brown to black and are sold in plastic bags in Chinese groceries.

Poultry

Chicken Breasts with Avocado

PREPARATION: 10 MINUTES   COOKING: 15 MINUTES

This is truly an excellent recipe that I developed one night when I was giving a dinner party and found out at the last minute that I would be detained at school until 7 P.M. This dish takes no time at all. The chicken is coated with a small amount of avocado cream and surrounded with avocado balls. The avocado should not be overripe.

1 large avocado	¼ pound small whole white
Juice of 1 lemon	mushrooms
1 tablespoon oil	3 tablespoons butter
Salt and pepper	1 tablespoon dried tarragon
2 whole chicken breasts, boned	Parsley for garnish

Peel the avocado. With a melon-ball cutter, scoop out small avocado balls. Set aside in a bowl.

Place the rest of the avocado in a blender jar or the container of a food processor. Add 1 tablespoon lemon juice, oil and a pinch of salt and pepper and run the machine for 30 seconds, or until the avocado is puréed. Set aside.

Cut the chicken breasts into 1-inch cubes. Wash and pat the mushrooms dry with paper towels. In a large saucepan, heat the butter and add the chicken cubes and mushrooms. Sauté rapidly over high heat until the chicken is browned. Sprinkle with salt and pepper and mix well. Add 1 tablespoon lemon juice and the tarragon; mix well. Correct the seasoning. Lower the heat and add the avocado purée. Mix well, then add the avocado balls. Stir gently and cook for 2 or 3 minutes, or until the balls of avocado are heated through. Gently lift the chicken cubes, mushrooms and avocado balls onto a warm platter. Garnish with parsley and serve immediately.

4 servings

Chicken Breasts with Figs and Watercress

PREPARATION: 25 MINUTES   COOKING: 45 MINUTES

As a child I spent the war years in Cairo. During the summer we used to go to a beach twenty miles from Alexandria. At that time there were only wooden shacks there with no running water (we bathed in the sea). All the houses were surrounded with hundreds of fig trees. Every morning a small Arab boy would come around with baskets full of golden ripe figs. We ate figs for breakfast, lunch and dinner. My mother's best recipe was chicken with figs.

3 bunches watercress	Salt and pepper
1 stick (¼ pound) butter	8 fresh figs*
4 chicken breasts	Juice of half a lemon
3 tablespoons Crème Fraîche (see p. xvi)	1 tablespoon tarragon

Preheat the oven to 375°. In a large saucepan, boil 1 quart water. Add the watercress and remove the saucepan from heat. Let the watercress stand in the hot water for 10 minutes. This will remove the bitterness.

Meanwhile, in a large skillet, heat 4 tablespoons butter and add the chicken breasts, skin side down. Sauté for 5 minutes first, then turn over and sauté for 10 minutes. Remove from heat and set aside.

Drain the watercress. With a fork, press the water out. Purée the watercress in a blender or a food processor. In a saucepan, heat 2 tablespoons butter and add the watercress. Sauté for 2 minutes, add the crème fraîche, salt and pepper to taste. Lower the heat and simmer for 5 minutes.

Make a cross cut on top of the figs. Place the chicken breasts in a buttered shallow baking pan and surround them with the figs. Add the lemon juice to the skillet, scrape the sides and the bottom of the skillet with a fork and pour the sauce over the chicken breasts. Sprinkle the chicken with tarragon, salt and pepper, and dot with the remaining butter. Bake for 20 minutes.

To serve, place the chicken breasts on a hot platter, surround with the figs and spread the watercress purée on top.

4 servings

*You can use dried figs soaked in hot water for 10 minutes as a substitute.

Chicken Breasts with Mangoes and Green Grapes

PREPARATION: 10 MINUTES   COOKING: 25 MINUTES

When I was born, my father planted a mango tree in front of our house in Garden City, Cairo. The tree grew along with me and I developed a passion for the fruit. One summer we had so many mangoes that my father, tired of being served sliced mangoes every evening for dinner, threatened to cut down the tree. I came up with this recipe and the tree was saved. Visiting Cairo many years later with my husband and son, I went back to see my old house. In front of it was the mango tree still standing guard.

1 stick (¼ pound) butter	2 mangoes
4 whole chicken breasts, boned	1 cup dry white wine
Salt and pepper	4 tablespoons vinegar
½ teaspoon thyme	½ pound seedless green grapes
1 bay leaf, crumbled	1 pint heavy cream

In a large skillet, heat half the butter and add the chicken breasts. Brown on all sides, reduce the heat and simmer for 15 minutes. Sprinkle with salt and pepper, thyme and bay leaf.

Meanwhile, peel the mangoes and cut into 3-inch slices. In another skillet, heat the remaining butter and add the mangoes. Sauté for 5 minutes and set aside.

Remove the chicken to a serving platter and keep warm in a turned-off oven. Add the wine to the skillet in which the chickens were cooked. Bring to a boil, add the vinegar and grapes. Cook for 5 minutes. Add the heavy cream, correct the seasoning and heat through. Do not let the sauce boil.

Arrange the mango slices around the chicken breasts. Pour the sauce over the chicken and serve immediately.

4 servings

Chicken-Breast Shish Kebab

PREPARATION: 15 MINUTES   COOKING: 15 MINUTES

1 clove garlic, chopped
1 bay leaf, crumbled
1 teaspoon thyme
Juice of 1 lemon
Salt and pepper
4 chicken breasts, boned

8 slices bacon
4 large tomatoes
1 large green pepper
3½-ounce can pitted black
  olives
1 tablespoon olive oil

In a bowl, make the marinade by mixing together the garlic, bay leaf, thyme, lemon juice, salt and pepper. Cut the chicken breasts into small pieces and add to the bowl. Mix well and set aside.

Just before broiling, wrap each piece of chicken with half a slice of bacon. Quarter the tomatoes and seed them by squeezing over a strainer set on top of a bowl. Cut the green pepper into 1-inch squares.

On each of 6 skewers put a piece each of chicken, tomato and green pepper, then a black olive. Brush with olive oil. Broil on one side for 6 minutes, then turn over, baste with some of the marinade and broil for 6 more minutes.

Serve with steamed vegetables and a green salad.

6 servings

Chicken Breasts with Straw Mushrooms and Avocado

PREPARATION: 15 MINUTES   COOKING: 25 MINUTES

This recipe was developed by a French friend, Elie Schulman, who was attached to the French embassy in New York. Elie loves to cook. After a month in New York he had discovered all the hidden treasures of Chinatown, Little Italy and Ninth Avenue vegetable and fruit stands. One day he made this delicate chicken dish using straw mushrooms, artichoke hearts and avocado—it was a meal in itself.

1 stick (¼ pound) butter
4 chicken breasts, boned and
  skinned
1 tablespoon dry Chinese wine
  or dry white vermouth
1 avocado
1-ounce can Chinese straw
  mushrooms*

1 can artichoke hearts
2 tablespoons Ginger Sauce
  (see p. 25)
1 teaspoon sesame oil
1 tablespoon soy sauce
Salt and pepper

In a large skillet, heat the butter and add the chicken breasts. Brown on all sides and add the wine or vermouth. Lower the heat and cook for 10 minutes.

Meanwhile, peel the avocado and slice into 1-inch-thick slices. Drain the straw mushrooms and artichoke hearts.

Add the ginger sauce, sesame oil and soy sauce to the skillet and mix well. Correct the seasoning by adding some salt and freshly ground pepper.

Add the mushrooms, avocado slices and artichoke hearts. Cover and cook for 5 minutes over medium heat until the mushrooms and avocados are heated through.

Carefully remove the chicken to a serving platter and surround it with the mushrooms, artichoke hearts and avocado. Pour the remaining sauce over the chicken. Serve immediately with steamed rice.

4 servings

*The Chinese straw mushroom is a delicate brown mushroom shaped like a closed umbrella. It is sold in the United States in cans in Chinese grocery stores and in some supermarkets.

Chaud-Froid of Chicken Breasts with Walnut Sauce

PREPARATION: 15 MINUTES   COOKING: 35 MINUTES

In this dish the chicken is cold but is served with a hot sauce.

1 quart chicken stock or broth
3 whole chicken breasts
Salt and pepper
¾ pound walnuts, very finely
  chopped
1 cup heavy cream
2 slices toasted white bread, cut
  into small pieces

Salt and pepper
SAUCE:
½ cup oil
¼ cup walnuts, coarsely
  chopped
1½ teaspoons paprika
Salt

In a large saucepan, bring the chicken stock to a boil. Add the chicken breasts and simmer, uncovered, for 20 minutes. Remove the chicken breasts to a serving platter. Remove the skin and sprinkle with salt and pepper. Refrigerate.

Boil the stock until it is reduced by half. Add the walnuts, cream and pieces of bread. Cook, stirring, for 5 minutes over low heat. Correct the seasoning. Purée the mixture in a blender or food processor and pour over the chicken. Refrigerate.

In a small saucepan, heat the oil and add the walnuts. Cook, stirring, until the walnuts are golden brown. Remove from heat and add the paprika and salt. Serve with the cold chicken.

4 servings

Spicy Chicken with Vinegar

PREPARATION: 15 MINUTES   COOKING: 45 MINUTES

The flavor of this recipe depends on the quality and richness of the vinegar. Choose a good Italian wine vinegar or dilute sharp vinegar with the leftover of a good burgundy.

4 tablespoons butter	1½ cup chicken stock or
1 tablespoon oil	bouillon
3½-pound chicken, cut into	1 teaspoon sugar
serving pieces	1 bay leaf
1 pound onions	2 sprigs parsley
1 teaspoon paprika	Salt and pepper
⅓ cup good wine vinegar	

In a kettle, heat the butter and oil. Add the chicken and brown on all sides. Remove to a platter.

Put the onions in the kettle and sauté for a few minutes—don't let the onions brown. Add the chicken, sprinkle with paprika and mix with a wooden spoon. Add the vinegar, stock, sugar, bay leaf, parsley, salt and pepper. Mix well and simmer for 40 minutes, or until the chicken is tender. Correct the seasoning.

Remove the chicken to a warm platter. Surround with the onions and discard the bay leaf and parsley. Pour the sauce over the chicken and serve.

4 servings

Chicken Fricassee

PREPARATION: 20 MINUTES   COOKING: 45 MINUTES

4 tablespoons butter
2 medium-size onions, chopped
1 clove garlic, chopped
3-pound chicken, cut into small
  serving pieces
Salt and pepper
3 tablespoons flour
1 cup dry white wine
½ cup chicken broth or bouillon

1 bay leaf
½ teaspoon nutmeg
1 teaspoon thyme
¼ cup Creme Fraîche (see
  p. xvi) or heavy cream
2 egg yolks
Juice of half a lemon
Chopped parsley for garnish

Preheat the oven to 375°. In a large skillet, heat the butter and add the onions and garlic. Sauté until transparent but not browned. Add the chicken pieces and brown on all sides; sprinkle with salt and pepper. Sprinkle the chicken with flour; mix well with a wooden spoon and cook for 5 minutes. Add the wine and broth and mix well. Add the bay leaf, nutmeg and thyme. Bring to a boil, then cover and bake 30 minutes.

Put the chicken on a warm platter. Strain the sauce through a very fine sieve set over a saucepan.

In a small bowl, beat the crème fraîche (or cream) with the egg yolks. Add the lemon juice and stir well. Slowly heat the sauce in the saucepan and add the creamy mixture, stirring constantly and making sure it doesn't come to a boil. Correct the seasoning with salt and pepper. Pour the sauce over the chicken. Sprinkle the chicken with the parsley and serve immediately with buttered turnips.

4 servings

Chicken with Cherries

PREPARATION: 30 MINUTES   COOKING: 1 HOUR AND 10 MINUTES

When my daughter Juliette was eight years old, she requested a cherry tree for her birthday. We planted what we thought was a dwarf cherry tree. In the years that followed, the cherry tree grew and grew. It flowered but had not produced any cherries in nine years. "No bees," someone said. "You need another cherry tree," my neighbor said. But I refused to plant a mate because the tree had taken over the garden. Last summer someone nearby must have had some bees in his or her garden, because we collected nearly thirty pounds of cherries. We ate cherries with everything, including chicken!

3 tablespoons butter
2½-pound roasting chicken
2 shallots, chopped
3 tablespoons chopped parsley
Pinch of nutmeg
Salt and pepper

Juice of 1 lemon
2 pounds cherries
¾ cup white wine
Pinch of cinnamon
2 tablespoons sugar

In a large saucepan, heat the butter and add the chicken. Brown on all sides, then remove the chicken to a platter.

Put the shallots and parsley in the saucepan and sauté over medium heat until the shallots are transparent. Return the chicken to the saucepan; sprinkle with nutmeg, salt, pepper and lemon juice, and simmer, covered, for 1 hour, or until the chicken is tender.

Meanwhile, pit the cherries. Put the wine, cinnamon and sugar in a saucepan and bring to a boil. Add the cherries and cook for 20 minutes. Transfer the chicken to a serving platter and pour the cherry sauce over it.

6 servings

Chicken Giblets with Garlic and Cream

PREPARATION: 20 MINUTES   COOKING: 35 MINUTES

This is an old Southern French recipe. As long as you are not the only one to eat garlic, don't be afraid to kiss your friends after they have also had this delicious dish.

2 whole bulbs garlic
2 pounds giblets (gizzards,
   hearts, wings)
1 pound turnips, diced
2 tablespoons butter
3 shallots, chopped
1 cup chicken stock or bouillon

1 cup white wine
Salt and pepper
1 teaspoon tarragon
Juice of 1 lemon
¼ cup heavy cream
Pinch of cayenne
Chopped parsley for garnish

Separate but do not peel the garlic cloves. Bring to a boil ⅓ cup water; add the garlic cloves and cook them until all the water has evaporated. Rinse with cold running water and drain. Peel and mash them with a fork. Set aside.

Slice the hearts and cut the wings in two pieces. In a saucepan, heat the butter and add the giblets. Brown on all sides. Add the turnips and shallots and cook for 3 minutes more. Add the stock and wine; add salt and pepper. Cover and cook over medium heat for 30 minutes, stirring from time to time.

Meanwhile, add the tarragon and lemon juice to the garlic purée. Mix well, then stir in the cream.

When the giblets are tender, remove them to a hot platter. Add the garlic-cream sauce to the cooking juice in the saucepan and cook, stirring all the while, until the sauce thickens. Correct the seasoning and add cayenne. Pour the sauce over the giblets, sprinkle with chopped parsley and serve immediately.

4 servings

Chicken Dodoma

PREPARATION: 20 MINUTES   COOKING: 1 HOUR

In Dodoma, Tanzania, the Indians make this chicken with cashew nuts. Trying the recipe again in New York, I found that using almonds gives it a more delicate flavor.

¼ cup fresh bread crumbs	¼ cup chopped almonds
1 pint heavy cream	1 teaspoon chopped fresh ginger
½ cup raisins	3-pound chicken
3½ tablespoons butter	Salt and pepper
2 egg yolks	½ cup chicken bouillon or stock

Preheat the oven to 375°. Soak the bread crumbs in the cream. Soak the raisins in 1 cup hot water. In a small saucepan, melt the butter and add to the cream, then pour the mixture back into the saucepan. Beat over medium heat with a whisk until the mixture is foamy—do not let it boil.

Remove from heat and add the egg yolks, one at a time, while continuing to beat. Add the almonds, ginger and raisins (drained), salt and pepper, and mix well.

Pat the chicken dry with paper towels. Sprinkle with salt and pepper. Stuff the chicken with the cream mixture and sew up the opening. Roast in a roasting pan with ½ cup bouillon for 1 hour.

Carve and arrange on a serving platter. Serve with Hot Leek Salad (see p. 226).

4 servings

Poulet à l'Ail (Chicken with Garlic)

PREPARATION: 20 MINUTES   COOKING: 1½ HOURS

Roasting a chicken on top of garlic gives the chicken an extraordinary flavor. Serve the chicken with the garlic (the garlic cloves will be smooth as a purée).

Ail au Four (see p. 191)
3½-pound roasting chicken
Juice and peel of half a lemon
Salt and pepper
2 tablespoons butter

4 ounces farmer cheese
3 tablespoons sour cream
3 scallions, chopped
Parsley for garnish

Preheat the oven to 375°. Make the ail au four (baked garlic) according to the recipe, but use a pan large enough to also hold the chicken and bake the garlic for only 45 minutes instead of 1¼ hours.

Meanwhile, prepare the chicken. Wipe the chicken inside and out with paper towels. Rub the cavity and outer skin with the lemon juice; rub the cavity with the lemon peel. Place 2 tablespoons butter under the breast skin and sprinkle the chicken with salt and pepper.

Place the chicken in the center of the baking pan and surround it with the garlic bulbs. Bake for 45 minutes, or until golden brown and when the chicken thigh is pierced with a fork the juice runs clear.

Carve the chicken and place on a warm platter. Surround with the garlic bulbs and garnish with parsley. In a small bowl, mix the cheese with the sour cream and scallions, and serve with the chicken.

4 servings

Roast Chicken in Beer

PREPARATION: 10 MINUTES   COOKING: 1 HOUR

While in Tanzania we lived in a community of expatriates of all nationalities. I became very friendly with a Bulgarian lady named Tremka. The roast chicken in beer she served us one night was delicious. It was her mother's recipe, which she was quite willing to share with me.

3½-pound roasting chicken

Salt and pepper

2 tablespoons butter

2 cups beer

1 bunch watercress for garnish

Preheat the oven to 375°. Wipe the chicken and sprinkle salt and pepper in the cavity and on the skin. Put 1 tablespoon butter under the breast skin and rub the remaining butter over the breast and thigh. Place the chicken in a roasting pan, pour the beer around it and bake for 1 hour, or until the juice runs clear when the thigh is pricked with a fork. Baste the chicken from time to time. If the beer dries out, add ½ cup more.

Carve the chicken and arrange on a serving platter. Pour the juice in the pan over the chicken. Garnish with watercress and serve.

4 servings

Roast Chicken with Juniper Berries

PREPARATION: REFRIGERATION   COOKING: 1 HOUR AND 20 MINUTES
OVERNIGHT; 15 MINUTES

This may seem like a strange recipe, but it transforms an ordinary chicken into a delicious dish. I was spending a weekend in the country in May when, taking a walk, I spotted a pine tree. The edges of its branches had a lot of new shoots, and the smell was lovely. I cut a small branch and brought it back home. I remembered eating in my childhood a chicken that was cooked wrapped in pine needles. I tried making a dish the same way, and added juniper berries. It turned out to be marvelous.

A handful of pine needles

4-pound roasting chicken

5 tablespoons butter

4 shallots, chopped

2 tablespoons juniper berries

Salt and pepper

Spread the pine needles over the chicken and wrap in foil. Refrigerate overnight.

The next day, remove the pine needles from the chicken. Preheat the oven to 375°.

In a saucepan, heat the butter and add the shallots. Crush the juniper berries and add to the butter. Cook, stirring, for 5 minutes over medium heat. Remove from heat.

Place the chicken in a roasting pan and spread the buttery mixture over the chicken. Sprinkle with salt and pepper.

Bake the chicken for 1 hour and 10 minutes, or until a thigh pricked with a fork gives off clear juice.

Carve the chicken and arrange on a warm serving platter. Add ½ cup water to the roasting pan, and stir over medium heat while scraping the pan. Correct the seasoning with salt and pepper and pour over the chicken. Serve with baked potatoes.

6 servings

Gratin of Chicken with Endives

PREPARATION: 15 MINUTES   COOKING: 45 MINUTES

3½-pound chicken	2 tablespoons sugar
6 tablespoons butter	4 slices Virginia ham
2 tablespoons oil	¼ pound grated Swiss cheese
8 endives	Salt and pepper
Juice of 1 lemon	

Preheat the oven to 375°. Wipe the chicken inside and out with paper towels. In a small bowl, mash 2 tablespoons butter with the oil. Spread the butter on the chicken breast and thighs and sprinkle with salt and pepper. Put the chicken in a roasting pan and bake for 40 minutes, or until the drumsticks are tender and move easily in their sockets. Baste the chicken with its own juice two or three times during the cooking.

Meanwhile, clean the endives under cold running water and dry them with paper towels.

In a large saucepan, heat 3 tablespoons butter and brown the endives on all sides. Pour the lemon juice over them and sprinkle with sugar. Lower the heat and simmer for 40 minutes, or until they are tender when pierced with a fork.

Remove the chicken from the oven and carve into serving pieces. Line a gratin dish with the ham. Put the endives on top of the ham and then the chicken. Add 3 tablespoons water to the roasting pan. Bring to a boil, then stir well while scraping the sides. Pour the juice over the chicken. Sprinkle the chicken with the cheese and dot with the remaining butter. Put the dish under the broiler for a few minutes. Serve with a green salad.

4 servings

Salt Chicken with Ginger Sauce

PREPARATION: 10 MINUTES   COOKING: 1¾ HOURS

I had this dish many years ago in Paris. My hostess told me that she had brought back the recipe from a trip to China. A large white mound that was brought to the table was quite impressive, and it was fun trying to guess what was hidden inside.

The dish requires large quantities of sea salt (found in natural-food stores but, unfortunately, very expensive), but kosher salt, available in all supermarkets, can be substituted. Chicken cooked this way is golden brown and not at all salty, just juicy and tender.

5½- to 6½-pound roasting   1 truffle (optional)
  chicken   4 pounds kosher salt or sea salt
Pepper   Ginger Sauce (see p. 25)
2 tablespoons cognac

Preheat the oven to 475°. Wipe the chicken inside and out with paper towels. Rub the inside of the chicken with pepper and cognac. If you have a truffle on hand, cut it into slices and slide the slices under the breast skin.

Pour two pounds of kosher salt into an ovenproof casserole and put the chicken on top. Cover the chicken with the remaining salt. Bake, uncovered, for 1¾ hours.

Remove the chicken from the oven and turn the casserole over onto a large tray. Break the salt crust and put the chicken on a warm platter. Carve the chicken and serve with ginger sauce.

6 servings

Chicken Sautéed with Beets

PREPARATION: 15 MINUTES   COOKING: 50 MINUTES

4-pound chicken, cut into   2 cloves
  serving pieces   1 onion, quartered
2 cups chicken stock or bouillon Salt and pepper
2 tablespoons cornstarch   4 medium-size canned beets
1 cup dry white wine   ½ cup heavy cream
2 bay leaves   Juice of 1 lemon
½ teaspoon thyme   1 sprig watercress for garnish
2 cloves garlic, crushed

Put the chicken pieces in a casserole and cover with chicken stock. Mix the cornstarch with wine and add to the chicken. Add the bay leaves, thyme, garlic, cloves and onion. Bring to a boil. Add salt and pepper and simmer, uncovered, for 35 minutes, or until the chicken is done.

Purée the beets with the cream in a blender or food processor.

Remove the chicken to a platter. Strain the cooking liquid into a saucepan and add the beet purée and lemon juice. Correct the seasoning and heat—do not let it boil. Pour the sauce over the chicken and garnish with watercress. Serve with steamed buttered potatoes.

4 servings

Sautéed Chicken with Celery

PREPARATION: 20 MINUTES   COOKING: 1 HOUR

4 tablespoons goose fat* or
  chicken fat
4-pound chicken, cut into
  serving pieces
½ pound tomatoes

½ pound onions, chopped
4 cloves garlic, peeled
6 celery stalks, cut into 4-inch
  pieces
Salt and pepper

In a casserole, heat the goose or chicken fat and add the chicken. Sauté until golden brown. Remove with a slotted spoon onto a plate and set aside.

Cut the tomatoes in half and seed them by squeezing over a strainer set on top of a bowl. Add the onions, tomatoes, garlic and celery to the fat. Add salt and pepper and stir with a wooden spoon. Reduce the heat and simmer for 30 minutes. Place the chicken on top of the vegetables and cook, covered, for another 30 minutes.

Remove the chicken to a serving platter and surround it with the celery. Pour the sauce over the chicken and serve immediately.

4 servings

*See p. 137 for rendering and preserving goose fat saved from preparing goose recipes.

Sautéed Chicken with Madeira and Tomatoes

PREPARATION: 20 MINUTES   COOKING: 45 MINUTES

This is a traditional recipe served in Italy and Spain. The best I ever had was in a small trattoria outside of Naples. I went back so many times that the cook, Augustina, finally gave me the recipe.

3 tablespoons butter	¾ cup Madeira
2 tablespoons oil	1 tablespoon tomato paste
3-pound chicken, cut into serving pieces	1 cup dry white wine
	6 tomatoes
1 onion, chopped	Salt and pepper
2 shallots, chopped	2 tablespoons chopped parsley

In a casserole, heat 1½ tablespoons butter and 1 tablespoon oil. Add the pieces of chicken and sauté until they are browned on all sides. Add the onion and shallots and stir with a wooden spoon. Add the Madeira and mix well. Mix together the tomato paste and the white wine and add to the chicken. Cover and simmer for 30 minutes, or until the chicken is tender.

Meanwhile, dip the tomatoes in boiling water. Cool and peel. Quarter the tomatoes and seed them by squeezing over a strainer set on top of a bowl.

In a skillet, heat the remaining butter and oil. Add the tomatoes and simmer for 15 minutes. Sprinkle with salt and pepper.

Place the pieces of chicken on a warm platter and strain the cooking sauce over them. Put the tomatoes on top of the chicken and sprinkle with parsley. Serve with steamed cauliflower.

4 servings.

Sautéed Chicken Livers with Egyptian Rice

PREPARATION: 10 MINUTES   COOKING: 30 MINUTES

My Egyptian grandmother always said that rice should be fried first and slightly browned before adding the water—it would then turn fluffy and never stick together. Her system never failed. Choose long-grain rice for best results.

1 tablespoon oil
1½ cups rice
4 cups boiling chicken stock or
  water
Salt
Freshly ground pepper

1 pound chicken livers
4 tablespoons butter
½ teaspoon cumin
½ cup heavy cream
Chopped parsley for garnish

Heat the oil in a heavy saucepan. Add the rice and, with a wooden spoon, stir continuously until the rice starts to brown and puff up. Add the boiling chicken stock or water, 1 teaspoon salt and pepper. Stir once more, cover and simmer for 20 minutes. If the rice is still a bit hard, add ¼ cup water and simmer until ready to serve.

Meanwhile, trim and pat the livers dry with paper towels. Dust lightly with flour. In a large skillet, heat the butter and add the livers. Sauté over high heat until browned. Sprinkle with salt, pepper and cumin and cook for a few minutes more, stirring gently so as not to break the livers. Add the cream, stir well and turn off the heat.

If you have a ring mold, fill it with the rice, pressing it down. If you don't have one, any bowl will do; place a cup upside down in the center of the bowl and place the rice all around. Unmold the rice on a round platter and fill the center with the livers. Sprinkle with parsley and serve.

4 servings

Chicken Stuffed with Boudin (Blood Sausage)

PREPARATION: 15 MINUTES   COOKING: 1 HOUR

In the neighborhood of les Halles in Paris at the time when the market still existed, you could go very late at night and have broiled boudin with French fries. Blood sausages, which are eaten in South America as well as in Europe, can be found in Italian or German butcher shops. If you have never had boudin, this is a way to try it the first time. The chicken stuffed with boudin becomes tender and juicy.

3½-pound roasting chicken
¾ pound blood sausage
3 tablespoons butter
1 onion, thinly chopped
2 tablespoons Crème Fraîche
  (see p. xvi)

1 egg yolk
Salt and pepper
2 tablespoons oil
Chopped parsley for garnish

Preheat the oven to 375°. Wash and pat the chicken dry with paper towels. Remove the skin of the sausage.

Put the butter in a skillet, and when the butter is foamy, add the onion and sauté until golden brown. Add the sausage and the crème fraîche. Mix well and cook over low heat for 5 minutes, stirring from time to time. Remove from heat and add the egg yolk. Mix well.

Sprinkle the chicken inside and out with salt and pepper and stuff it with the sausage meat. Brush the skin with oil and wrap in foil. Bake for 1 hour.

Unwrap the chicken, carve and place on a serving platter with the sausage in the center. Sprinkle with parsley and serve.

4 servings

Chicken Stuffed with Garlic Cloves

PREPARATION: 15 MINUTES   COOKING: 1½ HOURS

1 large roasting chicken
20 cloves garlic
1 bay leaf
¼ teaspoon thyme

2 pounds coarse salt
2 tablespoons oil
1 cup Mayonnaise (see p. 29)

Preheat the oven to 375°. Wash and pat the chicken dry with paper towels. Peel the garlic cloves. Place the garlic, bay leaf and thyme inside the cavity and close with skewers or sew with a needle and thread.

Pour half the salt in a large casserole (preferably earthenware), big enough to hold the chicken. Sprinkle the oil on the chicken and place the chicken on top of the salt. Cover with the remaining salt. Bake, uncovered, for 1½ hours.

Meanwhile, make the mayonnaise.

Remove the casserole from the oven and discard the salt. Cut the chicken into serving pieces and keep it warm. Remove the garlic cloves from the cavity and set aside.

Put the mayonnaise in the top of a double boiler and heat through. Purée the garlic cloves and add to the mayonnaise. Serve the chicken with the mayonnaise.

6 servings

Stuffed Chicken with Lemon Sauce

PREPARATION: 20 MINUTES   COOKING: 1 HOUR 15 MINUTES

4½-pound roasting chicken
3 slices Italian bread
¾ cup milk
¾-inch-thick slice ham
2 tablespoons butter
¼ pound chicken livers
1 shallot
2 cloves garlic
3 sprigs parsley
1 egg

Salt and pepper
¼ teaspoon nutmeg
2 quarts chicken stock or
   bouillon
SAUCE:
3 tablespoons butter
2 tablespoons flour
3 egg yolks
¼ cup heavy cream
Juice of 1 lemon

Wipe the chicken with paper towels and remove all loose fat. Soak the bread in the milk. Cut the ham into small pieces.

In a skillet, heat the butter and add the livers. Sauté for 2 or 3 minutes over high heat to sear them, then turn off the heat.

Put the livers, shallot, parsley, ham, egg, bread in the container of a food processor or blender. Run the machine for 30 seconds. Add salt, pepper and nutmeg and process for 20 seconds more. Stuff the chicken with the mixture and close the cavity by sewing or using skewers. Place the chicken in a large ovenproof casserole, cover with the stock and cook for 1 hour.

Take the casserole out of the oven and remove 1 quart stock. Put the chicken back in the oven and cook for 30 minutes more. Strain the quart of stock through a very fine sieve and pour it into a saucepan over high heat and boil until it is reduced by half.

Meanwhile, make the sauce. In another saucepan, melt 2 tablespoons butter; add the flour and cook over low heat for a few seconds. Slowly add the reduced stock, stirring all the while, and simmer for 5 minutes. Add salt and pepper. In a bowl, mix the egg yolks with the cream and add to the sauce, stirring with a wooden spoon. Add lemon juice and mix well.

Remove the chicken from the casserole and carve it. Place it on a warm platter with the stuffing in the center and serve with the sauce in a sauceboat and a bowl of steamed rice.

6 servings

Cornish Hens with Glazed Turnips

PREPARATION: 20 MINUTES   COOKING: 50 MINUTES

You can use squabs instead of Cornish hens. The dish would then be more expensive, but it will be superb.

10 tablespoons butter	1 teaspoon flour
4 slices bacon, diced	1 bay leaf
4 Cornish hens	2 sprigs parsley
Salt and pepper	6 small onions
3 tablespoons brandy	1 pound small turnips
¾ cup dry white wine	1 teaspoon sugar
1 cup chicken stock or bouillon	

In a large skillet, heat 5 tablespoons butter and add the bacon. Sauté for a few minutes. Add the Cornish hens and brown on all sides. Sprinkle with salt and pepper. Pour the brandy over the hens and ignite. Transfer the hens to a platter. Add the wine and chicken stock to the skillet. Sprinkle with flour and mix well. Put the hens back in the skillet and add the bay leaf and parsley. Cover and simmer for 30 minutes.

Meanwhile, heat 5 tablespoons butter in another skillet. Add the onions and turnips and sauté for 5 minutes. Sprinkle with sugar, and while shaking the skillet, cook over medium heat for 10 minutes, or until the onions and the turnips are caramelized.

Add the onions and turnips to the skillet containing the hens. Cook for 15 minutes, checking from time to time to see that there is enough liquid—add some chicken stock if necessary. Correct the seasoning. The dish is ready when the turnips are tender.

Serve the hens surrounded with the onions and turnips.

4 servings

Canard aux Oignons   (Duck with Onions)

PREPARATION: 20 MINUTES   COOKING: 1 HOUR AND 20 MINUTES

Ducks in America are fatter than those in Europe. In order to avoid having layers of fat remaining under the duck's skin when it is cooked, remove the excess fat* found around the opening to the cavity; fill the cavity with paper towels and refrigerate, uncovered, for two days. This will dry the skin. This procedure is excellent for whatever recipe for cooking duck you may want to use. In this recipe the bread inside the cavity will also absorb much of the remaining fat while the duck is cooking.

3 cloves garlic
3 slices stale French or Italian
  bread
3-pound duck
12 slices bacon
3 tablespoons butter
2 16-ounce cans or 2 pounds
  small white onions

1 tablespoon granulated sugar
2 tablespoons wine vinegar
1 cup chicken stock or bouillon
Salt and pepper
Watercress for garnish

Peel the garlic cloves and crush them with the flat side of a knife. Rub the slices of bread with the garlic. Remove excess fat from the duck and dry the duck with paper towels. Stuff with the slices of bread and set aside. Roll the slices of bacon and tie them with string.

In a saucepan large enough to hold the duck, heat 1 tablespoon butter and slowly brown the bacon over medium heat. Remove and drain on paper towels. Prick the duck skin all over with a fork. Put the duck in the bacon fat and brown on all sides. Cover and cook over low heat for 30 minutes.

Meanwhile, heat the remaining 2 tablespoons butter in a saucepan and sauté the onions over medium heat; when heated through, add the sugar and vinegar. Stir with a wooden spoon and cook for 5 minutes more over high heat.

Remove most of the fat from the saucepan containing the duck. Put the onions and stock in the saucepan and simmer for 30 minutes. Correct the seasoning.

Remove the duck from the saucepan and cut into serving pieces. Place on a warm platter and surround with the onions.

Heat the bacon in a skillet for a few minutes. Remove the string and place the bacon around the duck. Garnish with watercress. Strain the sauce and pour over the duck.

4 servings

*The fat can be rendered, cooked with chopped onion and strained to keep refrigerated for future use, as when cooking cabbage or Brussels sprouts.

Capon Stuffed with Chestnuts

PREPARATION: CHESTNUTS SOAKED   COOKING: 1 HOUR AND 40 MINUTES
OVERNIGHT; 25 MINUTES

The stuffing in this recipe can be used for duck, goose* or turkey. I use dried Italian chestnuts, which are already peeled. These are readily available in Italian grocery stores.

Place the chestnuts the night before in a bowl and cover with boiling water.

¼ pound dried Chinese mushrooms
¾ pound dried chestnuts, soaked the night before
1 stick (¼ pound) butter
2 tablespoons brandy
2 cups chicken stock or bouillon
Salt and pepper
5-pound capon

2 tablespoons soy sauce
1 bag ready-made bread crumbs for stuffing or 2 cups fresh bread crumbs
2 medium-size onions, chopped
2 celery stalks, chopped
1½ teaspoons thyme
½ cup heavy cream
Watercress for garnish

Soak the mushrooms for 20 minutes in a bowl of hot water. Drain the chestnuts. In a large saucepan, heat 4 tablespoons butter and add the chestnuts. Mix well. Add the brandy and ignite. Add 1 cup chicken stock, salt and pepper and cook, covered, for 20 minutes over medium heat, stirring once in a while.

Preheat the oven to 375°. Wash the capon and pat dry with paper towels. Put 1 tablespoon butter under the breast skin. Rub the capon with the soy sauce inside and out.

Drain the mushrooms and save the water in which they have been soaked. Cut off the stems and cut each mushroom into two or more pieces depending on their size.

Put the bread crumbs in a bowl. Add the mushrooms and their water, the chestnuts with the liquid in the saucepan, onions, celery, thyme, salt, pepper and cream. Mix well and correct the seasoning.

Stuff the capon with the bread-crumb mixture. Close the cavity by sewing or skewering. Rub the skin with the remaining butter and bake for 1 hour and 20 minutes, or until a thigh pricked with a skewer gives off clear juice. Baste from time to time with the remaining chicken stock.

Remove the capon from the oven and place on a heated platter. Garnish with watercress. Remove the fat from the sauce and serve the sauce in a sauceboat along with the capon.

6 servings

*If you are using goose, stuff the neck according to the recipe on p. 139.

Braised Duck with Green Peppers

PREPARATION: 15 MINUTES   COOKING: 1½ HOURS

4- to 5-pound duck
3 tablespoons butter
4 tomatoes
2 onions
4 green peppers

1 tablespoon flour
2 cups dry white wine
1 teaspoon paprika
Salt and pepper

Dry the duck inside and out with paper towels. Remove any excess fat.*
Heat the butter in a large saucepan and brown the duck, breast side first,
for 10 minutes over medium heat, then turn it over and brown for
another 10 minutes.

Meanwhile, prepare the vegetables. Cut the tomatoes in half and seed
them by squeezing over a strainer set on top of a bowl, then chop them.
Peel and chop the onions. Slice and seed the green peppers.

Put the duck on a platter and keep it warm in a turned-off oven.

Pour out the fat from the saucepan, leaving 2 tablespoons of fat in
the pan. Add the onions and sauté over medium heat until they are
transparent. Add the tomatoes and stir well. Sprinkle the mixture with
the flour and mix well. Slowly add the wine, stirring all the while with
a wooden spoon, and bring to a boil. Add the paprika and the salt and
pepper to taste, then simmer for 5 minutes. Strain the sauce over a bowl
through a very fine sieve. Pour the sauce back into the saucepan and add
the duck. Simmer, covered, for 50 minutes, or until the juice from the
thigh runs clear when it is pricked with a fork. Ten minutes before the
duck is ready, add the peppers. Cook for 10 more minutes.

Remove the duck from the saucepan and cut into four serving pieces.
Put the duck on a warm platter and surround with the peppers. Pour
3 tablespoons of the sauce over the duck and serve with the remaining
sauce in a sauceboat, accompanied by fresh buttered noodles.

4 servings

*The excess fat from the duck can be slowly melted in a heavy-bottomed saucepan
along with some chopped onion. You can add to it the fat from browning the duck. Strain
the fat and store it in a tightly sealed container in the refrigerator. This fat is excellent
(if you are not on a diet!) for cooking Brussels sprouts, cabbage or home-fried potatoes.

Duck with Apples

PREPARATION: 15 MINUTES   COOKING: 1 HOUR

Bob Morris is a sculptor who is also an excellent hunter. Once he brought back ten ducks. We all sat in the kitchen to pluck them, and for weeks we would find duck feathers in the most unusual places. We cooked each duck differently. The general consensus was that the following recipe was by far the best. We tried it again with regular duck and found the dish even more delicious, because wild ducks have a tendency to be tough.

3½-pound duck   8 cloves
1 stick (¼ pound) butter   6 tablespoons Scotch
4 apples   Salt and pepper
½ cup orange marmalade

Preheat the oven to 450°. Dry the duck with paper towels and prick the skin all over with a fork. Sprinkle the duck inside and out with salt and pepper. Spread half a stick of butter all over the duck and bake for 1 hour, turning it over several times and basting it with the melted butter.

Meanwhile, peel and core the apples. Cut in half and stick each half with a clove. In a skillet, heat the remaining butter. Add the apple halves and sauté until golden brown.

Remove the duck to a warm serving platter. Surround the duck with the apple halves. Remove the fat from the juice in the baking pan.

Add to the apples in the skillet the marmalade, Scotch and the drippings from the roasting pan. Bring to a boil while stirring. Correct the seasoning, pour into a sauceboat and serve with the duck.

4 servings

Michel Warren's Duck with Cucumber

PREPARATION: 15 MINUTES   COOKING: 1½ HOURS

Michel Warren was an eccentric cook; he once served us a duck cooked with cucumbers, whisky and wine. What a sumptuous meal for four people!

Prepare the duck two days in advance: Fill the cavity with paper towels and refrigerate, uncovered.

6 tablespoons butter
3½-pound duck
1 large cucumber
6 cloves
½ teaspoon thyme

Salt and pepper
4 onions, quartered
1 tablespoon flour
1 tablespoon Scotch
1 cup white wine

In a large saucepan, heat 2 tablespoons butter and add the duck. Brown on all sides. Reduce the heat and continue cooking while preparing the cucumber.

Peel the cucumber and cut into 6 pieces. Put the cucumber in a saucepan of boiling water and boil for 10 minutes. Drain. Stick a clove in each piece of cucumber and place the cucumber pieces around the duck. Add 2 tablespoons butter, thyme, and salt and pepper. Add the onions and 2 tablespoons water. Cook for 1 hour over medium heat, turning the duck from time to time.

Remove the duck to a platter and cut into serving pieces. Surround with the cucumbers and onions. Keep warm while preparing the sauce.

In a small saucepan, heat 2 tablespoons butter and add the flour. Cook over medium heat, stirring all the while, until the flour takes on a golden color.

Remove the fat from the duck sauce and pour the sauce into the saucepan containing the flour, stirring all the while. Add the Scotch and wine. Mix well, correct the seasoning and cook for 5 minutes.

Cover the duck with the sauce and serve immediately. Serve with steamed new potatoes and a salad.

4 servings

Fricassee of Goose

PREPARATION: 25 MINUTES   COOKING: 2 HOURS AND 20 MINUTES

Winter is the time to eat goose. For a flavorful fricassee, choose a small goose no larger than 6 pounds.

6-pound goose
1 stick (¼ pound) butter
3 onions, quartered
3 green Delicious apples, peeled,
  cored and quartered
Salt and pepper
1 teaspoon sugar

3 tablespoons apple brandy or
  brandy
3 cups hard cider
1 teaspoon thyme
1 bay leaf
3 sprigs parsley

Have the butcher cut the goose into serving pieces. Remove excess fat (save it so that you can render it by following the recipe below).

Heat the butter in a large casserole. Add the pieces of goose and sauté over high heat until they are golden brown, then transfer them to a platter.

Put the onions and apples in the casserole and sauté until the onions are golden brown. Pour off all but 3 tablespoons of the fat.

Put the goose back in the casserole. Sprinkle with salt, freshly ground pepper and sugar. Add the brandy and ignite. Reduce the heat and cook for 20 minutes, stirring from time to time. Add the cider, thyme, bay leaf and parsley. Cover and simmer for 2 hours. Add more cider if the sauce reduces too much. Remove the goose to a serving platter, pour the sauce over it and serve.

6 servings

Goose Fat

PREPARATION: 10 MINUTES   COOKING: 20 MINUTES

Goose fat cut into ½-inch cubes   Salt and pepper
3 onions, chopped with their
  skins

Put the goose fat in a heavy saucepan over medium heat. When it is half melted, add the onions and cook for 20 minutes, or until they are dark brown. Strain through a very fine sieve. Add salt and freshly ground pepper to taste. Cool and pour into a glass jar. Tightly seal the jar and refrigerate.

Goose fat is excellent for cooking vegetables such as cabbage.

About 1½ cups

Christmas Goose with Sauerkraut

PREPARATION: 1 HOUR   COOKING: 2 HOURS

In France, goose is traditionally served for Christmas dinner. In my family, my grandmother—and later, my mother—served a goose that had been rubbed with coarse salt and garlic, then roasted and served with sauerkraut cooked in champagne. I still use this recipe for our Christmas dinner, and I keep the goose fat to cook some vegetables for the remaining winter months.

9- to 10-pound goose
¼ cup kosher salt
6 cloves garlic, finely chopped
3 pounds sauerkraut
¼ pound smoked bacon
10 peppercorns

1 bottle champagne
2 cups chicken bouillon or stock
4 large cloves garlic, slivered
Salt and pepper
Parsley for garnish

Preheat the oven to 350°. Wash the goose under cold running water and pat it dry with paper towels. Mix the salt with the chopped garlic and rub the goose inside and out with the mixture. Let the goose stand for 1 hour.

Meanwhile, wash the sauerkraut and drain well. Cut the bacon into small cubes. In a large saucepan, sauté the bacon over medium heat until it is browned. Remove with a slotted spoon. Put the sauerkraut and peppercorns in the saucepan and mix well. Add the champagne and simmer for 1 hour.

Meanwhile, wipe the salt off the goose, inside and out. Prick the skin all over with a fork, then cut slits in the skin with the sharp point of a knife and insert slivers of garlic. Place the goose on a wire rack in a roasting pan and add 1 cup bouillon. Bake for 1 hour, basting the goose from time to time.

Remove all the juice from the roasting pan and add another cup of chicken stock. Cook the goose, basting frequently, for 1 hour more, or until golden brown.

Remove the goose from the pan, carve and arrange on a serving platter. Heat the sauerkraut through. Surround the goose with the sauerkraut and garnish with parsley. Remove the fat from the liquid in the roasting pan. Add ½ cup water, salt and pepper and heat through. Serve the sauce with the goose along with braised Brussels sprouts and braised endives.

6 to 8 servings

Stew of Goose Giblets with Dried Fruit

PREPARATION: 15 MINUTES   COOKING: 1½ HOURS

When cooking a goose for Christmas or New Year's, set aside the neck, gizzard, heart and wing tips for making this dish. Keep the liver for stuffing the neck (see below).

1 tablespoon goose fat
1 goose neck, cut into 1-inch
  pieces
1 heart, cut in two
1 gizzard, cut into several pieces
2 wing tips
6 medium onions, quartered
1 tablespoon brandy

1 tablespoon flour
2 cups chicken stock or bouillon
Salt and pepper
1 bay leaf
1 teaspoon thyme
1 cup mixture of dried apricots,
  apples, pears

In a heavy saucepan, heat the goose fat and add the giblets. Brown on all sides. Add the onions and brown them. Add the brandy and ignite. When the flame dies down, sprinkle with the flour, mix well, and cook for 3 minutes. Add the stock, salt, pepper, bay leaf and thyme. Bring the stock to a boil, lower the flame and simmer for 1½ hours, stirring from time to time.

Meanwhile, put the dried fruit in a bowl and cover with boiling water. Let stand for 15 minutes. Half an hour before the stew is ready, drain the fruit and add to the stew. Just before serving, correct the seasoning.

Serve with boiled potatoes and a green salad.

2 generous servings

Stuffed Goose Neck

PREPARATION: 20 MINUTES   COOKING: 1 HOUR

This dish is probably the best reason to buy a goose for Christmas or New Year's. It is delicious hot or cold.

1 goose neck skin
2 sweet Italian sausage
1 goose liver, coarsely chopped
1 clove garlic, finely chopped
1 tablespoon chopped parsley

2 tablespoons bread crumbs
2 shallots, finely chopped
½ tablespoon brandy
½ tablespoon tarragon
Salt and pepper

Preheat the oven to 375°.

If you order a fresh goose, ask the butcher to keep the neck skin intact while removing the neck itself. When buying a frozen goose, first cut off the neck and then carefully separate the neck from the skin so as not to rip the skin. Lay the skin flat and remove the veins and fat. Fold the skin in two, and using a needle with heavy thread, sew it up, starting from the narrow end and leaving an opening for the stuffing.

Put all the remaining ingredients in a bowl and mix well. Stuff the neck and sew up the opening.

Roast the neck in a small baking pan with 1 tablespoon goose fat for 1 hour, or until the skin is dark brown.

Remove from the oven and cool at room temperature. If served hot, slice the neck when it is cold, then heat it in the oven for 5 minutes. If served cold, refrigerate for 1 hour and serve on a bed of lettuce along with French mustard.

4 servings

Turkey Fondue

PREPARATION: 30 MINUTES   COOKING: 45 MINUTES

Around Thanksgiving you can often find slices of uncooked turkey breast in supermarkets. This recipe is quick and easy to make. Serve it with a good red wine.

2 tea bags
12 pitted prunes
2 medium-size eggplants
Salt
1 stick (¼ pound) butter
½ pound mushrooms

2 teaspoons tarragon
Salt and pepper
12 slices turkey breast
3 tablespoons chicken stock or
    bouillon

Bring 2 cups water to a boil and steep the tea bags. Add the prunes and soak for 15 minutes. Drain.

Meanwhile, peel the eggplants and cut them into large cubes. Sprinkle with salt and let stand for 10 minutes and drain. Wash and trim the mushrooms.

In a large skillet, heat 3 tablespoons butter; add the eggplant and sauté over medium heat for 5 minutes. Add the mushrooms. Brown for 2 or 3 minutes, then sprinkle with tarragon, salt and pepper. Cover and simmer for 15 minutes.

In another skillet, heat 3 tablespoons butter and add the turkey. Brown on both sides and sprinkle with salt and pepper. Add the turkey to the eggplant; add chicken stock and cook over low heat for 10 minutes—don't overcook.

Heat 2 tablespoons butter in the skillet in which the turkey was browned, and sauté the prunes. Remove the turkey to a warm platter and surround it with the eggplant, mushrooms and prunes. Serve immediately.

6 servings

Turkey Pie with Fresh Clams

PREPARATION: 15 MINUTES   COOKING: 50 MINUTES

Pâte Brisée I (see p. 10)
2 dozen fresh clams or canned
  whole clams
8 ounces mushrooms, trimmed
  and quartered
3 tablespoons butter
2 tablespoons chopped shallots
1½ teaspoons sage
1½ cups cubed leftover turkey
  meat

1 tablespoon brandy
½ cup clam juice
Salt and pepper
Juice of half a lemon
1 tablespoon flour
1 egg
2 sprigs parsley for garnish

Preheat the oven to 350°. Wash and scrub the clams under cold running water, then soak in cold water for about 30 minutes. Make the pâte brisée. Butter a 9-inch pie pan. Cut the ball of dough in two and set one half aside. Roll the dough on a floured board and fit it into the pie pan. Prick the dough with a fork and bake for 15 minutes, or until the dough is cooked but not browned. Remove from the oven and set aside.

Put the clams in a large saucepan; cover and steam until all of them are open. Put them in a bowl to cool. Strain the juice and save it. Shell the clams.

Heat 2 tablespoons butter in a skillet, add the shallots and sauté until transparent. Add the mushrooms and sauté for 2 minutes. Add the salt and pepper; mix well. Add the turkey and sauté for about a minute. Add the clams and sage and mix well. Put the brandy in the skillet and ignite. Correct the seasoning. Add the clam juice and lemon juice and mix well. Simmer for 2 to 3 minutes. Mix 1 tablespoon butter with the flour and add to the skillet. Cook for 2 more minutes, stirring all the while.

Fill the pie shell with the turkey-clam mixture. Roll the remaining dough on a floured board and cover the pie with it, sealing the edges. Beat the egg with 1 tablespoon water and brush the dough with it. Bake for 20 minutes, or until the top is golden brown. Serve with a green salad.

6 servings

Gratin of Turkey

PREPARATION: 15 MINUTES   COOKING: 1½ HOURS

Turkey is generally thought of as a holiday bird, but it is available all year round, and if you can find a small turkey of about 4 pounds, here is a recipe that is a far cry from the traditional roast turkey.

Instead of the tiny turkey, which may be impossible to get, you can use capon.

3 tablespoons butter
1 carrot, finely chopped
1 onion, finely chopped
1 turkey liver
Salt and pepper
1 tablespoon flour

¼ cup port
4-pound turkey, cut into serving
   pieces
3½ ounces heavy cream
4 tablespoons grated Swiss
   cheese

Preheat the oven to 450°.

In a skillet, heat the butter and add the carrot, onion and liver; stir with a wooden spoon. Sprinkle with salt, pepper and flour. Stir well and add the port and ½ cup water. Mix well and simmer while preparing the turkey.

Sprinkle the pieces of turkey with salt and pepper and place in a baking pan without any fat or water. Bake for 50 minutes.

Purée the vegetables and sauce in a food processor. Add the cream, correct the seasoning and pour over the turkey. Sprinkle with the grated cheese.

Lower the oven temperature to 375° and bake for about 30 minutes, or until the cheese is golden brown.

Serve in the baking pan with stewed tomatoes.

8 servings

Turkey Scallops with Asparagus

PREPARATION: 15 MINUTES   COOKING: 25 MINUTES

2½ pounds asparagus
4 tablespoons butter
4 turkey scallops*

4 tablespoons brandy
3½ ounces heavy cream
Salt and pepper

*These are slices of turkey cut from the breast and are available in supermarkets.

Wash and trim the asparagus and pat dry with paper towels. Steam over 1½ cups water for 5 minutes. Set aside.

In a large skillet, heat the butter, add the turkey and sauté until golden brown on both sides. Sprinkle with salt and pepper. Put the asparagus on top, cover and cook for 15 minutes. Uncover the skillet, add the brandy and ignite.

Arrange the asparagus and turkey on a serving platter. Add the cream to the skillet and scrape the sides and bottom with a wooden spoon. Add salt and pepper. Pour the sauce over the turkey and serve.

4 servings

Fish and Shellfish

Fresh Bluefish with Pistachios

PREPARATION: 30 MINUTES   COOKING: 30 MINUTES

This dish is unusual because the fish is wrapped in vine leaves before being broiled. If you are in the country, you may be able to find fresh vine leaves. Soak them in hot water for an hour, then wrap the fish in them. Vine leaves can also be found preserved in brine in jars at any Middle Eastern grocery store or in some supermarkets. Soak them in cold water before using them.

2 2-pound bluefish	2 sticks (½ pound) butter
8 ounces shelled pistachios	5 lemons
1 tablespoon brandy	Salt and pepper
4 ounces slivered almonds	Vine leaves

Have the fishmonger clean and bone the fish, leaving the head and tail intact.

Dip the pistachios in boiling water for 2 minutes. Drain and place them on a dish towel. Rub them against one another in the dish towel to remove as much skin as possible. Put them in a bowl and add the brandy.

Put the almonds on a cookie sheet and toast in a 400° oven for 5 minutes and remove to a bowl.

Put the butter, juice of 1 lemon, the pistachios with the brandy, salt and pepper to taste in the container of a food processor. Run the machine until the butter is smooth and most of the nuts are finely chopped. Add the almonds and run the machine for 1 second just to mix them with the butter.

Sprinkle some salt and pepper in the cavity of each fish and fill with half the butter.

Spread the vine leaves, overlapping them. Place each fish in the center and wrap it, then tie with a string. Place the fish on a grill over charcoal and cook 15 minutes on each side.

Serve the fish still wrapped in the leaves on a large platter and surround with lemon quarters. Unwrap the fish at the table and discard the leaves. Cut each fish into three or four pieces. Serve the remaining butter alongside in a sauceboat.

6 to 8 servings

Baked Dried Cod

PREPARATION: OVERNIGHT SOAKING; 15 MINUTES   COOKING: 30 MINUTES

1 dried cod	5 medium potatoes, diced
6 tablespoons butter	3 tablespoons grated Parmesan
3 onions, sliced	6 hard-boiled eggs
8-ounce can tomato paste	¼ pound pitted black olives
Salt and pepper	

Wash the cod under cold running water and soak it overnight in cold water. The next day, drain it and pat dry with paper towels. Cut it into 1-inch pieces.

Preheat the oven to 350°. Heat the butter in a large skillet and add the onions. Sauté until golden brown. Add the cod, tomato paste and salt and pepper to taste. Stir well and cook for 10 minutes over low heat.

Put the potatoes in a saucepan and cover with water. Bring to a boil and boil for 10 minutes, or until the potatoes are barely done. Drain. In a buttered 1½-inch-deep ovenproof pan, spread a layer of potatoes, then a layer of the cod mixture. Cover with another layer of potatoes. Sprinkle with the cheese and dot with the remaining butter. Put slices of hard-boiled egg all around the edge of the pan, leaving ¼ inch between each slice.

Bake for 30 minutes, or until the cheese is golden brown. Just before serving, put black olives between the slices of egg. Serve with a green salad.

6 servings

Filets of Fluke with Green Peppercorns

PREPARATION: 10 MINUTES   COOKING: 20 MINUTES

Green peppercorns are fresh peppercorns preserved in water. They are soft and dark green; crushed and mixed with crème fraîche, they add a spicy touch to fish or meat. They are sold in jars or cans in most specialty stores.

12 large mushrooms
1 tablespoon green peppercorns
3 tablespoons butter
2 shallots
4 filets of fluke

½ bottle of dry white wine
Salt
2 tablespoons Crème Fraîche
 (see p. xvi)
2 sprigs parsley

Wash and pat dry the mushrooms with paper towels. Remove the stems. Set aside the mushroom caps.

Finely chop the mushroom stems, peppercorns, butter and shallots in a blender or food processor. Spread the mixture in a large skillet and put the filets on top, cover with the wine and sprinkle with salt. Bring to a boil, then simmer, covered, for 5 minutes. Add the mushroom caps and cook for 8 minutes more.

Using a spatula, carefully transfer the filets onto a serving platter. Cover them with the mushroom caps.

Boil the sauce to reduce it to 2 cups. Add the crème fraîche, mix well and pour over the fish.

Garnish with the parsley and serve right away.

4 servings

Filets of Flounder with Marjoram

PREPARATION: 30 MINUTES   COOKING: 35 MINUTES

4 tablespoons butter
1½ cups mushrooms, sliced
2 cloves garlic, chopped
2 shallots, chopped
Salt and pepper
1 cup white wine
1 teaspoon marjoram

6 filets flounder
3 tomatoes, sliced
½ cup chopped black olives
½ cup grated Swiss cheese
2 tablespoons chopped parsley
 for garnish

Preheat the oven to 375°. In a skillet, heat 2 tablespoons butter and add the mushrooms, garlic and shallots. Reduce the heat and cook over low heat for 10 minutes. Add salt and pepper, white wine and marjoram and mix well.

Line a gratin dish with half the mushroom mixture and put the filets on top. Cover with the remaining mushroom mixture, then a layer of tomatoes and olives. Sprinkle with the cheese. Dot with the remaining butter and bake for 25 minutes. Sprinkle with parsley and serve with noodles.

6 servings

Filets of Flounder with Swiss Chard

PREPARATION: 20 MINUTES   COOKING: 1 HOUR AND 20 MINUTES

1 carrot, cut into 1-inch slices
1 onion, quartered
1 fish head and fish bones
2 cups dry white wine
1 bay leaf
¼ teaspoon thyme
4 filets of flounder

Salt and pepper
½ pound Swiss chard
3 tablespoons butter
2 tablespoons flour
4 tablespoons heavy cream
Juice of 1 lemon
3 tablespoons capers

Put the carrot, onion, fish head and bones in a large saucepan and cover with 4 cups water and wine. Add the bay leaf and thyme, salt and pepper to taste. Bring to a boil, skim off the froth and simmer for 45 minutes.

Meanwhile, preheat the oven to 375°. Put the filets in a buttered ovenproof dish and sprinkle them with salt and pepper. Set aside.

Wash and trim the Swiss chard. Put it in a large saucepan and cover with water. Bring to a boil and simmer for 10 minutes. Drain and squeeze out all the water, then chop in a blender or food processor. Set aside.

Strain the stock over a saucepan or a bowl. Pour 1½ cups stock over the fish and bake for 10 minutes. Turn off the oven and keep the fish warm in it.

In a saucepan, heat the butter and add the flour. Mix well and cook slowly for a few minutes. Slowly add 2 cups stock, stirring all the while. Add salt and pepper and simmer for 5 minutes. Add the Swiss chard and mix well. Add the cream and lemon juice. Correct the seasoning. Add the capers. Pour the sauce over the fish and serve immediately.

4 servings

Poached Filets of Flounder with Morels

PREPARATION: 1 HOUR   COOKING: 40 MINUTES

Morels can be found in the United States if you are lucky while searching through the woods in the spring. They are available dried in specialty stores. They are quite expensive, but what a treat!

When buying the fish, ask the fishmonger to give you a fish head and some bones for the stock.

6 ounces dried morels	8 filets of flounder or lemon sole
1 cup dry white wine	6 tablespoons butter
2 onions, sliced	2 tablespoons flour
3 sprigs parsley	2 onions, chopped
1 fish head and fish bones	1 pint heavy cream or Crème
Salt and pepper	Fraîche (see p. xvi)

Wash the morels and soak them for 1 hour.

Meanwhile, make the stock. Put in a saucepan 2 cups water, wine, sliced onions, parsley, fish head and bones, salt and pepper and bring to a boil. Skim off the froth and simmer for 10 minutes.

Poach the filets in the stock for 7 minutes. With a slotted spoon in each hand, remove carefully onto a warm platter. Keep warm in a turned-off oven while making the sauce.

Strain the stock and keep 2 cups for making the sauce.

In a saucepan, heat 2 tablespoons butter and add the flour all at once. Mix well with a wooden spoon and slowly add the stock, stirring all the while. Simmer the sauce for 5 minutes. Drain the morels and add the liquid to the sauce. Mix well.

In a skillet, heat the remaining butter and sauté the morels with the chopped onions. When the onions are golden brown, add to the sauce. Add salt and pepper to taste and the cream. Pour the sauce over the fish and serve very hot with sautéed spinach.

6 servings

Halibut with Avocado

PREPARATION: 20 MINUTES   COOKING: 20 MINUTES

Last spring I spent a week in Maine with a friend, an English teacher turned fisherman. One evening he came home with a large piece of halibut and made this wonderful dish. The fish is served at room temperature with an avocado sauce. The halibut can be replaced with grey sole or flounder filets.

1 pound halibut
2 cups milk
1 bay leaf
1 sprig thyme
Salt and pepper
1 large tomato
1 avocado

1 clove garlic
¼ cup olive oil
2 tablespoons vinegar
1 egg yolk
5 Boston lettuce leaves
1 lemon, cut into wedges

Wash and pat dry the fish with paper towels. Put the milk, bay leaf and thyme in a saucepan large enough to hold the fish and bring to a boil. Add the fish and enough water to cover. Add salt and pepper and simmer for 20 minutes, or until the flesh flakes easily. Let the fish cool in the saucepan.

Meanwhile, prepare the sauce. Seed the tomato by cutting it in half and squeezing over a strainer set on top of a bowl. Peel the avocado and the garlic. Thoroughly mix the avocado, tomato and garlic in a food processor. Remove to a bowl and add salt and pepper to taste. Mix the oil, vinegar and egg yolk and pour over the avocado.

Line a platter with lettuce leaves. Drain the fish and place on top of the leaves. Pour the sauce over the fish and serve with lemon wedges.

4 servings

Mackerel with Aïoli

PREPARATION: 25 MINUTES   COOKING: 10 MINUTES

Mackerel is a fish often ignored in the United States, probably because it is quite fatty. But when absolutely fresh, it is delicious.

2 mackerel, central bone
   removed
1 tablespoon kosher salt
Aïoli (see p. 171)
1 tablespoon chopped parsley

2 tablespoons chopped basil
1 tablespoon chopped Chinese
   parsley (coriander)
¼ teaspoon lemon juice
Bunch of watercress

Place the mackerel side by side in a long fish poacher and cover with cold water. Add kosher salt. Bring to a boil, then remove from heat and let the mackerel cool to room temperature.

Make the aïoli. Add to it the parsley, basil, Chinese parsley and lemon juice.

Drain the mackerel (they should be lukewarm) and place on a serving platter. Remove the skin. Cover with the aïoli and decorate with watercress. Serve with a purée of string beans.

3 to 4 servings

Mullet with Lime

PREPARATION: 15 MINUTES   COOKING: 20 MINUTES

6 small mullets
1 can anchovy filets
1 cup chopped parsley
3 tablespoons dried basil

3 tablespoons dried chives
6 limes
Salt and pepper

Preheat the oven to 400°. Wash the mullets and pat them dry with paper towels. Drain the anchovies.

Put the anchovies, parsley, basil, chives and juice of 1 lime in the container of a food processor and run the machine until the mixture becomes a paste.

Slice the remaining limes. Make 4 slits on each fish and place a lime slice in each slit.

Spread the anchovy paste on the fish and sprinkle with salt and pepper. Wrap the fish individually in pieces of foil. Bake for 20 minutes.

Unwrap the fish and arrange on a serving platter. Surround them with slices of lime. Serve with steamed potatoes or rice.

6 servings

Clafoutis de Moules

PREPARATION: MUSSELS SOAKED 1 HOUR; 20 MINUTES   COOKING: 25 MINUTES

Clafoutis is really a French dessert, a kind of pancake made with fruits such as cherries or peaches. Made with mussels, it is unusual and delicious.

3 quarts mussels
1 pound fish filets (flounder, cod)
2 cups cider
Salt and pepper

¼ cup heavy cream
½ cup flour
2 egg yolks
3 tablespoons brandy
2 tablespoons butter

Preheat the oven to 425°. Clean the mussels thoroughly.* Cut the filets into 3-inch pieces. Put the filets in a large skillet and cover with the cider. Sprinkle with salt and freshly ground pepper. Bring to a boil and reduce the heat. Simmer for 5 minutes. Then set aside while preparing the mussels.

Drain the mussels and put them in a large saucepan. Add ¾ cup water, cover and cook over high heat for about 15 minutes, or until the mussels open. Transfer the mussels to a bowl to cool and strain the broth through a very fine sieve.

With a slotted spoon, remove the filets onto a gratin dish. Take the mussels out of their shells and put on top of the filets.

Add ½ cup of the mussel broth to the cider and bring it to a boil. Lower the heat, add the cream beaten with the egg yolks and flour and then brandy. Mix well with a whisk. Slowly add the butter—do not let the sauce boil. Correct the seasoning and pour over the mussels.

Bake for 10 minutes and serve immediately.

4 servings

*Wash and scrub the mussels with a stiff brush under cold running water. Discard those that feel too heavy (they may contain nothing but sand) and those that are not tightly closed. Soak the mussels in cold water for at least 1 hour.

Fish Stew with Garlic Bread

PREPARATION: MUSSELS SOAKED 1 HOUR; 40 MINUTES   COOKING: 30 MINUTES

I am no fisherman, but last summer a friend, Dick Cornuelle, insisted that I go fishing off Montauk Point. "We are going for fluke, Colette; it is very easy to catch them," he said. "All you have to do is lower your fishing line with a weighted hook and they will bite. Fluke lie at the bottom of the sea." My children and I spent the day fishing while Dick, the fisherman, was lying in the cabin feeling seasick for the first time. We caught four fluke, one large flounder, and one striped bass. To cheer him up, on the way back home we picked up some shrimp and mussels and made him this great fish stew.

2 pints mussels
1 pound shrimp
5 tablespoons olive oil
2 onions, chopped
1 fish head
2 cloves garlic, peeled and
  crushed
1 bay leaf
2 sprigs thyme
Half a bottle of dry white wine

1 tablespoon tomato paste
Salt and pepper
½ teaspoon dried hot red pepper
1 teaspoon saffron
2 pounds fresh fish filets
½ cup flour
3 tablespoons oil
1½ cups sliced scungilli (conch)*
1 loaf Italian or French bread
2 cloves garlic, peeled

Clean the mussels thoroughly (see footnote on p. 154 for instructions on how to do this). Set aside in a large bowl of cold water.

Shell and devein the shrimp. Set aside.

In a large saucepan, heat two tablespoons olive oil and add the onions, fish head and garlic. Sauté for 5 minutes. Add the bay leaf, thyme, wine, tomato paste and 1 quart water. Add salt and pepper to taste. Bring to a boil, then lower the heat and add the hot red pepper and saffron. Mix well, cover and simmer over medium heat for 45 minutes.

Meanwhile, drain the mussels. Place them in a large saucepan, cover and cook over high heat for about 15 minutes, or until they open. Drain them over a bowl and reserve the broth. When the mussels are cool enough to touch, remove them from their shells and set aside. Strain the reserved broth.

Preheat the oven to 300°.

Dredge the fish filets with flour, and sauté in oil for 3 minutes on each side. Drain on paper towels.

Strain the soup in the saucepan. Place the fish filets, shrimp, scungilli and mussels in a large ovenproof casserole. Cover with the soup and some of the mussel liquid.

Slice the bread, rub with garlic and place enough slices on top of the stew to cover it. Cover the casserole with foil and bake for 30 minutes. Toast the remaining slices of bread.

Bring the casserole to the table and serve the toast on the side.

6 servings

*Scungilli, or conch, can be found already cooked in most fish stores. If you buy uncooked scungilli, they must be washed carefully, as they may be sandy. Boil for at least 6 hours, then drain.

Mussels Cooked in Hard Cider

PREPARATION: MUSSELS SOAKED 1 HOUR; 15 MINUTES   COOKING: 15 MINUTES

2 quarts mussels
1 tablespoon oil
2 tablespoons chopped parsley

½ cup hard cider
2 cloves garlic, finely chopped
Freshly ground pepper

Clean the mussels thoroughly (see footnote on p. 154 for instructions on how to do this). Drain and place the mussels in a large saucepan. Add the oil, parsley, cider, garlic and freshly ground pepper.

Shaking the pan from time to time, cook over high heat for 15 minutes, or until the mussels are all open.

Serve in soup bowls with the broth from the saucepan and fresh French or Italian bread.

4 servings

Prawns with Asparagus

PREPARATION: 20 MINUTES   COOKING: 25 MINUTES

2 pounds large prawns
2 pounds asparagus
1 bunch broccoli
3 cups chicken stock or bouillon

6 tablespoons butter
1 tablespoon Crème Fraîche
   (see p. xvi)
Salt and pepper

Clean and devein the prawns. Trim the asparagus, cutting off the tough ends. Cut off the thick main stalk of the broccoli and separate the smaller stalks with the buds.

Heat the chicken stock in a large skillet. Put the broccoli on the bottom layer of a steamer and the asparagus on the top layer. Place the steamer in the skillet, cover and steam for 10 minutes, or until the broccoli is done but still firm.

Carefully remove the asparagus and broccoli onto a platter. Purée half the asparagus, 1 tablespoon butter and ½ cup chicken stock (taken from the skillet). Pour the purée into a saucepan, add salt and pepper to taste and the crème fraîche. Mix well. Keep warm while cooking the prawns.

Discard the remaining stock in the skillet. In the same skillet, heat the remaining butter and add the prawns. Sauté for 4 to 5 minutes over high heat, then turn over and sauté for another 5 minutes. Sprinkle with salt and pepper. Add the broccoli and the remaining asparagus. Reduce the heat and simmer, covered, for 5 minutes.

Pour the asparagus purée on a platter and cover with the prawns, asparagus and broccoli. Serve with steamed rice.

5 servings

Broiled Prawns

PREPARATION: 20 MINUTES   COOKING: 20 MINUTES

12 whole large prawns
12 slices bacon
Pepper
6 tablespoons white vinegar

3 tablespoons chopped shallots
1 stick (¼ pound) butter
6 lettuce leaves

Shell the prawns. Wrap each prawn with a slice of bacon and put 3 prawns apiece on 6 small skewers. Sprinkle with freshly ground pepper. Heat the broiler.

In a saucepan, heat the vinegar and shallots until all the vinegar has evaporated, then place the saucepan over a larger saucepan of simmering water and add the butter, cut into small pieces. Beat the butter with a whisk to make it light and fluffy. Keep warm.

Broil the prawns for 6 minutes on each side. Serve piping hot on a bed of lettuce with the butter on the side.

4 servings

Prawns with Vegetables

PREPARATION: 40 MINUTES   COOKING: 30 MINUTES

Instead of prawns, you can use lobsters. If you are using lobsters, choose small ones and allow one per person; remove the legs and the claws, which you can use for a salad.

16 large prawns
4 carrots, cut into strips
4 turnips, cut into strips
4 stalks celery, cut into strips
2 cups string beans, strings
  removed
¾ cup oil
1 clove garlic, peeled and
  crushed
2 shallots, chopped

1 onion, chopped
3 tomatoes
¾ cup white vermouth
1 cup dry white wine
2 cups fish stock or water
Salt and pepper
1 tablespoon tarragon
1 teaspoon thyme
Mayonnaise (see p. 29)

Steam the carrots, turnips, celery and string beans over 1 cup water for 8 minutes. Keep warm.

In a deep skillet, heat 2 tablespoons oil and add the prawns. Sauté for 5 minutes, then add the garlic, shallots, onion, and tomatoes. Cook for 5 minutes, then add the vermouth, wine and stock. Add the salt and pepper, tarragon and thyme. Bring to a boil and reduce the heat. Simmer for 10 minutes more.

Meanwhile, make the mayonnaise. Slowly add to it ½ cup strained liquid from the stew, stirring all the while. Keep the sauce warm over a double boiler. Correct the seasoning.

Arrange the carrots, turnips, celery and string beans on a warm platter and place the prawns on top. Purée in a food processor the remaining liquid containing the onions, tomatoes and shallots and pour over the vegetables. Serve with warm mayonnaise on the side.

4 servings

Red Snapper with Peaches

PREPARATION: 20 MINUTES   COOKING: 45 MINUTES

This recipe is also excellent with striped bass.

1 large red snapper
4 large peaches
1½ cups Béchamel (see p. 201)
Juice of 1 orange
1 tablespoon Crème Fraîche (see
  p. xvi) or heavy cream

1 tablespoon capers
4 slices bacon
Parsley for garnish
Salt and freshly ground pepper

Have the fishmonger remove the head and center bone of the fish. Keep the head and the bone for a fish stock. Cut the fish in two, lengthwise. Set aside.

Dip the peaches in boiling water for a couple of seconds, or if they are hard, for 5 minutes. Cool under running water, peel and slice. Drain and set aside.

Preheat the oven to 375°. Make the béchamel and add to it the orange juice, crème fraîche, capers, salt and pepper. Fry the bacon and drain on paper towels.

Oil a baking pan. Place on it one piece of fish, skin side down. Cover with the sliced peaches and then the bacon. Cover with the other piece of fish, skin side up. Cover the fish with the béchamel and sprinkle with freshly ground pepper. Bake for 25 minutes. Serve garnished with parsley.

4 servings

Salmon Baked in Champagne

PREPARATION: 10 MINUTES   COOKING: 55 MINUTES

I live not too far from Chinatown in New York and I often do my shopping there. Down Canal Street are endless sidewalk stands selling fish and fresh vegetables. In the spring the salmon is small, but a whole one will feed about six people. I always ask the fishmonger to remove the center bone, for my husband refuses to this day to eat fish that has a bone in it. With the salmon I serve small steamed buns stuffed with a sweet lotus paste. They are white and round, and have a red lotus flower printed on top. Their sweet taste is delightful in combination with the flavor of the fish. If you can't find these buns, use biscuits instead.

6 tablespoons butter	1 bay leaf
5 shallots, chopped	6 egg yolks
4-pound fresh salmon, center bone removed	1½ cups heavy cream
	¼ teaspoon thyme
1 bottle dry champagne	Salt and pepper
1 sprig parsley	6 Chinese steamed buns

Preheat the oven to 400°. In an ovenproof dish big enough to hold the whole salmon, heat half the butter and add the shallots and salmon. Sauté until golden brown for 5 minutes, then with a spatula in each hand, turn over the fish and sauté for another 5 minutes. Add the champagne and the remaining butter (cut into small pieces), parsley and bay leaf. Bake for 40 minutes, basting frequently.

Remove the fish onto a platter and keep warm in a turned-off oven while making the sauce. Strain the juice into a saucepan and reduce by half over high heat, then lower the heat. In a bowl, beat the egg yolks with the cream and thyme and slowly pour into the sauce, stirring all the while. Add salt and pepper and pour over the fish.

Steam the buns for 5 minutes and serve with the fish.

6 servings

Saumon en Croûte   (Salmon Baked in a Crust)

PREPARATION: 25 MINUTES   COOKING: 1 HOUR

Pâte Brisée I (see p. 10), made
  with 2 eggs plus 1 yolk
1 cup dry white wine
1 onion, chopped
1 clove
1 bay leaf
¼ teaspoon thyme
Salt and pepper
½ pound fresh salmon

5 tablespoons butter
⅓ cup rice
2 hard-boiled eggs
¼ pound mushrooms, coarsely
  chopped
2 shallots, chopped
Juice of 1 lemon
½ cup heavy cream
3 tablespoons chopped parsley

Make the pâte brisée using 2 eggs plus 1 egg yolk instead of only 1 egg. Refrigerate.

Put the wine, 2 cups water, onion, clove, bay leaf and thyme in a large saucepan. Bring to a boil and add 1 teaspoon salt and ¼ teaspoon pepper. Lower the heat and simmer for 10 minutes. Add the salmon and bring to a boil. Immediately turn off the heat, cover the saucepan and let the salmon cool in the broth.

In a small saucepan, bring 1 cup water to a boil and add ¼ teaspoon salt and the rice. Lower the heat and simmer for 12 minutes, or until done. Peel the eggs and coarsely chop with a fork.

Preheat the oven to 375°.

In a skillet, heat the butter and add the mushrooms. Cook for 2 or 3 minutes. Add the shallots and parsley. Mix well and turn off the heat.

Remove the salmon from the broth and discard the skin and bones. With a fork, flake the salmon and place in a bowl. Add the mushrooms, rice and eggs to the salmon. Mix gently with a wooden spoon.

On a floured board, roll the dough in a rectangle. Place the salmon mixture in the center and form into a long sausage-like shape. Roll the dough around it and seal the edges with a drop of water. Place the roll on a floured baking pan.

Add 1 tablespoon water to the egg yolk and beat with a fork. Brush the dough with this mixture and bake for about 20 minutes, or until the pastry is golden brown.

Meanwhile, melt the remaining butter. Add the lemon juice and slowly add the heavy cream, stirring all the while. Add the parsley and salt and pepper to taste.

Serve with the sauce on the side.

6 servings

Cold Sardines or Smelts

PREPARATION: 20 MINUTES   MARINATING: 24 HOURS   COOKING: 30 MINUTES

This dish is quick to prepare, but the fish must marinate in the refrigerator for 24 hours. You could use large smelts or even any small whole fish if you cannot find sardines.

2 pounds sardines or smelts	1 tablespoon chopped parsley
Salt and pepper	3 bay leaves
3 tablespoons flour	½ teaspoon thyme
2 cups oil	1 teaspoon paprika
6 cloves garlic, chopped	½ teaspoon cayenne
1 small onion, chopped	2 slices lemon
8 fresh mint leaves, chopped	6 tablespoons wine vinegar

Clean and wipe the fish. Sprinkle with salt and pepper and dredge with flour.

In a skillet, heat 1 cup oil and add the fish, four or five at one time. Fry until golden brown. Remove with a slotted spoon onto a serving platter. Set aside.

In a skillet heat the remaining oil. Add the garlic, onion, mint, parsley, bay leaves and thyme. Reduce the heat and add paprika and cayenne. Simmer for 5 minutes, then add the sliced lemon and vinegar. Simmer for 10 minutes more and pour over the fish. Cover with foil and refrigerate for 24 hours to marinate thoroughly.

Serve with steamed new potatoes.

6 servings

Grilled Sardines with Lemon

PREPARATION: 25 MINUTES   MARINATING: 1 HOUR   COOKING: 10 MINUTES

Fresh sardines are delicate in taste, and quickly broiled, they make an excellent dinner in the spring. If sardines are not available, you can substitute smelts. Choose large ones.

2 dozen sardines or smelts,
 heads left on
Pinch of paprika
Salt and pepper
⅓ cup olive oil
Juice of 2 lemons

6 tablespoons butter
2 tablespoons chopped parsley
6 cloves garlic, finely chopped
1 teaspoon grated lemon rind
1 lemon, sliced

Wash and pat the sardines dry with paper towels. Place them side by side in a baking pan and sprinkle with paprika, salt and pepper. Add the oil, and lemon juice. Refrigerate for at least 1 hour.

In a small saucepan, heat the butter and add parsley, garlic, salt and pepper, and lemon rind.

Broil the fish for 5 minutes on each side. Arrange on a serving platter and pour the garlic butter over them. Garnish with lemon slices.

6 servings

Phyllo Stuffed with Fish Filets and Spinach

PREPARATION: 40 MINUTES   COOKING: 25 MINUTES

Phyllo is paper-thin dough used in Middle Eastern cooking. It can be found in specialty shops, where it is sold rolled in sheets and kept under plastic wrap. It can keep for weeks in sealed plastic bags.

1 package phyllo
1 pound fish filets
1 pound spinach
Salt and pepper
1 stick (¼ pound) butter

Paprika
3 tablespoons Crème Fraîche (see
 p. xvi) or sour cream
1 egg
3 tablespoons chopped chives

Cut the phyllo into strips 4 inches wide. Wash the fish filets and pat dry with paper towels. Wash and trim the spinach.

In a large saucepan, add 1 tablespoon salt to 4 cups water and bring to a boil. Add the spinach, bring to a boil, cover and turn off the heat. Let the spinach stand for 5 minutes, then drain and cool under cold running water. Chop coarsely with a knife and set aside.

Meanwhile, heat 4 tablespoons butter in a skillet and add the fish. Sauté for 4 minutes over high heat. Sprinkle with salt, pepper and paprika. Add the spinach, mix well and remove from heat.

Preheat the oven to 375°.

Melt the remaining butter in a small saucepan and remove from heat. With a pastry brush, brush some melted butter on each phyllo strip.

Add the crème fraîche to the spinach and fish and mix well. Correct the seasoning. Place some of the spinach-fish mixture at one end of each phyllo strip; fold the dough in a triangle and continue to fold until the stuffing is enclosed (see illustration, p. 14).

Beat the egg with 1 tablespoon water and brush on each triangle. Sprinkle some chives on top and bake for 20 to 25 minutes, or until the phyllo is golden brown. Serve piping hot with a chilled dry white wine.

6 servings

Gratin of Shad Roe with Sorrel Purée

PREPARATION: 30 MINUTES   COOKING: 30 MINUTES

Shad roe, which has a very short season, is a great delicacy in the United States. It can be sautéed in butter or poached accompanied by a butter sauce or served cold with mayonnaise. Served on a purée of sorrel, it is a very elegant dish.

Sorrel Purée (see p. 201)	Salt and pepper
2 pairs of shad roe	1 cup fresh bread crumbs
4 cups fish stock or water	4 tablespoons butter

Preheat the oven to 475°. Make the sorrel purée and set aside.

Carefully wash the roe and pat dry with paper towels. Remove any little blood vessels. Poach the roe in the fish stock for 10 minutes. Carefully transfer to a plate.

Put the sorrel purée in a gratin dish. Place the shad roe on top and sprinkle with salt and freshly ground pepper. Sprinkle with the bread crumbs and dot with butter. Bake for about 5 minutes, or until golden brown.

4 servings

Poached Shad with Beurre Blanc

PREPARATION: 15 MINUTES   COOKING: 30 MINUTES

Shad is a delicate fish that is available only during the spring. The Hudson River was once famous for its shad, but for many years its waters were so polluted that the fish nearly disappeared. Today, thanks to the environmentalists, the shad has begun to reappear in the New York fish market.

1- to 3-pound shad
1 large onion stuck with 2
    cloves
1 carrot, cut into 1-inch pieces
1 bay leaf

Salt and pepper
6 shallots, finely chopped
⅓ cup vinegar plus 1 tablespoon
12 tablespoons butter
Parsley for garnish

Buy very fresh shad; its eyes should be bright and shiny. Wash it quickly and pat dry with paper towels.

Put 6 cups water, onion, carrot and bay leaf in a large saucepan big enough to hold the fish and bring to a boil. Add salt and pepper to taste. Lower the heat and simmer for 15 minutes. Add the shad and poach for 15 minutes. Carefully transfer to a platter and keep warm in a turned-off oven.

Meanwhile, prepare the sauce. Put the shallots and ⅓ cup vinegar in a saucepan and boil until all the vinegar has evaporated. Add 1 teaspoon cold water, then lower the heat and add the butter, 1 tablespoon at a time, stirring all the while with a wooden spoon—do not let the sauce boil. Add salt and pepper to taste and 1 tablespoon vinegar. Beat the sauce with an electric beater until it becomes very light and fluffy.

Serve the shad, garnished with parsley, with the sauce in a sauceboat. Serve with steamed potatoes.

6 servings

Shrimp Beignets   (Fritters)

PREPARATION: 20 MINUTES   COOKING: 20 MINUTES

In France most shellfish are sold with their heads on. In the United States one can find small shrimp that are as good as the French *crevettes grises.* This dish is delicious served with saffron rice and a crisp green salad.

1 pound very small shrimp	3 sprigs parsley
2 limes	1 egg
¾ cup flour	Salt and pepper
1 tablespoon oil	Pinch of cayenne
⅓ cup beer	Oil for deep frying
1 medium-size onion	2 limes for garnish

Shell and devein the shrimp. Put them in a bowl and add the juice of 1 lime. Toss well and set aside while preparing the batter.

In the container of a food processor or blender, place the flour, oil, ⅓ cup water, beer, onion, parsley and egg. Run the machine until the ingredients are well mixed. Add salt, pepper and cayenne and run the machine for 30 seconds. Pour the batter in a bowl and let it stand for 15 minutes.

In a deep fryer, heat the oil to 360°. Pour the batter over the shrimps and mix well. Drop the mixture by tablespoonfuls in the oil and fry for less than 2 minutes, or until browned. Drain on paper towels and serve very hot with slices of lime.

6 servings

Profiteroles with Shrimp

PREPARATION: 40 MINUTES   COOKING: 40 MINUTES

Profiteroles are small puffs of pastry usually filled with chocolate for dessert. Here they are filled with shrimp. Instead of shrimp, you can use mussels, lobster or crab meat.

PUFFS:

Pinch of salt

6 tablespoons butter

1 cup flour

4 eggs

FILLING:

2 tablespoons butter

3 tablespoons flour

2½ cups milk

6 tablespoons grated Swiss
cheese

½ pound small shrimps, shelled
and deveined

Salt and pepper

Pinch of cayenne

1 head Boston lettuce for
garnish

Preheat the oven to 425°. Put 1 cup water in a saucepan and bring to a boil. Add the salt and butter. When the butter has melted, add the flour all at once. Stir the mixture very rapidly until the dough becomes a mass that is completely free from the sides of the pan. Remove from heat. Add 1 egg and mix until completely incorporated into the dough. Repeat the procedure with the remaining eggs. The dough will be thick and shiny. Using a pastry bag or two tablespoons dipped in cold water, make 1-inch balls and drop them on a buttered baking sheet, leaving a 2-inch space between them. Bake for 20 minutes, or until golden brown.

Meanwhile, prepare the sauce for the filling. In a saucepan, heat the butter and add the flour all at once. Cook over low heat while stirring with a wooden spoon. Slowly add the milk while continuing to stir. Bring slowly to a boil, then turn the flame very low and simmer for 10 minutes, stirring from time to time.

Remove the puffs from the oven. Slit the side of each puff with a sharp knife. Place the puffs back in the oven and turn the heat off.

Add to the sauce the shrimp, salt, pepper and cayenne. Add 4 table-spoons grated cheese. Mix well and simmer until the shrimp are cooked.

Fill the puffs with the shrimp mixture. Place them on a buttered baking dish and sprinkle the remaining cheese over the puffs. Bake for a couple of minutes, or until the cheese has melted. Serve on a bed of lettuce.

6 servings

Filets of Sole in a Shrimp-Filled Boat

PREPARATION: 20 MINUTES   COOKING: 1 HOUR AND 20 MINUTES

In late September at the seaside we ate fish nearly every day. One day my young son had the idea for this dish, which would look like a boat with a sail.

Ask your fish store to set aside for you half a dozen large shrimps with their heads on—shrimp are usually sold in the United States without their heads, but it is possible to get them if you order them in advance.

6 Idaho baking potatoes	2 tablespoons flour
1 stick (¼ pound) butter	½ cup half-and-half
Salt and pepper	½ cup grated Swiss cheese
2 shallots, chopped	8 ounces small shrimps, shelled
¾ cup dry white wine	and deveined
6 filets of sole	
6 large shrimps with their heads	
on	

Preheat the oven to 400°. Scrub the potatoes clean and bake for 45 minutes. Remove from the oven and make a 4-inch slit on top. With a spoon, remove 4 tablespoons of flesh from each potato and, in a bowl, mash with 6 tablespoons butter. Add salt and pepper to taste. Stuff each potato shell with the mixture and keep warm in a turned-off oven.

In a large skillet, heat 1 tablespoon butter and add the shallots. Sauté until cooked but not browned, then add the wine. Mix well. Add the filets of sole, lower the heat, and simmer for 8 to 10 minutes—do not let it boil. Remove with a slotted spoon and keep warm in the oven. Add both large and small shrimps to the skillet and cook over medium heat for 5 to 8 minutes. Remove with a slotted spoon. Set aside the large shrimps.

Strain the broth through a very fine sieve and cook over high heat until reduced to 5 tablespoons.

Remove the potato shells and filets of sole from the oven and preheat the oven to 400°.

In a saucepan, heat 1 tablespoon butter, add the flour and mix well. Stirring all the while with a wooden spoon, add the half-and-half and then the broth. Correct the seasoning. Pour half the sauce into another saucepan. Add the small shrimps and heat through. Fill the potato shells with the creamed shrimp. Put a filet of sole on top of each potato and cover with the remaining sauce. Sprinkle with cheese and dot with a small piece of butter. Bake for about 15 minutes, or until browned. Just before serving, place a large shrimp at one end of each potato.

6 servings

Broiled Filets of Sole with Lemon-Butter Sauce

PREPARATION: 15 MINUTES   COOKING: 10 MINUTES

This is a very simple recipe, quick to make. I always find that broiled fresh fish served with a lemony sauce is one of the best ways to cook fish when your time is limited but your guests are important.

8 filets of sole
1 teaspoon butter
2 tablespoons olive oil
1 tablespoon tarragon

Salt and pepper
2 lemons, cut in wedges for
   garnish
Parsley for garnish

Preheat the broiler.
   Pat the filets dry with paper towels. Butter a shallow baking pan and put the filets in it side by side. Brush them with olive oil mixed with tarragon and sprinkle with salt and pepper. Broil for 5 minutes or until the filets are golden brown. Remove to a warm platter and garnish with lemon wedges and parsley. Serve with lemon-butter sauce (see below).
   8 servings

Lemon-Butter Sauce

PREPARATION: 10 MINUTES

1 stick (¼ pound) butter
¼ cup lemon juice
4 tablespoons chicken bouillon

Salt and pepper
10 capers, cut into small pieces

Cut the butter into 8 pieces and refrigerate. In a small saucepan, boil the lemon juice until it is reduced to 1 tablespoon. Remove from heat, and with a whisk, beat in 2 pieces of butter. Place the saucepan over very low heat and add a piece of butter at a time, beating continuously with the whisk. Stir in the bouillon; add the salt, pepper and capers.

Noodles with Stingray and Capers

PREPARATION: 15 MINUTES   COOKING: 25 MINUTES

I always thought that ray was not found in the United States, but according to my friend Paul O'Rourke, who is a fisherman, it does exist.

Exploring Chinatown, I found that Paul was right—ray was being sold in most fish markets. You eat the pectoral fins, which look like wings, of this rather large fish. The skin has a sort of slimy film, which can be easily wiped off.

2 pounds ray
1 onion, quartered
½ teaspoon thyme
1 bay leaf
Salt and pepper
1 pound fresh noodles

1 egg yolk
¼ cup heavy cream
2 tablespoons butter
2 tablespoons capers
Chopped parsley for garnish

Wipe the ray clean with paper towels. Place it in a large skillet and cover with hot water. Add the onion, thyme, bay leaf, salt and pepper and bring to a boil. Reduce the heat and simmer for 10 minutes. With a spatula, transfer the ray to a plate and carefully remove the skin. Then remove the flesh with a small spatula and keep warm over a saucepan of simmering water.

Add 1 tablespoon salt to several quarts of boiling water in a large saucepan and add the noodles. Cook for 5 minutes. Drain and place in a large bowl.

Beat the egg yolk with the cream and slowly add 1 cup of the fish stock. Correct the seasoning.

In a small saucepan, heat the butter, add the capers and heat through. Pour over the noodles and toss well.

Put the noodles on a serving platter and place the fish on top. Pour the cream sauce over the fish. Sprinkle with chopped parsley and serve.

4 servings

Striped Bass with White Wine

PREPARATION: 15 MINUTES   COOKING: 30 MINUTES

Save the bones and ask the fishmonger for an extra head. They will make a marvelous fish stock that can be kept frozen for a long time.

1- to 3-pound striped bass
½ teaspoon salt
¼ teaspoon pepper
2 tablespoons butter
3 shallots, chopped

3 ripe tomatoes, sliced
3 cups dry white wine
2 tablespoons chopped parsley
1 lemon, cut into wedges for
    garnish

Preheat the oven to 375°.

Clean and bone the bass (or have the fishmonger do it), leaving the head on. Sprinkle the cavity and the skin with salt and pepper.

Butter a baking pan with ½ tablespoon butter. Sprinkle the bottom with the shallots and place the tomatoes on top. Put the fish on top of the tomatoes and slowly pour the wine into the baking pan. Bake for 20 minutes, basting three or four times.

To serve, remove the fish from the pan with a spatula in each hand and put it on a warm platter. Strain the sauce over a saucepan and heat it. Correct the seasoning. Just before serving, add the remaining butter to the sauce. Garnish the bass with parsley and lemon wedges, and serve the sauce alongside.

4 servings

Fresh Tuna in White Wine

PREPARATION: 15 MINUTES   COOKING: 45 MINUTES

1 stick (¼ pound) butter
½ cup oil
2-pound fresh tuna steak
3 tablespoons brandy
⅛ teaspoon four-spices
 (see p. xv)
⅛ teaspoon nutmeg
⅛ teaspoon cayenne

⅛ teaspoon curry
1 onion, chopped
1 shallot, chopped
1 clove garlic, chopped
4 cups dry white wine
3 tablespoons tomato paste
Salt and pepper
¼ cup heavy cream

In a large skillet, heat the butter and oil. Add the tuna and fry on each side for 5 minutes. Pour the brandy over the tuna and ignite. Sprinkle with the four-spices, nutmeg, cayenne and curry. Add the onion, shallot and garlic. Cover with the wine and add the tomato paste. Add salt and pepper. Mix the sauce well with a wooden spoon and simmer for 30 minutes.

With a spatula in each hand, transfer the tuna to a warm platter. Strain the sauce through a fine sieve into a saucepan and slowly heat through. Add the cream, correct the seasoning, and pour over the tuna. Serve with steamed rice.

6 servings

Tuna with Aïoli

PREPARATION: 30 MINUTES   COOKING: 25 MINUTES   REFRIGERATION: 3 HOURS

Aïoli is a sauce made the same way as a mayonnaise, but garlic gives it its distinctive flavor and aroma. It is delicious served with boiled beef, chicken or fish.

This recipe requires 3 hours of refrigeration. Make it on a Friday night so you can spend the next day at the beach not worrying about dinner.

6 potatoes	Pepper
9½-ounce can tuna in oil	2 tomatoes for garnish
½ teaspoon salt	2 lemons for garnish
Aïoli (see below)	1 cup black Greek olives for
1 head Boston lettuce for	garnish
garnish	Parsley sprigs for garnish

Wash and peel the potatoes. Place them in a saucepan of boiling water to which salt has been added. Cook over medium heat for 20 minutes, or until they are tender when pierced with a fork.

Meanwhile, make the aïoli, reducing the ingredients by half.

Drain the potatoes. Purée the potatoes and tuna with its oil in a blender or food processor.

In a bowl, mix together the tuna purée and the aïoli. Add salt and pepper to taste. Pour the mixture into a 1½-quart loaf pan and press down with a spoon. Cover with foil and refrigerate for 3 hours.

To serve, unmold the tuna on a bed of lettuce leaves. Surround it with sliced tomatoes alternating with lemon slices, the olives and parsley. Serve with a cold string bean salad.

6 servings

Aïoli
PREPARATION: 15 MINUTES

8 cloves garlic	Juice of 1 lemon
2 egg yolks	Salt and pepper
2 cups olive or vegetable oil	

Peel the garlic and pound it in a mortar with a pestle until it becomes a paste.

Place the egg yolks and the garlic in the container of a blender or a food processor and run the machine until the eggs are frothy.

With the machine still running, slowly add the oil until the sauce thickens. Add the lemon juice and run the machine for a few seconds. Put the sauce in a bowl. Add salt and pepper to taste and mix well. Use immediately or refrigerate.

2 cups

Trout with Garlic Cream

PREPARATION: 15 MINUTES   COOKING: 20 MINUTES

I very seldom cook frozen fish. The only frozen fish that is excellent is mountain trout. I always have some in my freezer for unexpected guests so that I can serve them this quick but elegant dish.

4 fresh or frozen trouts
4 tablespoons butter
Salt and pepper
3 cloves garlic, finely chopped

1 cup heavy cream
1 tablespoon brandy
Parsley for garnish

Preheat the oven to 475°.
You can use frozen trout without thawing it out. Wash and pat the trouts dry with paper towels. Put them side by side in a baking dish and dot with bits of butter. Sprinkle with salt and pepper. Bake for 15 minutes or until the flesh flakes easily.
Remove the trouts from the oven and arrange on a serving platter. Keep warm on top of a saucepan of boiling water.
Meanwhile, pour the juice in the baking dish into a saucepan. Add 1 tablespoon water and cook over high heat for 3 minutes, then add the garlic and cream, beating constantly with a whisk. Just before the cream starts to boil, remove from heat and add the brandy. Mix well and strain through a fine sieve over the fish. Garnish with parsley and serve.
4 servings

Tilefish with Capers

PREPARATION: 40 MINUTES   COOKING: 30 MINUTES

I didn't even know that such a thing as tilefish existed until one Sunday winter morning when we went fishing out of Sheepshead Bay with a group of people. We spent the day on a boat a hundred miles from shore. I caught nothing, but my son Thomas caught a fish. Everyone admired it, and I learned it was a tilefish. The captain of the fishing boat told me to poach it with potatoes and capers. I tried it and found the dish superb.

2 pounds medium-size potatoes
1 teaspoon salt
2 pounds tilefish
¾ cup vinegar
1 onion stuck with 2 cloves
1 bay leaf
1 carrot cut in three pieces

2 tablespoons butter
2 tablespoons flour
2 cups milk
Salt and pepper
Pinch of nutmeg
3 tablespoons heavy cream
½ cup capers

Peel the potatoes and put them in a saucepan. Cover with boiling water, add 1 teaspoon salt and bring to a boil. Reduce the heat and simmer for about 30 minutes, or until the potatoes are cooked.

Preheat the oven to 425°.

Meanwhile, in a deep skillet large enough to hold the fish, put 2 quarts water. Add vinegar, the onion stuck with cloves, the bay leaf and carrot. Boil for 5 minutes. Add salt and pepper. Add the fish and poach for 15 minutes.

Meanwhile, heat the butter in a skillet. Add the flour and brown it, then add the milk. Add salt and pepper to taste and the nutmeg. Stir with a wooden spoon until the milk comes to a boil; reduce the heat, add the cream and capers. Mix well and simmer until ready to use.

Drain the fish. With a fork and knife, remove the skin and the center bone. Cut into several slices.

Drain the potatoes and slice them. In a gratin dish arrange the potatoes and fish. Pour the sauce over them and bake for 10 minutes. Serve with a chilled white wine.

4 servings

Tilefish with Prawns

PREPARATION: 15 MINUTES   COOKING: 20 MINUTES

2 carrots, sliced
1 bay leaf
1 sprig parsley
⅓ cup white wine
4 large prawns
4 tilefish steaks, ¾ inch thick

2 tablespoons butter
2 tablespoons flour
1 tablespoon Crème Fraîche
  (see p. xvi)
12 fresh mint leaves
Salt and pepper

Put the carrots, bay leaf and parsley in a large saucepan. Cover with the wine and 1 quart water. Add salt and pepper and bring to a boil. Reduce the heat and let it simmer.

Meanwhile, shell the prawns but do not remove the tails. Put them in the simmering broth for 8 minutes. Remove with a spatula and keep warm on top of the stove or in a turned-off oven.

Wipe the tile steaks clean. Add them to the broth and simmer for 10 minutes. Carefully remove to a warm platter and keep warm along with the prawns. Strain the broth over a bowl and set aside 2 cups.

In a small saucepan, heat the butter, add the flour and mix well. While continuing to stir, slowly add the broth. Simmer for 5 minutes, stirring all the while. Correct the seasoning, add the crème fraîche and mix well.

Set aside 4 mint leaves for garnish and chop the remaining leaves. Add the chopped mint to the sauce. Pour the sauce over the fish and surround with the prawns. Decorate the fish with the mint leaves and serve.

4 servings

Vegetables

Braised Artichokes

PREPARATION: 30 MINUTES   COOKING: 1 HOUR

6 artichokes
1 tablespoon flour
1 cup oil
1 tablespoon sugar
Salt and pepper

3 carrots
4 medium-size onions
1 large potato
Juice of 2 lemons

Cut off the tips of the artichoke leaves so that they are only 1½ inches long. Spread apart the center leaves, and with a teaspoon, remove the center choke.

Mix the flour with 2 tablespoons water, then add the oil, sugar, salt and pepper. Pour into a casserole and bring to a boil.

Peel the carrots, onion and potato and finely chop in a food processor.

Place the artichokes in the boiling oil and put the chopped vegetables on top. Pour the lemon juice over the artichokes and add boiling water to cover. Cook, covered, over medium heat for 30 minutes. Uncover, correct the seasoning and simmer, uncovered, for 20 minutes more. The liquid should have disappeared almost completely. Remove the artichokes with a slotted spoon. Arrange on a serving platter and surround with the vegetables.

Serve right away with roast chicken or beef.

6 servings

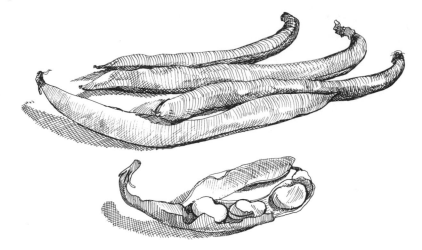

Braised Fava Beans and Artichokes

PREPARATION: 20 MINUTES   COOKING: 50 MINUTES

Chinese restaurants in New York often have the dishes of the day written in Chinese on sheets of paper hanging on the walls. As I cannot read Chinese and I haven't been able to persuade any of my children to learn Chinese for the specific purpose of deciphering Chinese menus, I often look around me when I am in a Chinese restaurant to see what the Chinese customers are eating so that if I don't see the dish on the English menu I can point out the food itself to the waiter. One day in a small Chinese restaurant I saw a man eating a mound of fresh green fava beans. They looked so appetizing that I ordered the dish. It turned out to be superb.

The season for fava beans is short, so if you live near an Italian or Chinese neighborhood, watch for them. They look like large string beans. They should feel full to the touch and the shells should be bright green.

4 pounds unshelled fresh fava
   beans
4 or 5 small purple Italian
   artichokes
Juice of 1 lemon

5 tablespoons butter
1 tablespoon savory
1 pound tiny frozen onions
Salt and pepper

Shell the fava beans. Wash the artichokes, remove the tough outer leaves and cut 1 inch off the top. Quarter them and remove the chokes in the center. Pour the lemon juice over them to prevent them from blackening.

In a large saucepan, heat 2 tablespoons butter. Add the artichokes and sauté over medium heat for 4 minutes. Add the onions and the savory, then the fava beans, salt and pepper and the remaining butter cut into small pieces. Add 2 tablespoons boiling water, cover and simmer for 40 minutes.

Serve with broiled chicken or veal.

4 to 5 servings

Steamed Broccoli

PREPARATION: 8 MINUTES   COOKING: 15 MINUTES

2 bunches broccoli	Juice of half a lemon
3 tablespoons butter	Salt and pepper

Wash the broccoli and cut off the tough lower part of the main stalk. Separate the budding stems and peel them.

Steam over high heat for 8 minutes or boil in a large kettle of boiling water. Drain immediately.

In a small saucepan, heat the butter and add the lemon juice and salt and pepper to taste.

Arrange the broccoli on a serving platter and pour the butter over it.

6 servings

NOTE: If you are serving a crown roast of pork, fill the center with the broccoli for a spectacular effect.

Broccoli with Blue Cheese Sauce

PREPARATION: 20 MINUTES   COOKING: 15 MINUTES

1 bunch broccoli	3 tablespoons heavy cream
2 ounces blue cheese	Pepper to taste
5 tablespoons ricotta	3 drops of Tabasco (optional)

Wash the broccoli and cut off the tough lower part of the main stalk. Separate the budding stems and peel them. Cut each lengthwise into 2 or 3 pieces.

Pour ½ cup water in a large skillet and place a steamer on top.

Arrange the broccoli stems so that they lie flat in the steamer's basket. Cover and steam over high heat for 6 minutes. (If you don't own a steamer, fill a saucepan with 1½ quarts salted water and boil until just tender.)

Meanwhile, mix together the blue cheese, ricotta and cream in a food processor. Add pepper and Tabasco. Serve in a bowl with the broccoli.

6 servings

NOTE: The leftover blue-cheese mixture, stored in a tightly sealed container, will keep for a week in the refrigerator. It can be served with steamed string beans, steamed new potatoes or boiled artichokes.

Brussels Sprouts with Bacon and Pine Nuts

PREPARATION: 10 MINUTES   COOKING: 20 MINUTES

2 pounds Brussels sprouts
¼ pound bacon, diced

½ cup pine nuts
Salt and pepper

Wash and trim the Brussels sprouts. Place in a steamer with 1½ cups water and steam for 15 minutes. Do not overcook.

Meanwhile, in a large skillet, sauté the bacon until golden brown. Remove with a slotted spoon and drain on paper towels.

Add the pine nuts and Brussels sprouts to the bacon fat. Sauté for a couple of minutes, or until the pine nuts are lightly browned. With a slotted spoon, transfer to a serving bowl. Sprinkle with freshly ground pepper and lightly with salt. Sprinkle the bits of bacon on top and serve.

6 servings

Cabbage Pie

PREPARATION: 20 MINUTES   COOKING: 1 HOUR

Pâte Brisée I (see p. 10)
1 head green cabbage
2 onions
4 tablespoons butter
¾ pound sweet Italian sausage
2 tablespoons chopped parsley

½ teaspoon allspice or
 four-spices (see p. xv)
Pinch of thyme
2 tablespoons heavy cream
Salt and pepper

Preheat the oven to 400°. Reduce by half the ingredients for the pâte brisée recipe and prepare the dough for the pie shell. Refrigerate.

Meanwhile, wash the cabbage, remove the core and cut into small pieces. Chop the cabbage and onions in a food processor or blender.

In a large skillet, heat the butter and add the sausage. Cook for 10 minutes, stirring all the while. Add the cabbage, parsley, allspice and thyme. Mix well and correct the seasoning with salt and pepper. Cook for 5 minutes and set aside.

Roll out the dough on a floured board. Butter a 9-inch pie pan and line it with the dough. Fill the pie shell with the cabbage and crimp the edges of the dough with a fork. Bake for 30 minutes, then pour the cream on top and bake for 15 minutes more. Serve piping hot.

6 servings

Red Cabbage with Granny Smith Apples

PREPARATION: 30 MINUTES   COOKING: 40 MINUTES

1 large head red cabbage   ¾ cup red wine
4 Granny Smith apples   Salt and pepper
4 tablespoons butter   1 tablespoon sugar
¼ cup wine vinegar

Wash the cabbage and remove the core. Peel, quarter and core the apples. Slice the cabbage in a food processor.

In a large saucepan, heat the butter and add the cabbage. Sauté for 5 minutes, stirring all the while. Add the vinegar and mix well. Add the wine, salt and pepper and mix well. Reduce the heat and cook, covered, for 15 minutes. Add the apples and cook for another 15 minutes. Add the sugar in the last 5 minutes of cooking.

6 servings

Spring Cabbage Purée

PREPARATION: 15 MINUTES   COOKING: 30 MINUTES

2-pound head green cabbage   Salt and pepper
6 tomatoes   1 tablespoon vinegar
¼ pound bacon   Pinch of thyme
4 tablespoons butter

Wash the cabbage and quarter it. Steam over 1½ cups water in a skillet for 10 minutes.

Meanwhile, quarter and seed the tomatoes by squeezing over a strainer set on top of a bowl. Reserve the juice. Dice the bacon. In a skillet, heat the butter and sauté the tomatoes for 20 minutes. Sprinkle with salt, pepper and thyme. In another skillet, sauté the diced bacon until crisp. Drain on paper towels and keep warm in the oven.

Purée the cabbage in a food processor with the tomato juice. Put the purée in a bowl and add 1 tablespoon bacon fat and the vinegar. Correct the seasoning and place the tomatoes and bacon on top. Serve right away.

4 servings

Glazed Carrots

PREPARATION: 15 MINUTES   COOKING: 30 TO 40 MINUTES

3 pounds carrots   Salt and pepper
1 stick (¼ pound) butter   Chopped parsley for garnish
2 tablespoons sugar

Wash and scrape the carrots. Cut into 1-inch pieces. Put the carrots in a large saucepan and barely cover with cold water. Add half the butter and bring to a boil. Cook rapidly over high heat, uncovered, until all the water has evaporated; stir the carrots once or twice, being careful not to break them. Add the remaining butter, salt and pepper to taste and the sugar. Lower the heat and cook gently for 20 minutes, or until the carrots are lightly glazed. Sprinkle with parsley and serve right away.

6 servings

Carrot Soufflé

PREPARATION: 20 MINUTES   COOKING: 40 MINUTES

2 pounds carrots   3 eggs
3 tablespoons butter   ¼ teaspoon nutmeg
2 tablespoons flour   Salt and pepper
1 cup milk

Preheat the oven to 325°.

Scrape and wash the carrots. Cut them into 1-inch slices. Put them in a large saucepan and cover with water. Add salt and bring to a boil. Cook over medium heat for about 15 minutes and drain. Purée the carrots in a food processor or blender. Set aside while making the sauce.

In a saucepan, heat the butter and add the flour. Stir well and cook for a few minutes. Slowly add the milk, stirring all the while, and simmer for 10 minutes. While the sauce is simmering, separate the eggs. Beat the whites with an electric beater until stiff but not dry. Add the yolks to the sauce, one at a time, stirring with a wooden spoon. Add the nutmeg, salt and pepper. Fold the sauce into the carrot purée, then fold in the egg whites. Pour the mixture into a buttered soufflé dish and bake for 30 minutes. Serve immediately.

6 servings

Cauliflower Cake with Pesto

PREPARATION: 15 MINUTES   COOKING: 1 HOUR

1 cauliflower
1 pound potatoes
1 stick (¼ pound) butter, cut
    into small pieces
4 eggs

2 tomatoes, sliced
Parsley sprigs for garnish
2 cups Pesto (see below)
Salt and pepper

Preheat the oven to 350°.

Remove the leaves of the cauliflower and separate the florets. Cut off and discard any thick stems. Peel the potatoes and quarter them.

Spread the potatoes and cauliflower on one layer of a steamer and place over 1 cup water in a skillet. Steam for 15 minutes, or until the potatoes are done.

Purée the cauliflower, potatoes, butter and eggs in a food processor. Add salt and pepper to taste.

Butter a 1½-quart loaf pan and fill it with the purée. Put the loaf pan in a roasting pan containing about 1½ inches of water and bake for 45 minutes.

Unmold on a serving platter. Garnish with tomatoes and parsley. Serve hot or cold with pesto.

6 servings

Pesto

PREPARATION: 15 MINUTES

½ cup grated Parmesan
1½ cups basil leaves
¼ cup pine nuts

2 cloves garlic
½ cup oil
Salt and pepper

Place all the ingredients in the container of a food processor or a blender and run the machine until the basil is finely chopped. Remove to a bowl. Add salt and pepper to taste.

2½ cups

Steamed Cauliflower with Beaumont Cheese

PREPARATION: 15 MINUTES   COOKING: 15 MINUTES

No vegetable has a better, more delicate taste than new cauliflower in the spring. In fact, steamed cauliflower needs nothing more than some salt and pepper and a touch of butter. But you can add some melted tangy cheese, such as Beaumont cheese, to give some extra zest to the dish.

1 large cauliflower
¼ pound Beaumont cheese
4 slices Swiss cheese

4 tablespoons heavy cream or
  milk
Pepper

Unless they are very tender, remove the leaves of the cauliflower and separate the florets; remove the center stem. Steam the florets (and the leaves) for 5 minutes over 1 cup water in a skillet.

Meanwhile, cut both cheeses into small pieces. Put the cream and the cheese in a small saucepan and stir with a wooden spoon over low heat until the cheese has melted and become creamy.

Remove the cauliflower (and the leaves) and arrange on a serving platter. Pour the melted cheese over them and sprinkle with freshly ground pepper.

4 servings

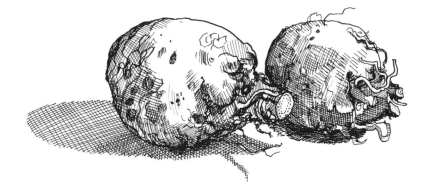

Celery Root with Smoked Bacon

PREPARATION: 25 MINUTES   COOKING: 1 HOUR

Celery root, also known as celeriac (see illustration), is a delicious vegetable often forgotten by Americans. It can be used for soup and is also
very good served with steak or duck, or braised with bacon.

3 large potatoes   1 onion, chopped
2 medium-size celery roots   3 tablespoons oil
¼ pound smoked bacon, diced   Salt and pepper

Peel the potatoes and celery roots and dice them. In a saucepan, heat the
oil and add the bacon. Cook until golden brown and drain on paper
towels.

Sauté the diced celery root in the bacon fat until golden brown.
Remove with a slotted spoon to a plate. Add the potatoes and the onion
to the fat and sauté until golden brown. Put the celery root and bacon
back into the saucepan. Sprinkle with freshly ground pepper and a little
salt (be careful—the bacon is salty). Pour 4 tablespoons water in the
saucepan and simmer for 30 minutes.

4 servings

Purée of Celery Root

PREPARATION: 15 MINUTES   COOKING: 45 MINUTES

3 celery roots
Juice of 2 lemons
2 pounds potatoes
1 tablespoon flour

½ cup milk
¼ teaspoon nutmeg
Salt and pepper
1 stick (¼ pound) butter

Peel the celery roots and sprinkle with lemon juice so that they will not darken. Slice them. Peel and slice the potatoes.

Bring 6 cups water to a boil and add 1 tablespoon salt. In a small bowl, mix the flour with 2 tablespoons water and add to the boiling water. Add the juice of half a lemon and then the celery root and potato. Cook over medium heat for 30 minutes, or until the celery root is tender when pierced with a fork. Drain.

Purée the celery root and the potato in a food processor or a blender. Pour the purée back into the saucepan and add milk, salt, pepper and nutmeg.

Just before serving, add the butter and mix well. Put the purée in a serving bowl and smooth the surface with a fork. Serve with roast meat or chicken.

6 servings

Chestnut Stew

PREPARATION: 30 MINUTES   COOKING: 1½ HOURS

1½ pounds chestnuts
4 ounces bacon
6 small onions
1½ cups chicken stock
2 tablespoons butter

Salt and pepper
1 bay leaf
¼ pound mushrooms
4 ounces small green olives

Make an incision in the shape of a cross in the flat side of each chestnut. Fry the chestnuts for a couple of minutes in very hot oil (360°), then drain on paper towels and let them cool. Remove the inner skins and shells. Dice the bacon and peel the onions. Heat the chicken stock.

In a casserole, heat the butter and add the onions and bacon. Cook until golden brown, then add the chicken stock. Add the chestnuts, mix well and add salt and pepper and the bay leaf. Simmer, covered, for 45 minutes, stirring from time to time and adding more liquid if necessary.

Wash, trim and slice the mushrooms. Add the mushrooms and green olives to the casserole and cook for 30 minutes more. Serve very hot.

4 servings

Steamed Eggplant with Ginger Sauce

PREPARATION: 10 MINUTES   COOKING: 5 MINUTES

One late spring afternoon I was walking through Chinatown's outdoor markets when I came across a beautiful purple vegetable—a long, narrow eggplant, about an inch in diameter and 6 inches long. I bought some of these eggplants and desperately tried to find some way of preserving their incredible color. I boiled them, steamed them and fried them. Everything I tried failed—when cooked, they turned brown. But what a marvelous taste! I decided that they were at their best steamed and served them with a ginger sauce.

6 long Chinese eggplants   1 cup Ginger Sauce (see p. 25)

Place the eggplants in a steamer over 1½ cups water in a saucepan. Steam for 5 minutes and set aside while making the sauce.

Put on a warm platter, cover with the sauce and serve.

6 servings

Broiled Eggplant

PREPARATION: 10 MINUTES   COOKING: 30 MINUTES

1 large eggplant   Dash of cumin
½ cup olive oil   Salt and pepper
1 cup Yogurt Sauce (see p. 90)   2 tablespoons chopped parsley
1 clove garlic, crushed

Cut the eggplant into ½-inch slices. Place in a shallow dish and brush with oil. Sprinkle with salt and pepper. Broil until golden brown on both sides.

Meanwhile, make the yogurt sauce, add garlic and mix well. Add cumin and correct the seasoning. Arrange the eggplant slices on a platter and pour the yogurt sauce over them. Sprinkle with parsley and serve.
6 servings

Eggplant Gratiné

PREPARATION: 20 MINUTES   COOKING: 15 MINUTES

1 large eggplant
1 pound tomatoes
6 tablespoons butter
6 tablespoons olive oil

Salt and pepper
¼ cup grated Parmesan
2 tablespoons thyme

Peel the eggplant and cut into thin slices. Dip the tomatoes in boiling water, then peel and cut into thin slices.

Heat 2 tablespoons butter and 3 tablespoons oil in a skillet; in another skillet heat 3 tablespoons butter and oil. Put the eggplant in one skillet and the tomatoes in the other. Sprinkle salt and pepper over both. Cook over high heat for 10 minutes, turning the eggplant once and stirring the tomatoes.

In a gratin dish, make a layer of eggplant, cover with tomatoes and sprinkle with Parmesan and thyme. Put another layer of eggplant on top of the tomatoes and sprinkle with Parmesan and thyme. Dot with the remaining butter and brown under the broiler. Serve immediately with hamburgers or steak.
4 servings

Stuffed Endives

PREPARATION: 30 MINUTES   COOKING: 45 MINUTES

6 large endives
3 onions, finely chopped
5 tablespoons butter
8 ounces sweet Italian sausage

¼ cup fresh bread crumbs
2 tablespoons chopped parsley
Salt and pepper
½ cup chicken stock

Wash the endives and cut in two lengthwise. Remove some of the inside leaves to make a cavity for the stuffing. Finely chop the inside leaves and set aside.

Preheat the oven to 450°.

In a skillet, heat 3½ tablespoons butter and add the onions. Cook for 5 minutes, then add the chopped endive leaves and sauté for 2 minutes. Remove the sausage from its casing and add it to the onions. Add the bread crumbs and parsley, and salt and pepper to taste. Cook, stirring with a fork, for 5 minutes.

Fill one half of each endive with some of the stuffing, forming a mound. Place the other half on top and tie with string.

Butter a gratin dish. Place the endives side by side. Melt the remaining butter and pour over them. Add the stock and bake, basting occasionally, for 15 minutes, or until the endives are golden brown. Serve in the dish in which they have cooked.

6 servings

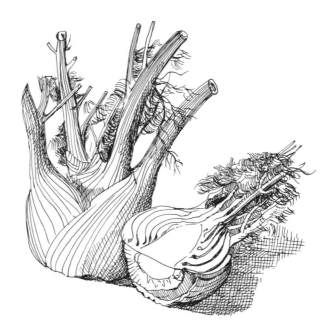

Fennel with Sherry

PREPARATION: 5 MINUTES   COOKING: 45 MINUTES

Fennel is a crisp white-and-green bulbous vegetable the Italians call *finocchio*. Similar to celery in texture but with the distinctive taste of anise, it is delicious both cooked and raw. Fennel seeds are often used as spices in many Italian and other European dishes.

4 bulbs fennel
Salt and pepper
4 tablespoons butter

½ cup dry sherry or port
3½ ounces heavy cream

Cut off the stalks of the fennel and split the bulbs in two lengthwise. Wash and pat dry with paper towels. Place the pieces of fennel side by side in a large skillet and sprinkle with salt and pepper. Put ½ tablespoon butter on top of each piece of fennel and add 1 cup water. Cover the skillet and cook over medium heat for 45 minutes.

When the fennel is cooked (test with a fork; it should be tender but not mushy) remove to a platter and keep warm in a turned-off oven.

Put the fennel liquid over high heat. Add the sherry or port and scrape the pan with a wooden spoon. Bring to a boil, then turn off the heat. Add the cream and pour over the fennel. Serve immediately with broiled steak or fish.

6 servings

Fricassee of Fennel

PREPARATION: 15 MINUTES   COOKING: 1 HOUR

4 bulbs fennels
6 small potatoes
¼ pound small onions
4 tablespoons butter

¼ pound bacon, diced
¼ cup oil
½ cup chicken stock or bouillon

Wash and quarter the fennel bulbs. Peel and quarter the potatoes. Peel the onions.

In a saucepan, heat the butter and add the onions and bacon. Sauté them until the bacon is nearly done. Remove with a slotted spoon and set aside. Add the fennel and sauté for 5 minutes. Add the bacon and onions and simmer for 10 minutes.

Meanwhile, heat the oil in a skillet and add the potatoes. Sauté for 10 minutes. Remove with a slotted spoon and add to the fennel. Sprinkle with salt and pepper. Add ½ cup stock or bouillon and simmer for 20 minutes, or until the potatoes are done. (Add more stock if necessary.) Serve with roast pork.

6 servings

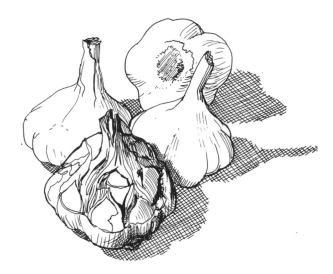

Ail au Four   (Baked Garlic Bulbs)

PREPARATION: 10 MINUTES   COOKING: 1¼ HOURS

This recipe may sound strange, but it's worth trying because it's quite extraordinary in taste. The garlic bulbs, protected by their skins, stay whole and become a golden brown color and the flesh acquires the consistency of a purée. The garlic loses its powerful aroma and you may have no fear kissing your friend after dinner!

6 whole bulbs garlic
4 tablespoons butter
¼ cup dry white wine
¼ cup chicken bouillon

4 ounces farmer cheese
3 tablespoons sour cream
3 scallions, chopped
Salt and pepper

Preheat the oven to 325°. With the point of a sharp knife, make an incision, 1½ inches from the top, all around the skin of the garlic bulbs. Remove the first layer of skin, but do not peel the garlic (see illustration).

Butter a baking pan large enough to hold the garlic bulbs side by side. Place them in the pan and dot each bulb with ½ tablespoon butter. Sprinkle with salt and pepper and pour the wine and bouillon over the bulbs. Cover the pan with foil and bake for 45 minutes. Remove the foil and bake for fifteen minutes more.

Just before serving, beat together the cheese and sour cream; add the chopped scallions and salt and pepper. Serve this sauce alongside the garlic with broiled steak or baked chicken. Serve each person a bulb of garlic. The way to eat it is to press the garlic flesh out of the skin of each clove with a fork and mix it with the cream cheese.

6 servings

Lentils with Bacon

PREPARATION: 10 MINUTES   COOKING: 30 MINUTES

2 pounds lentils	6 slices bacon
2 bay leaves	Salt and pepper
3 cloves garlic	Parsley for garnish

Put the lentils in a large saucepan and cover with 2 quarts water. Bring to a boil, lower the heat and add the bay leaves and salt and pepper. Simmer for 30 minutes.

Meanwhile, peel and slice the garlic cloves. Cut the bacon into 1-inch pieces. In a skillet, fry the bacon until crisp and remove with a slotted spoon onto paper towels. Add the garlic to the hot bacon fat and cook for several minutes.

Test the lentils to see if they are cooked. If they are still slightly hard, cook for about 15 minutes more—do not overcook. Put them in a colander to drain.

Put the lentils back in the saucepan. Pour the hot bacon fat and garlic over the lentils and mix gently with a wooden spoon. Heat slowly and correct the seasoning.

Place the lentils in a serving dish. Sprinkle them with the bacon and garnish with parsley. Serve with roast pork.

8 servings

Purée of Mushrooms

PREPARATION: 10 MINUTES   COOKING: 35 MINUTES

2 pounds firm white mushrooms	1 egg
6 tablespoons butter	1 cup heavy cream
3 tablespoons flour	Salt and pepper
1 cup milk	⅛ teaspoon nutmeg

Preheat the oven to 350°.

Cut off the ends of the mushroom stems under running water; drain and pat dry with paper towels. Set aside 4 mushroom caps for garnish. Purée the mushrooms in a food processor or a blender.

In a large skillet heat 3 tablespoons butter and add the mushroom purée. Cook over medium heat, stirring occasionally, for about 15 minutes, or until the mushrooms have lost their juice.

Meanwhile, prepare the sauce. In a saucepan, melt 3 tablespoons butter and add the flour all at once. Mix well with a wooden spoon, then slowly add the milk, stirring all the while. Simmer the sauce for 10 minutes, then add it to the mushrooms.

Beat the egg with the cream and add to the mushrooms. Add salt, pepper and nutmeg. Pour the mixture in an ovenproof serving dish and bake for 10 minutes. Just before serving, garnish with the raw mushroom caps. Serve with broiled steak or roast chicken.

8 servings

Mushrooms with Cider

PREPARATION: 10 MINUTES   COOKING: 15 MINUTES

2 pounds firm white mushrooms   Salt and pepper
2 cups hard cider   1 cup Crème Fraîche (p. xvi)
1 tablespoon butter

Wash the mushrooms and pat dry with paper towels. Place the mushrooms in a saucepan and cover with the cider; bring to a boil, lower the heat and simmer for 6 minutes. Drain the mushrooms over a bowl and reserve ½ cup of the liquid.

In a skillet, heat the butter and add the mushrooms. Sauté for 3 minutes; add salt and pepper to taste.

Mix the reserved liquid with the crème fraîche. Pour the mushrooms in a serving bowl and pour the crème fraîche over them. Serve with buttered white toast.

6 servings

Braised Onions

PREPARATION: 20 MINUTES   COOKING: 3 HOURS

This is an old Alsatian recipe. Years ago my grandmother lived in Alsace the first years of her marriage. She used to tell us that in making this dish, the onions would be baked in a coal oven all day long and the results were worth waiting for. Today, I make this dish during the holidays, using leftover goose fat from the Christmas goose and baking it for 3 hours.

12 large onions   2 tablespoons goose fat
Salt   Pepper

Preheat the oven to 250°.

Peel the onions and slice them without slicing them through (see illustration). Sprinkle the onions with salt and place them upside down on a platter for 20 minutes.

Dry the onions with paper towels. In a large ovenproof casserole, heat the goose fat and place the onions side by side. Sprinkle generously with freshly ground pepper. Cover and bake for 3 hours.

Serve with roast pork or goose stew.

6 servings

Stuffed Onions

PREPARATION: 20 MINUTES   COOKING: 40 MINUTES

Martha Enson is seventeen years old and has been my student for three years. On my birthday she bakes me a cake and waits anxiously for the verdict, but it is always superb. She tested the following recipe for me and added the spices. I tried it her way and found she had improved the recipe.

12 large red onions	Salt and pepper
¾ pound leftover beef, lamb or pork	5 tablespoons olive oil
¼ teaspoon thyme	1 cup cooked rice
¼ teaspoon tarragon	3 tablespoons butter
¼ teaspoon chives	2 cups Green Sauce (see p. 31)

Preheat the oven to 400°. Peel the onions and put them in 1 quart boiling salted water. Cook over medium heat for 20 minutes. They should be cooked but still firm.

Meanwhile, prepare the stuffing. Chop the meat and add the thyme, tarragon, chives and salt and pepper to taste.

Remove the onions and drain them on a rack. When cool to the touch, cut off 2 inches from the top. With a teaspoon, remove some of the inner layers. Chop the cut-off part of the onions and half of the part that was removed. Add to the stuffing (it should be a scant cup of chopped onions).

In a large skillet, heat the olive oil and add the meat. Sauté for 5 minutes, then add the cooked rice and mix well. Correct the seasoning, adding salt and pepper if necessary.

Fill the onions with the stuffing. Place them in an ovenproof dish and put ½ tablespoon butter on top of each onion. Bake for 5 minutes. Serve right away with green sauce on the side.

6 servings

Green Peas with Romaine

PREPARATION: 20 MINUTES   COOKING: 15 MINUTES

3 tablespoons butter
1 tablespoon flour
3 pounds fresh peas, shelled, or
   2 boxes frozen young peas
Salt and pepper
6 small scallions, cut into 1-inch
   pieces

1 small head romaine, shredded
2 eggs, lightly beaten
4 sprigs parsley, chopped, for
   garnish

In a saucepan, heat the butter and add the flour all at once. Mix well with a wooden spoon, then slowly add ½ cup water, stirring all the while. Bring to a boil and add the peas. Add salt and pepper to taste. Add the scallions and romaine. Cook, covered, for 10 minutes.

Just before serving, add the eggs and mix well. Correct the seasoning. Sprinkle with parsley and serve.

   6 servings

Snow Peas with Pine Nuts

PREPARATION: 6 MINUTES   COOKING: 10 MINUTES

Snow peas look like regular unshelled peas, but unlike the other kind, their pods are very tender and edible. They are delicious simply steamed and served with a pat of fresh butter, or used in soup or cooked with meats and chicken. The secret is not to overcook them.

6 ounces snow peas
1 teaspoon sesame oil
3 tablespoons pine nuts
2 tablespoons soy sauce

2 tablespoons chicken stock or
   bouillon
Parsley sprigs for garnish

String the snow peas and steam them for 4 minutes. Remove to a serving bowl and keep warm.

Heat the sesame oil in a saucepan and sauté the pine nuts for 3 minutes. Add the soy sauce and bouillon. Heat through, but do not boil.

Surround the snow peas with parsley and pour the sauce over them. Serve immediately.

   4 servings

Galettes de Pommes de Terre

PREPARATION: 20 MINUTES   COOKING: 20 MINUTES

5 large potatoes	½ cup grated Swiss cheese
(about 1¾ pounds)	¼ teaspoon nutmeg
2 eggs	Salt and pepper
2 tablespoons flour	Oil for frying

Peel and wash the potatoes; pat dry with paper towels. Shred the potatoes in a food processor. Take three layers of paper towels and place the potatoes in the center; twist both ends of the paper towels to squeeze the water out of the potatoes.

In a bowl, beat together the eggs and flour. Add the cheese, nutmeg and salt and pepper to taste. Add the potatoes and mix well.

Heat the oil in a large skillet and add the potato mixture by spoonfuls to make pancakes, each about 5 inches in diameter. Fry both sides until golden brown. Stack the pancakes on a hot platter as you cook them and keep them warm in a turned-off oven. Serve hot with roast chicken or duck.

10 pancakes

Paul Bocuse's Potato Pancake

PREPARATION: 10 MINUTES   COOKING: 15 MINUTES

A few years ago I translated Paul Bocuse's cook book from French into English. One of the happy results was that the following summer he invited my husband and me for a tour of his friends' restaurants. Our first stop was Paul's own restaurant at Collonges-au-Mont d'Or. We arrived by suppertime tired from our trip, so I asked Paul to make us a light dinner. Following him into the kitchen, I watched him prepare our dinner. Using a 10-inch crêpe pan, he made us a marvelous potato pancake that he served with an entrecôte and an apple pie. He told me that in order to make a good pancake the potatoes had to be peeled at the last moment and not soaked beforehand because potatoes that are soaked in water lose all their taste.

1 pound potatoes	1 large egg
2 tablespoons chopped parsley	Salt and pepper
2 cloves garlic, finely chopped	2 tablespoons olive oil
Pinch of nutmeg	

Peel and wash the potatoes; pat dry with paper towels. Grate the potatoes in a food processor and remove to a bowl. Add the parsley, garlic, nutmeg and egg. Mix well with a spoon. Add salt and freshly ground pepper (three turns of the pepper mill, according to Paul). Mix well.

In a large crêpe pan, heat the oil and add the potato mixture, spreading and flattening it with a spatula. Cook for about 5 minutes on each side, or until it is golden brown.

Slide the pancake onto a warm round platter. Cut it in four and serve with broiled steak.

4 servings

Potato Pancakes with Mushrooms

PREPARATION: 20 MINUTES   COOKING: 20 MINUTES

½ pound potatoes
½ pound mushrooms
1 egg
Pinch of nutmeg
Salt and pepper

1 tablespoon Crème Fraîche
(see p. xvi)
½ cup oil
1 stick (¼ pound) butter

Peel and wash the potatoes; pat dry with paper towels.

Grate them in a food processor.

Wash and pat the mushrooms dry with paper towels. Chop finely in a food processor or a blender and add to the potatoes. Add 1 egg, nutmeg, salt and pepper to taste and the crème fraîche. Mix well.

In a skillet, heat some of the oil with 2 tablespoons butter. Drop the potato mixture by tablespoonfuls into the oil and flatten the pancakes with a spatula. Brown on each side for 5 minutes. Add some butter and oil for frying each batch of pancakes. Remove to a serving platter as you cook the pancakes and keep warm in a very low oven.

6 servings

Baked Potatoes with Anchovies

PREPARATION: 15 MINUTES   COOKING: 45 MINUTES

A few years ago I took forty students to France in January. We rented a bus and traveled along the Loire Valley. A snowstorm hit France that winter; the weather was cold and damp and we were miserable as we trudged from one castle to another. At Chinon we stopped for lunch at a small inn, and we were served this delicious potato dish with a broiled entrecôte. Our spirits were raised, our feet no longer felt frozen, and it was with great pleasure that we continued our trip.

8 large potatoes, julienned
1 stick (¼ pound) butter
5 onions, finely chopped
2 cans anchovy filets

8 tablespoons Crème Fraîche (see p. xvi)
Freshly ground pepper

Preheat the oven to 425°.

Keep the julienned potatoes covered with water until ready to use.

In a skillet, heat 2 tablespoons butter and add the onions. Cook until golden brown and set aside.

Drain the anchovies, reserving the oil. Cut each anchovy in half.

Butter a gratin dish. Drain the potatoes and pat dry with paper towels. Place a layer of potatoes at the bottom of the gratin dish, cover with a layer of onions and then a layer of anchovies. Finish with a layer of potatoes and sprinkle with pepper. Melt the remaining butter. Add to it the oil from the anchovies and pour over the potatoes. Spread half of the crème fraîche on top and bake for 30 minutes. Add the remaining crème fraîche and bake for 15 minutes more. Serve right away with broiled steak and a green salad.

6 servings

Baked Potatoes with Ricotta

PREPARATION: 15 MINUTES   COOKING: 45 MINUTES

4 large Idaho potatoes
2 cloves garlic
2 teaspoons chopped chives
½ pound ricotta

2 tablespoons Crème Fraîche (see p. xvi)
Salt and pepper

Preheat the oven to 400°. Scrub and pat dry the potatoes with paper towels. Bake for 40 minutes, or until they are easily pierced with a fork.

Meanwhile, peel and mince the garlic. Add the garlic and chives to the ricotta and mix well. Add the crème fraîche and salt and pepper to taste. Mix well.

Remove the potatoes from the oven and split the center with a knife. With a tablespoon, remove 2 tablespoons of the flesh from each potato, forming a hole in the center. Fill the hole with the cheese and make a mound. Place the potatoes on an ovenproof serving platter and heat in the oven for 4 minutes.

Serve piping hot with cold chicken and a green salad.

4 servings.

Sautéed New Potatoes

PREPARATION: 5 MINUTES   COOKING: 25 MINUTES

18 new potatoes, washed and
  scrubbed
1 tablespoon salt
3 tablespoons butter

3 tablespoons chopped fresh
  parsley
Salt and pepper

Place the potatoes in a large saucepan and cover with boiling water; add salt. Cook for about 20 minutes, or until they are pierced easily with a fork. Drain the potatoes.

In a large skillet, heat the butter and add the potatoes. Sauté at high heat for 3 or 4 minutes, or until the potatoes are golden brown. Sprinkle with parsley and serve immediately.

6 servings

Hot Pumpkin Mousse

PREPARATION: 20 MINUTES   COOKING: 20 MINUTES

Pumpkin in France is always served as a vegetable or used for soup, never as a dessert, as in pumpkin pie. I never liked pumpkin as a child, but when I came to the United States I started to enjoy Thanksgiving pumpkin pie and took a fresh look at pumpkin as a vegetable. Last Christmas I made an unsweet pumpkin mousse in small cupcake cups and served it with the goose. It was an instant success. All you need is an unsweetened can of pumpkin purée (to make it from scratch would take hours) and foil cupcake cups $2\frac{7}{8}$ inches in diameter and $1\frac{1}{4}$ inches deep.

1 cup Béchamel (see below)
1 cup pumpkin purée
2 egg yolks
3 eggs
4 tablespoons grated Swiss
 cheese

6 tablespoons heavy cream
¼ teaspoon cayenne
¼ teaspoon nutmeg
1 clove garlic
Salt and pepper
Watercress for garnish

Preheat the oven to 425°. Make the béchamel. In a food processor, mix it with the pumpkin purée, egg yolks, eggs, cheese, cream, cayenne, nutmeg, garlic, salt and pepper.

Butter 8 foil cupcake cups about 3 inches in diameter and 1¼ inches deep and fill them three quarters full with the mixture. Bake in a pan filled with about 1 inch of water for 20 minutes.

Unmold each pumpkin mousse on a serving platter. Garnish with watercress and serve immediately.

8 servings

Béchamel

PREPARATION: 5 MINUTES   COOKING: 20 MINUTES

This is a basic sauce that can be used as a base for other sauces by adding tomato paste, cheese or spices, such as mustard and paprika.

2 tablespoons butter
3 tablespoons flour

2½ cups milk
Salt and freshly ground pepper

In a small saucepan, heat the butter and add the flour all at once. Stir with a wooden spoon and cook slowly over low heat, stirring all the while, until the flour has absorbed all the butter. Slowly add the milk in a stream, stirring all the while to avoid lumps. Add salt and pepper. Simmer, stirring frequently, for about 15 minutes.

To keep warm, place the saucepan over another, larger saucepan of simmering water. If the sauce has to keep for more than 20 minutes, cover it with a piece of buttered waxed paper.

2½ cups

Sorrel Purée

PREPARATION: 20 MINUTES   COOKING: 25 MINUTES

Sorrel is a wonderful vegetable that has only recently begun to appear in American vegetable markets, where it is sometimes called sour grass.

It has dark green leaves. When cooked, it has a slightly bitter taste, so a little sugar should always be added.

If sorrel is unavailable, use young small spinach leaves as a substitute and omit the sugar.

3 pounds sorrel	1 cup chicken broth
3 tablespoons butter	Salt and pepper
2 tablespoons flour	2 egg yolks
1 teaspoon sugar	½ cup heavy cream

Wash the sorrel well and discard some of the larger stems. Put the sorrel in a saucepan and add 1 cup water. Cook over medium heat for 5 to 8 minutes, or until the sorrel has wilted. Drain and press the leaves with your hands to squeeze out the water.

In a saucepan, melt the butter and add the flour. Cook over low heat, stirring constantly with a wooden spoon, until the flour turns golden. Continue stirring while adding the sorrel, sugar, chicken broth and salt and pepper to taste. Cook, covered, over medium heat for 15 minutes, stirring from time to time.

Purée the contents of the saucepan in a food processor. Add the egg yolks and run the food processor for 5 seconds.

Transfer to a saucepan and heat the sorrel through, but do not boil. Just before serving, add the cream and stir with a wooden spoon. Serve at once.

6 servings

Stuffed Spinach Roll

PREPARATION: 50 MINUTES   COOKING: 45 MINUTES

2 ounces dried mushrooms	2 tablespoons ice water
2 pounds fresh spinach	6½ tablespoons butter
1 tablespoon salt	½ pound lean pork, chopped
1¼ cups flour	¼ pound beef round, chopped
2 eggs	¼ cup grated Parmesan
1 tablespoon oil	Salt and pepper

Soak the mushrooms in warm water. Wash and trim the spinach. In a large saucepan, bring 2½ quarts water to a boil and add the salt. Add the spinach and bring to a second boil. Remove from heat and drain. Set aside to cool.

Put the flour, eggs, oil and a pinch of salt in the container of a food processor and run the machine for 15 seconds. With the machine still running, add 2 tablespoons ice water. Run the machine for 10 seconds more, or until the dough forms a ball. Roll the dough on a floured board and make a rectangle about ⅛ inch thick. Sprinkle the dough with flour and cover it with a damp paper towel while preparing the stuffing.

In a skillet, heat 1½ tablespoons butter and add the pork and beef. Sauté for 5 minutes. Drain the mushrooms and cut them into two or three pieces if they are too large. Add the mushrooms to the meat. Add salt and pepper to taste (the meat should be quite spicy). Simmer for 10 minutes while chopping the spinach.

Press the spinach with a fork or your hands to remove all the water. Chop coarsely with a sharp knife. In a skillet, heat 2 tablespoons butter and add the spinach. Cook, stirring all the while over very high heat, until all the water has evaporated.

With a spatula, spread a layer of spinach on the dough, then a layer of the stuffing. Roll the dough to enclose the stuffing, forming a sausage-like shape. Put the stuffed roll on a piece of cheesecloth slightly larger than the roll itself, and enclose it very tightly. Twist and tie the ends with string. Bring 3 quarts water to a boil in a large saucepan and add the stuffed roll. Lower the heat and simmer for 40 minutes. Drain and remove the cheesecloth. Melt the remaining butter. Slice the roll and serve very hot with the butter and grated Parmesan.

This dish is excellent reheated and served with a purée of fresh tomatoes.

6 servings

Steamed Spinach with Lemon Sauce

PREPARATION: 10 MINUTES   COOKING: 4 MINUTES

2 pounds fresh spinach   3 tablespoons soy sauce
Salt and freshly ground pepper 1 tablespoon sugar
2 tablespoons lemon juice

Wash and trim the spinach. Place the spinach in a steamer over 1 cup water. Steam for 3 minutes and remove immediately.

In a small bowl, mix together a pinch of salt, pepper, lemon juice, soy sauce and sugar. Mix well and pour over the spinach. Serve right away.

6 servings

Roulade d'Epinards

PREPARATION: 20 MINUTES   COOKING: 1 HOUR

1 pound potatoes
2 pounds spinach
2 tablespoons butter
Salt and pepper
¼ teaspoon nutmeg

2 eggs
¼ cup grated Parmesan
8 tablespoons flour
1 stick (¼ pound) butter, melted

Scrub the potatoes and put them in a saucepan of salted boiling water. Cook, covered, for about 30 minutes, or until they are easily pierced with a fork.

Meanwhile, wash and trim the spinach. Put in another saucepan of boiling water and bring to a boil, then turn off the heat. Let stand for 5 minutes, then drain. Squeeze all the water out with a fork and coarsely chop.

In a skillet, heat the butter and add the spinach, salt, pepper and nutmeg. Sauté over high heat for 5 minutes. Remove from heat and add 1 egg and the Parmesan. Mix well and set aside.

Drain the potatoes and cool under running water. Peel them and mash with a fork or in a food mill. Add 6 tablespoons flour and 1 egg, salt and pepper. Mix well.

Cut a double 12-inch-square piece of cheesecloth and sprinkle with the remaining flour. Put the mashed potato on the cheesecloth and roll with a floured rolling pin until it is about ½ inch thick. Spread the spinach on the potato with a spatula. Roll the potato as you would a jelly roll and enclose in the cheesecloth. Tie both ends with string.

In a pan wide enough to hold the roll, bring 1½ quarts water to a boil and add the roll. Lower the heat and simmer for 25 minutes. Remove the roll with a spatula in each hand. Untie the cheesecloth and slice the roll. Arrange on a serving platter and serve with melted butter.

6 servings

Spaghetti Squash

Spaghetti squash is a vegetable that looks like a honeydew melon. It should be either boiled or baked. When boiled—which is the faster method—the squash is cut in two and the flesh scooped out with a fork —it will come out as long spaghetti-like strands. The squash can be eaten hot with any of your favorite spaghetti sauces or cold in a vinai-grette as an hors d'oeuvre. I like to serve it hot with a clam sauce or cold with a mustard sauce.

Spaghetti Squash with Clam Sauce
COOKING: 30 MINUTES   PREPARATION: 35 MINUTES

1 spaghetti squash
1 dozen large clams
6 tablespoons olive oil
3 cloves garlic, chopped

6 sprigs parsley, chopped
Pinch of oregano
Grated Parmesan
Freshly ground pepper

Place the squash, unpeeled, in a large kettle; cover with water, bring to a boil and cook for 20 minutes over medium high heat, or until a fork will easily pierce the skin. Drain.

While the squash is cooking, wash and scrub the clams and rinse them several times to remove all sand. Put them in a large kettle, cover, and cook until the clams open. Remove to a bowl and strain the broth and reserve it. When the clams are cool enough to handle, remove them from their shells and mince them.

In a skillet, heat the olive oil and add the garlic. Cook slowly for 5 minutes, stirring all the while. Add the clams and parsley and the strained broth. Add pepper and oregano. Simmer the sauce while pre-paring the squash.

Cut the squash in two, and with a fork, scrape out the flesh. Put the squash in a large bowl and pour the clam sauce in. Serve with grated Parmesan.

4 servings

Spaghetti Squash Rémoulade
COOKING: 30 MINUTES   PREPARATION: 15 MINUTES

1 spaghetti squash
1 teaspoon lemon juice
4 tablespoons Dijon mustard
3 tablespoons boiling water

½ cup olive oil
2 tablespoons vinegar
Salt and pepper
1 teaspoon dried tarragon

Following the directions in the above recipe, cook the squash and let it cool.

Cut the squash in two and scrape out the flesh with a fork. Put the squash in a bowl and add the lemon juice. Toss well and refrigerate.

Meanwhile, prepare the rémoulade sauce. Put the mustard in the container of a food processor, and with the machine running, slowly add the boiling water drop by drop, and then the olive oil, vinegar, and tarragon. The sauce will be thick and creamy. Add salt and pepper.

Pour the sauce over the squash; toss well and refrigerate until ready to serve.

4 servings

String Beans with Anchovies

PREPARATION: 20 MINUTES   COOKING: 20 MINUTES

2 pounds young fresh string
   beans, strings removed
8 anchovy filets preserved in
   brine (available at Italian
   grocery stores)

2 eggs
2 cloves garlic
½ cup olive oil
Salt and pepper

In a saucepan, uncovered, boil the string beans for 15 minutes. Drain immediately.

Wash the anchovies under cold running water. Cut in two lengthwise and remove the center bone. Soak them in cold water for 10 minutes. Put the eggs (at room temperature) in a pan of hot water and simmer for about 15 minutes. Cool under running water, peel, and cut in two. Remove the yolks and set aside. (Save the whites for some later use.)

Mix the egg yolks and garlic in a blender or a food processor until the garlic is puréed. With the machine still running, add the oil in a stream. Remove to a bowl and add a pinch of salt and pepper. The sauce will have the consistency of mayonnaise.

Arrange the string beans in a serving bowl and place the anchovy filets on top. Serve the sauce in a separate bowl or, for a special touch, fill a pastry bag, fitted with a fluting tube, with the mayonnaise and decorate the string beans. Serve with cold chicken or boiled beef.

4 to 6 servings

String-Bean Pancakes with Ham

PREPARATION: 20 MINUTES   COOKING: 40 MINUTES

1 pound string beans
½ pound boiled ham, cut into
  small pieces
3 tablespoons chopped parsley
½ cup ricotta
Salt and pepper

4 tablespoons flour
4 tablespoons Italian bread
  crumbs
2 eggs
Oil for frying
Parsley sprigs for garnish

String the string beans. In a saucepan, uncovered, boil the string beans for 15 minutes. Drain well.

Purée in a food processor the string beans, ham, parsley, cheese and salt and pepper.

With your hands, form flat pancakes with the puréed mixture. Put the flour in one plate, the bread crumbs in another, and beat the eggs on a third plate.

Roll the pancakes first in flour, then in eggs and last in bread crumbs. In a deep fryer, heat the oil to 360° and fry the pancakes until golden brown. Drain on paper towels. Arrange on a serving platter, garnish with parsley and serve.

4 servings

String Bean Purée

PREPARATION: 10 MINUTES   COOKING: 15 MINUTES

2 pounds string beans
¼ cup plus 3 tablespoons
  chicken stock
1 tablespoon cornstarch

3 tablespoons Crème Fraîche
  (see p. xvi)
Salt and freshly ground pepper
¼ teaspoon nutmeg

String the beans and put them in 1½ quarts salted boiling water. Boil for 8 minutes, or until tender. Drain.

Purée the string beans with the stock in a blender or food processor. Pour the purée into a saucepan.

In a small bowl, dilute the cornstarch with 3 tablespoons stock and add to the purée. Add the crème fraîche, salt and pepper. Mix well, add the nutmeg and cook the purée over medium heat until it thickens. Keep warm over simmering water until ready to serve.

4 servings

Swiss Chard with Beef Marrow

PREPARATION: 20 MINUTES   COOKING: 25 MINUTES

Once the marrow is used, the bones can be used to make a beef stock for soups or sauces.

3 pounds beef marrow bones	Salt and pepper
2 bunches Swiss chard	Juice of 1 lemon
3 tablespoons butter	3 tablespoons chopped parsley

Wash and scrub the bones. Place in a large kettle, cover with cold water; bring to a boil and simmer for 15 minutes. Remove the bones and let them cool. Remove the marrow by tapping them. Set aside until ready to use.

Wash the Swiss chard and cut into 2-inch pieces. Steam over 1 cup water for 5 minutes. Meanwhile, melt the butter. Slice the marrow, add to the butter and heat through.

Place the Swiss chard in a serving bowl and sprinkle with salt and pepper and lemon juice. Toss well and pour the butter and marrow on top. Sprinkle with chopped parsley and serve.

4 servings

Swiss Chard Pie

PREPARATION: 40 MINUTES   COOKING: 1 HOUR

In France, during Lent or on Fridays when meat is not eaten, a favorite dish is Swiss chard pie with hard boiled eggs.

Pâte Brisée I (see p. 10)	½ pound boiled ham, thinly
5 hard-boiled eggs	sliced
1¾ pounds Swiss chard	1 tablespoon flour
4 tablespoons butter	½ cup cream
Salt and pepper	1 egg
½ teaspoon nutmeg	

Make the pâte brisée and refrigerate. Cut off the green part of the Swiss chard and keep it whole. Discard the stems. Wash under running water to remove sand, and drain.

In a skillet, heat 3 tablespoons butter and add the Swiss chard, salt, pepper and nutmeg. Sauté for 5 minutes. Remove from heat and cool.

Preheat the oven to 400°.

Divide the dough in two. On a floured board, roll half the dough to fit a 9-inch pie pan with a removable bottom. Butter the pie pan and line with the dough. Cover the bottom with a layer of ham. Cover the ham with Swiss chard, then a layer of ham, then Swiss chard. Cover the Swiss chard with the eggs cut in two lengthwise.

In a small saucepan, heat 1 tablespoon butter and add the flour. Stir with a wooden spoon until all the flour has been absorbed but not browned. Slowly add the cream, stirring all the while. If the sauce is too thick, add 2 or 3 tablespoons water. Add salt and pepper to taste and simmer for 5 minutes.

Pour the sauce over the eggs. Roll the remaining dough and fit it on top of the pie. Crimp the edges.

Beat an egg with 1 tablespoon water and brush it on the dough. Bake for 20 minutes. When the dough is golden brown, cover with foil and cook for 30 minutes more. Serve immediately.

6 servings

Baked Tomatoes with Bacon

PREPARATION: 25 MINUTES   COOKING: 40 MINUTES

8 tomatoes	¾ cup plus 2 tablespoons fresh
8 slices bacon	bread crumbs
3 medium-size onions	Salt and pepper
2 scallions	6 eggs
2 tablespoons butter	5 tablespoons oil

Preheat the oven to 375°. Wash and dry the tomatoes. Slice off the top and set aside. With a teaspoon, carefully remove all the flesh and seeds. Sprinkle the inside with salt and set aside on a plate.

Dice the bacon and set aside.

Peel and chop the onions and scallions. In a skillet, heat the butter and add the onions, scallions and bacon. Sauté until the onions are golden brown, then remove from heat. Add the bread crumbs and salt and pepper to taste. Set aside.

Beat the eggs lightly and add to the mixture in the skillet. Mix well.

Drain the tomatoes. Fill with the mixture and put the tops back on the tomatoes.

Oil a baking dish and put the tomatoes side by side on it. Sprinkle with the remaining bread crumbs and pour the remaining oil over the tomatoes. Bake for 30 minutes.

Serve hot with roast chicken or broiled steak.

4 servings

Stuffed Tomatoes with Fresh Mint

PREPARATION: 15 MINUTES   COOKING: 30 MINUTES

8 round firm small tomatoes	1 can deviled ham
2 slices white bread	1 egg
¼ cup milk	¼ cup chopped fresh mint
2 shallots, chopped	¼ cup olive oil
2 tablespoons chopped parsley	Salt and pepper
1 tablespoon dried tarragon	

Cut off the top of the tomatoes, and with a teaspoon, remove all the seeds. Place the tomatoes upside down on a cake rack to drain.

Soak the bread in the milk, then squeeze the bread and set aside.

Mix the shallots, parsley and tarragon with the deviled ham. Add the bread, egg, mint and 1 tablespoon olive oil. Add salt and pepper and mix well. Stuff the tomatoes with the mixture.

In a skillet, heat the remaining oil and add the tomatoes. Cook, covered, over medium heat for 30 minutes. Serve with veal.

4 servings

Purée of Watercress with Bean Curd Sauce

PREPARATION: 15 MINUTES   COOKING: 10 MINUTES

Every so often my husband and I go to the Bronx Terminal market, a wholesale produce center in New York, around five in the morning. We love to walk around in the market watching the trucks unload case after case of fresh vegetables. We go from store to store, pricing the vegetables and fruits, buying a ten-pound bag of garlic, a case of endives or lettuce to share with friends. One morning we saw watercress, bright dark green and so fresh that he insisted I buy a case. What to do with so much watercress? He came up with this recipe, which turned out to be the best watercress dish we ever had.

15 bunches watercress	4 tablespoons soy sauce
6 tablespoons sesame seeds	3 tablespoons sugar
2 squares fresh bean curd	Freshly ground pepper

Preheat the oven to 350°.

Wash and cut off the stems of the watercress. Put the watercress in a large saucepan with 2 cups boiling water and boil for 4 minutes. Drain and let it cool.

Meanwhile, place the sesame seeds on a cookie sheet and toast in the oven until golden brown.

Purée in a food processor the bean curd, sesame seeds, soy sauce, sugar and pepper. Remove to a bowl.

Squeeze all the water from the watercress and chop in the food processor. Transfer the watercress back into the saucepan. Add the bean curd sauce, mix well, and heat just before serving. Correct the seasoning by adding a pinch of salt if necessary.

8 servings

Five-Layer Vegetable Cake

PREPARATION: 20 MINUTES   COOKING: 40 MINUTES

All the vegetables are julienned and stacked one on top of the other in a heavy saucepan. The vegetables are cooked slowly without any liquid or fat or salt and served with herb butter. Guests will add their own salt, since cooking the vegetables with salt would draw water from them and make the dish too soggy.

1 box tiny frozen peas	1 stick (¼ pound) butter
4 potatoes, peeled and washed	1 cup chopped parsley
6 turnips, peeled and washed	1 tablespoon tarragon
6 carrots, scraped and washed	Salt and pepper
1 pound string beans	

Defrost the peas by running them under hot water. Drain.

In a food processor, julienne first the potatoes, then the turnips and then the carrots. Cut the string beans into ½-inch pieces.

Line the bottom of a heavy saucepan or casserole with the carrots (you should have a 1-inch layer). Cover the carrots with string beans, then a layer of turnips, then the peas and finally the potatoes. Cover and cook over very low heat for 40 minutes.

Meanwhile, in a food processor, mix the butter, parsley and tarragon. Add salt and pepper to taste and refrigerate until the vegetables are done.

Unmold the vegetables onto a round platter and sprinkle with salt and freshly ground pepper. Cut the vegetable cake as you would a pie with a sharp knife and a spatula. Serve with the herb butter. More salt and pepper should be added individually at the table.

6 servings

Green Pudding

PREPARATION: 20 MINUTES   COOKING: 45 MINUTES

2 pounds spinach	1 cup milk
2 tablespoons butter	4 egg yolks
1 tablespoon flour	4 egg whites
Salt and pepper	¼ cup grated Parmesan

Preheat the oven to 375°. Wash the spinach and cut off the stems. Drop the spinach in a saucepan full of boiling water. Bring to a boil, turn off the heat and let the spinach stand in the water for 5 minutes. Drain and cool.

Meanwhile, make the sauce. In a saucepan, heat the butter and add the flour. Mix well until the flour has been absorbed by the butter, then slowly add the milk, stirring all the while.

Add salt and pepper to taste. The sauce should be rather thin. Squeeze all the water out of the spinach and chop finely. Add the spinach to the sauce, then the egg yolks. Mix well.

Beat the egg whites until stiff but not dry. Slowly fold the spinach mixture into the egg whites. Pour into a buttered 1½-quart round pan and put it in a pan filled with about 2 inches of water. Bake for 20 minutes.

Serve in the pan in which the pudding was cooked (it cannot be unmolded).

Just before serving, sprinkle the top with the Parmesan. Serve with pork roast.

6 servings.

Sauces for Cooked Vegetables

Garlic Sauce (for cold beets, cauliflower, potatoes)
PREPARATION: 10 MINUTES

3 tablespoons wine vinegar
3 tablespoons tomato juice
1 tablespoon olive oil
2 cloves garlic, chopped

1 teaspoon tarragon
1 teaspoon chives
Salt and pepper

Put all the ingredients in a food processor or blender. Run the machine for 30 seconds. Pour in a bowl and refrigerate until ready to use.
   ¾ cup

Mayonnaise with Yogurt (for string beans, cold spinach, broccoli)
PREPARATION: 15 MINUTES

1 hard-boiled egg
2 egg yolks
¼ cup plain yogurt

1 teaspoon Dijon-style mustard
1 teaspoon lemon juice
1 teaspoon chopped chives

Put all the ingredients in a food processor or blender and run the machine for 30 seconds. Pour in a bowl and refrigerate until ready to use.
   ¾ cup

Black Olive Vinaigrette (for shredded carrots, shredded celery, sliced cold Brussels sprouts)
PREPARATION: 10 MINUTES

½ cup plain yogurt
1 egg yolk
1 tablespoon wine vinegar
1 tablespoon Dijon-style
   mustard

4 pitted Greek black olives
2 gherkins
Pinch of paprika
Salt and pepper

Put all the ingredients in a food processor or blender and run the machine for 30 seconds, or until all the ingredients are well mixed. Pour in a bowl and refrigerate until ready to serve.

1 cup

Tomato and Yogurt Sauce (for boiled cold potatoes, boiled artichokes, cold parsnips)
PREPARATION: 10 MINUTES

This sauce is excellent with a bland-tasting vegetable, such as potatoes or parsnips. The kosher pickle gives it a piquant flavor.

½ cup plain yogurt
1 large kosher pickle
2 tablespoons tomato paste

1 tablespoon chopped chives
Pepper

Cut the kosher pickle into three or four pieces. Put all the ingredients in a food processor or blender and run the machine for 1 minute, or until the pickle is puréed. Pour in a bowl and refrigerate until ready to use.

¾ cup

Pasta

Macaroni with Anchovies

PREPARATION: 5 MINUTES   COOKING: 35 MINUTES

1½ pounds large macaroni
¼ cup olive oil
1 large can peeled tomatoes
2 cloves garlic
¼ teaspoon thyme

2 sprigs parsley
Salt and freshly ground pepper
2 cans anchovies, rolled, in oil
½ cup grated Parmesan

Put 2 quarts salted water with 2 tablespoons oil in a large saucepan and bring to a boil. Add the macaroni, stir, and boil for about 15 minutes.

Drain the tomatoes. In a skillet, heat the remaining oil and add the tomatoes, garlic, thyme, parsley, salt and pepper. Cook, uncovered, for 20 minutes, or until the sauce thickens. Remove the parsley.

Drain the macaroni and put in a large bowl. Add the butter and mix well. Garnish with the anchovies. Serve with the sauce on the side and the grated Parmesan in a bowl.

6 servings

Baked Macaroni

PREPARATION: 15 MINUTES   COOKING: 1 HOUR

1 pound macaroni
¾ pound mushrooms
4 egg yolks
1 cup grated Swiss cheese

1 cup chopped ham
4 egg whites
5 tablespoons butter
Salt and pepper

Preheat the oven to 350°.

Put the macaroni in a large saucepan of boiling water with 1 table-spoon salt and boil for about 10 minutes. While the macaroni is cooking, wash the mushrooms.

In a bowl, mix together the egg yolks, Swiss cheese, ham, and half the mushrooms. Drain the macaroni and add to the mixture. Toss well.

Beat the egg whites in another bowl until stiff; fold them into the macaroni. Pour the macaroni into a buttered 1½-quart mold. Put the mold in a pan with 2 inches of water and bake for 45 minutes.

Meanwhile, heat the butter in a skillet and add the remaining mush-rooms and salt and pepper. Simmer for 10 minutes, or until the mush-rooms are quite soft. Unmold the macaroni on a serving platter and pour the mushroom sauce on top.

6 servings

Fresh Noodles with Leek Sauce

PREPARATION: 15 MINUTES   COOKING: 35 MINUTES

2 cups Béchamel (see p. 201)   1 cup grated Swiss cheese
1 pound leeks   Salt and freshly ground pepper
1 pound fresh flat noodles

Make the béchamel and keep warm over a saucepan of simmering water. Wash the leeks carefully to remove sand and tie them with string.

In a large saucepan, bring to a boil 1½ quarts salted water and add the leeks. Cook for 15 minutes. Drain and squeeze all the water out, then cut into thin slices.

Put 1½ quarts salted water in the saucepan and bring to a boil. Add the noodles and cook for 5 minutes, or until the noodles are done. Drain.

Put the noodles in a serving bowl. Add the leeks and mix well. Add the cheese to the béchamel, correct the seasoning, and pour over the noodles. Mix well and serve with roast veal.

4 servings

Fresh Tagliatelle with Walnuts

PREPARATION: 10 MINUTES   COOKING: 20 MINUTES

In my neighborhood there is a fresh-pasta store that is run by three Italian brothers. Their fresh pasta is the best I have ever had. One of the brothers liked French cooking. He had spent some time after the war in France and would tell me stories about his adventures in France and the food he ate. He gave me this recipe in exchange for my book. It is an excellent hors d'oeuvre or a main course for lunch.

1 pound fresh tagliatelle (flat noodles)
1 tablespoon olive oil
1 cup shelled walnuts
1 stick (¼ pound) butter, cut into small pieces

¼ teaspoon cinnamon
2 teaspoons sugar
Salt and pepper

In a large saucepan, bring to a boil 2 quarts water with 1 tablespoon salt. Add the tagliatelle and the oil (it prevents the noodles from sticking together). Boil, uncovered, for 8 minutes, or until the tagliatelle are done.

Meanwhile, chop the walnuts coarsely in a food processor.

Drain the tagliatelle. Place in a large salad bowl, add the butter, cinnamon, sugar, walnuts and freshly ground pepper. Mix well and serve right away.

6 servings

Salads

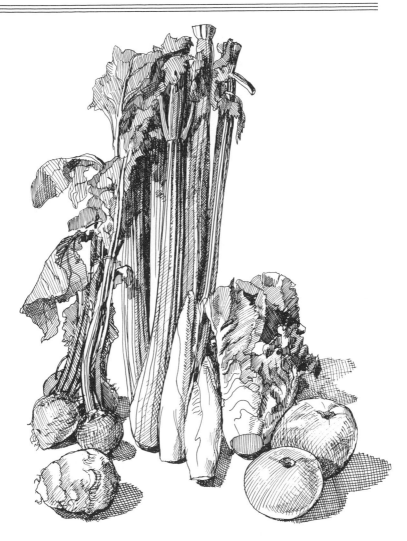

Asparagus Salad with Mussels

PREPARATION: MUSSELS SOAKED 1 HOUR; 20 MINUTES   COOKING: 20 MINUTES

2 pints mussels
2 pounds asparagus
3 hard-boiled eggs
2 tablespoons wine vinegar

5 tablespoons oil
2 shallots, finely chopped
Salt and pepper
1 tablespoon chopped fresh basil

Scrub the mussels well under cold running water. Discard those that are open or feel too heavy (they may be full of mud). Soak the mussels in cold water for 1 hour.

Put the mussels in a saucepan, cover and boil for about 5 minutes, or until they open. Drain over a bowl and keep the broth for other uses.

Remove the mussels from their shells and set aside. Wash and trim the asparagus, removing the tough ends. Steam over ½ cup water for 10 minutes, or until tender. Remove to a platter and cool.

Finely chop the eggs. Combine the vinegar, oil, shallots, salt and pepper, and add the mussels. Pour over the asparagus and sprinkle with the egg and basil. Serve at room temperature.

4 servings

Beet Salad with Walnuts

PREPARATION: 15 MINUTES

1-inch piece fresh ginger, sliced
1 can whole small beets, sliced
1 tablespoon vinegar
3 tablespoons oil

Salt
Freshly ground pepper
1 cup shelled walnuts, broken
  into pieces

In a salad bowl, mix together the vinegar, oil, salt and pepper. Add the sliced ginger and the beets. Mix well. Sprinkle the walnuts on top and serve.

4 servings

Brussels Sprouts Salad with Sesame Seeds

PREPARATION: 10 MINUTES   COOKING: 10 MINUTES

Last summer, when I was in Tanzania, I went into a small Indian spice store to buy fresh mustard seeds. While waiting for my turn, I saw an Indian woman buying sesame seeds. I was reminded of the taste of roasted sesame seeds on fresh Italian bread in New York and felt homesick. I decided then and there to bake some bread with sesame seeds. So when my turn came to be served, I asked for a half pound of sesame seeds. To my amazement, the Indian shook his head. "Sesame seed is the food of the gods," he said. "We use it for offerings. I may give you just a handful."

In the United States, sesame seeds are available in most supermarkets, but my Indian friend was right: mixed with vegetables, in salads, with meat, the seeds transform a simple recipe into a dish fit for the gods.

2 pints Brussels sprouts	3 tablespoons vinegar
2 tablespoons oil	1 teaspoon soy sauce
2 tablespoons white sesame	3 tablespoons sugar
seeds	Salt and pepper

Wash and trim the Brussels sprouts. Place them in a steamer over 1 cup water and steam for 10 minutes. Remove to a salad bowl and set aside.

Heat the oil in a skillet. Add the sesame seeds and cook until the sesame seeds are light brown. Remove from heat and let cool.

In a bowl, mix together the oil, sesame seeds, vinegar, soy sauce and sugar. Add salt and pepper to taste.

Pour the sauce over the Brussels sprouts, toss well and serve.

6 servings

Carrot Salad

PREPARATION: 20 MINUTES

½ pound mushrooms
Juice of 2 lemons
6 carrots
Salt and pepper

4 tablespoons any type of oil
¼ teaspoon sesame oil
¼ pound bean sprouts
Parsley for garnish

Wash the mushrooms and pat dry with paper towels. Slice them and put them in a bowl. Pour half of the lemon juice over them.

Scrape and wash the carrots and shred them in a food processor.

In a small bowl, beat together with a fork 1 teaspoon salt, pepper to taste, the remaining lemon juice and the oil. Add the sesame oil and mix well.

Put the carrots, mushrooms and bean sprouts in a salad bowl and pour the sauce over them. Toss well, garnish with parsley and serve.

4 servings

Celery, Apple and Walnut Salad

PREPARATION: 15 MINUTES

2 bunches celery
2 Golden Delicious apples
20 walnuts, shelled
Juice of 2 lemons

4 tablespoons oil
Salt and pepper
3½ ounces Roquefort cheese

Separate the celery stalks and wash them. Cut off the leaves (save them for making a soup). Cut the celery into 1-inch pieces but leave the tiny stalks in the center whole. Peel, core and slice the apples.

In a salad bowl, mix together the celery, apples and walnuts. Combine the lemon, oil and salt and pepper to taste. Mix well and crumble the Roquefort cheese into the dressing. Pour the dressing over the salad, toss lightly and refrigerate until ready to serve.

6 servings

Crab and Rice Salad

PREPARATION: 30 MINUTES   COOKING: 20 MINUTES

½ cup raisins
¾ cup rice
Salt
1 green bell pepper
1 red bell pepper
2 cans crab meat
2 shallots

Pinch of cayenne
2 tablespoons wine vinegar
6 tablespoons oil
1 tablespoon soy sauce
1 tablespoon chopped parsley
1 head romaine

Put the raisins in a bowl and pour some boiling water over them. Set aside.

Put the rice and ¼ teaspoon salt in a saucepan and cover with 2½ cups boiling water. Simmer for 20 minutes, or until the rice is done.

Meanwhile, cut the peppers into ¼-inch strips, then cut each strip in two. Peel and chop the shallots.

Drain the crab meat and set aside 6 large pieces for garnish.

Make the dressing. In a bowl, combine the cayenne, vinegar, oil, soy sauce and ½ teaspoon salt. Add the shallots and mix well.

Drain the raisins and wash the romaine.

Line a salad bowl with the romaine leaves. Mix together the rice, crab meat, raisins and peppers. Add the dressing and mix well.

Put the salad on top of the romaine leaves and garnish with the crab meat. Refrigerate until ready to serve.

6 servings

Chinese Duck Salad

PREPARATION: 20 MINUTES

3 ounces dried Chinese black
   mushrooms
¼ pound fresh mushrooms
3 white celery stalks
2 tomatoes
1 cucumber
2 tablespoons lemon juice
1 tablespoon brandy

4 mint leaves, chopped
2 tablespoons soy sauce
Salt and pepper
2 cloves garlic
1 cup thinly sliced cooked duck
4 ounces fresh bean sprouts
Chinese parsley (coriander) or
   regular parsley

Cook the dried mushrooms in boiling water for 15 minutes.

Meanwhile, wash and trim the fresh mushrooms. Pat dry with paper towels and slice thinly. Chop the celery. Slice the tomatoes. Peel the cucumber and slice thinly.

In a bowl, mix the lemon juice, brandy, mint and soy sauce. Add salt and pepper. Peel the garlic and slice thinly. Add to the dressing. Correct the seasoning.

Drain the dried mushrooms, cut off the stems and slice thinly.

In a salad bowl mix together all the ingredients except the dressing. Pour the dressing over the salad, garnish with Chinese parsley and serve.

4 servings

Endive Salad with Kiwis

PREPARATION: 15 MINUTES

This is a beautiful salad. The endive leaves form the petals and the kiwis the heart of the flower.

6 endives	½ teaspoon salt
3 kiwis	½ teaspoon Dijon-style mustard
2 tablespoons wine vinegar	Freshly ground pepper
6 tablespoons oil	

Wash the endives and pat dry with paper towels. Separate the leaves. Peel and slice the kiwis.

In a bowl, combine the remaining ingredients to make the dressing.

On a large round platter, place the endive leaves in a circle, the tips of the leaves pointing outward. Make a second circle of endives and continue until all the leaves have been used up. Make a tight circle in the center with the sliced kiwis. Just before serving, pour the dressing over the endives.

6 servings

Endive Salad with Fresh Peas

PREPARATION: 20 MINUTES

4 endives	1 tablespoon lemon juice
Salt	Freshly ground pepper
1 cup fresh peas (¾ pound	3 tablespoons olive oil
unshelled)	1 clove garlic, chopped

Wash and pat the endives dry with paper towels. Cut 1 inch off the top, then cut in four lengthwise. Cut each strip into 1-inch pieces and place in a salad bowl.

Bring to a boil 2 cups water and add 1 teaspoon salt. Add the peas, bring to a boil, then turn off the heat. Let stand in the hot water for 5 minutes. Drain and cool under cold running water. Add to the endives and refrigerate until ready to serve.

Meanwhile, make the dressing. Mix the lemon juice with pepper and ¼ teaspoon salt. Add the olive oil and garlic and mix well. Just before serving, add the dressing and toss well.

4 servings

Hot Leek Salad

PREPARATION: 10 MINUTES   COOKING: 20 MINUTES

12 leeks	Salt
1 tablespoon vinegar	Freshly ground pepper
3 tablespoons oil	1 teaspoon chopped dill

Trim the leeks. Wash the leeks well to remove all the sand. Drain. Tie the leeks with a string so that they don't fall apart.

Put the leeks in a large skillet and cover with boiling water. Add 1 teaspoon salt. Simmer for 20 minutes. Then with two slotted spoons, remove the leeks to a serving platter. Untie the leeks.

In a small bowl, mix together the salt, pepper, vinegar and oil and pour over the leeks. Sprinkle with the dill and serve hot.

4 servings

Okra Salad

PREPARATION: 10 MINUTES

Here is a simple recipe that is delicious as an hors d'oeuvre served with poached eggs or a thin slice of pâté.

Okra (illustrated above) is at its best in the spring—small, crisp and bright green. Mixed with dried fish flakes (available at Japanese grocery stores), its flavor is delicate and unusual.

1 pound okra
1 tablespoon dried fish flakes

½ cup soy sauce
Salt and pepper

Wash and pat the okra dry with paper towels. Thinly slice the okra in rounds and place in a bowl.

In another bowl, mix the soy sauce and fish flakes. Add to the okra and mix well. Correct the seasoning by adding salt and pepper. Refrigerate until ready to serve.

6 servings

Pomegranate Salad

PREPARATION: 30 MINUTES

Choose a very red pomegranate. Before removing the seeds (which are edible), rub your hands with lemon juice. Pomegranate blackens your fingers, and the lemon juice will prevent this from happening. Cut the pomegranate in two and remove the seeds over a bowl so as not to lose the juice, which will be used for the dressing.

2 large red bell peppers
1 head Boston lettuce
4 medium-size tomatoes
1 small cucumber
1 pomegranate
2 leftover chicken breasts,
  skinned and diced

4 ounces black Italian olives
3 tablespoons oil
Salt and pepper
Pinch of cayenne
Juice of 1 lemon
Parsley sprigs for garnish

Roast the peppers on top of the stove over an open flame. When their skin is black, remove to a bowl and cool under cold running water. Dry them with paper towels and remove the skins. Cut into long, thin strips.

Wash the lettuce; dry and cut into bite-sized pieces. Quarter the tomatoes. Peel and cut the cucumber in two lengthwise. Remove the seeds and dice. Cut the pomegranate in two and remove the seeds over a bowl.

Line a salad bowl with the larger lettuce leaves. Mix together the chicken, tomatoes, lettuce, cucumbers and pomegranate seeds. Garnish with the red pepper and the olives.

In a bowl, make the dressing by combining the oil, salt and pepper, cayenne and pomegranate juice. Mix well and add lemon juice to taste. Pour the dressing over the salad, garnish with parsley and serve.

6 servings

Rice Salad with Prawns and Tuna

PREPARATION: 10 MINUTES   COOKING: 25 MINUTES

Salt
¾ cup rice
1 onion stuck with a clove
1 pound large prawns
1 cup Mayonnaise (see p. 29)

Heart of Boston lettuce
1 can tuna in water
4 hard-boiled eggs, quartered
4 small cornichons (French
  pickled gherkins), chopped

In a saucepan, bring to a boil 2 cups water with ½ tablespoon salt. Add the rice and cook for 15 minutes, or until it is barely tender. Drain and cool under cold running water. Set aside.

Meanwhile, in another saucepan, bring to a boil 2 cups water with ½ teaspoon salt and the onion. Add the prawns and simmer for 5 minutes, then drain. Remove the shells and devein the prawns. Set aside to cool.

Make the mayonnaise.

Wash the lettuce and pat dry with paper towels. Drain the can of tuna and cut the tuna into small pieces. Mix together the rice and tuna. Add the mayonnaise and mix well. Line a salad bowl with the lettuce and fill with the rice. Arrange the prawns on top of the rice and garnish with the eggs. Sprinkle the chopped cornichons on top of the eggs. Refrigerate until ready to serve.

4 servings

Fresh Spinach Salad with Hard-Boiled Eggs

PREPARATION: 10 MINUTES   COOKING: 10 MINUTES

2 pounds spinach
2 eggs
1 tablespoon lemon juice

2 tablespoons oil
Salt and pepper

Wash the spinach and cut off the stems. Drain and pat dry with paper towels. Boil the eggs for 10 minutes or more. Cool under cold running water. Peel and mince the eggs.

In a salad bowl, combine the lemon juice, oil and salt and pepper to taste. Add the spinach just before serving, toss well and sprinkle the egg on top.

4 servings

String Bean and Mussel Salad

PREPARATION: MUSSELS SOAKED 1 HOUR; 25 MINUTES   COOKING: 20 MINUTES

2 pounds young string beans
2 pints mussels
1½ tablespoons lemon juice

2 tablespoons oil
¼ teaspoon chopped fresh sage
Salt and pepper

Wash and cut the ends off the string beans. Steam over 1 cup water for 6 minutes. Set aside in a bowl to cool.

Scrub the mussels under cold running water. Discard those that are open or feel too heavy (they may be full of mud). Soak the mussels in cold water for 1 hour to make sure they are free of sand.

Place the mussels in a large saucepan and boil, covered, until they are all open. Drain over a bowl and reserve the juice for other uses.

Remove the mussels from the shells and add to the string beans.

In a small bowl, mix together the lemon juice, oil, sage, salt and pepper. Mix well and add to the string beans and mussels. Toss well and serve.

6 servings

Radish and Fennel Salad

PREPARATION: 20 MINUTES

1 bunch large, firm radishes	2 tablespoons olive oil
1 bulb fennel	Salt and pepper
1 tablespoon lemon juice	6 black olives for garnish

Trim and wash the radishes; discard the leaves. Trim and wash the fennel. Slice the radishes and fennel in a food processor.

In a salad bowl, mix together the lemon juice, oil, salt and pepper. Add the radishes and fennel and toss well. Garnish with the black olives. Refrigerate until ready to serve.

4 servings

Walnut-Ball Salad

PREPARATION: 25 MINUTES

In the fall, when walnuts are gathered, their flesh is tender and pale in color and the shell not quite as hard as it is later. If you are lucky enough to own a walnut tree, autumn is the best time to try this recipe.

1 head romaine	½ cup finely chopped walnuts
5 ounces blue cheese	1 tablespoon lemon juice
1 tablespoon plain yogurt	4 tablespoons olive oil
Pinch of cayenne	Salt and pepper
½ cup coarsely chopped walnuts	

Wash the romaine and dry with paper towels.

In a bowl, mash with a fork the blue cheese with the yogurt and cayenne, and add the coarsely chopped walnuts. Mix well. (The mixture should be firm.)

Make balls the size of marbles and roll them in the finely chopped walnuts. Refrigerate until ready to serve.

In a salad bowl, combine the lemon juice, olive oil, salt and pepper. Tear the romaine leaves in two or three pieces and add to the dressing. Toss well. Add the cheese-walnut balls and serve.

6 servings

Carrot, String Bean and Cucumber Salad

PREPARATION: 20 MINUTES   COOKING: 15 MINUTES

1 cucumber
½ pound carrots
½ pound string beans
3 cloves garlic
3 tablespoons wine vinegar
1 teaspoon cumin
1 teaspoon Chinese parsley
    (coriander)

Salt and pepper
1 container plain yogurt
1 tablespoon Dijon-style
    mustard
½ cup olive oil

Peel and slice the cucumber. Put in a bowl and sprinkle with salt to draw out the water.

Peel and dice the carrots. String the beans and cut in thirds.

Put in a saucepan of boiling water the carrots, string beans, garlic, vinegar, cumin, parsley, salt and pepper. Cook for 15 minutes over medium heat. Drain and let them cool at room temperature.

Drain the cucumbers and pat dry with paper towels. Place the yogurt and mustard in the container of a food processor. With the machine running, add the oil in a stream. Add salt and pepper.

Put the carrots, string beans and cucumbers in a bowl. Add the yogurt, toss well and refrigerate until ready to serve. Serve as an appetizer with Italian salami.

6 servings

Desserts

Apple and Apricot Tart

PREPARATION: 10 MINUTES   COOKING: 50 MINUTES

Pâte Brisée II (see below)
3 pounds McIntosh apples
4 tablespoons butter
⅔ cup apricot jam

¼ cup sugar
1 teaspoon vanilla extract
⅔ cup slivered almonds

Preheat the oven to 350°. Make the pâte brisée.* Refrigerate while preparing the apples.

Peel, core and quarter the apples. In a large skillet, heat 3 tablespoons butter and add the apples. Sauté for 5 minutes, then add the jam, sugar and vanilla. Mix well and simmer for another 5 minutes. Turn off the heat and let the apples cool.

Butter a 9-inch pie pan. Roll out the dough and line the pie pan. Press the edges with a fork. Fill the shell with the apples and spread evenly. Bake for 40 minutes, then sprinkle the almonds on top of the apples and bake for 10 minutes more, or until the almonds are golden brown. Serve at room temperature.

8 servings

*The pâte brisée recipe makes enough dough for 2 pie shells. This tart requires only 1 shell, so refrigerate the remaining dough for future use.

Pâte Brisée II (for desserts)

1½ cups flour
3 tablespoons sugar
9 tablespoons butter, cut into
   1-inch pieces

2 eggs
1 tablespoon oil
¼ cup ice water

In a food processor or a blender, mix the flour, sugar and butter; add the eggs and oil and mix well. With the machine still running, slowly add the ice water. Remove the dough and shape it into a ball. Dust with flour and chill for 30 minutes in the refrigerator before using it.

This dough can be frozen or kept for several days in the refrigerator. Makes 2 9-inch pie shells

Apple Mousse

PREPARATION: 20 MINUTES   COOKING: 45 MINUTES

2 pounds McIntosh apples   Peel of 1 lemon
1 cup sugar   6 egg whites
6 egg yolks   ½ teaspoon salt

Preheat the oven to 350°.

Peel and core the apples; cut them into thin slices. Put them in a saucepan and cover with 1½ cups water. Bring to a boil, then simmer for 10 minutes, or until the apples are tender. Drain and purée them in a food processor or a blender; add the sugar, egg yolks, and lemon peel and run the machine until all ingredients are blended. Set aside.

Put the egg whites and ½ teaspoon salt in a large bowl. Beat the egg whites with an electric beater until quite stiff. Gently fold the apple mixture into them.

Butter a 2-quart mold and pour the mixture into the mold. Put the mold in a pan with 2 inches of water and bake in a 350° oven for 10 minutes, then raise the heat to 400° and bake for 30 minutes more, or until golden brown. Serve immediately.

6 generous servings

NOTE: Because this dessert has no flour and will "fall" very quickly, the timing is important. Start baking the mousse as you serve your first course. The dessert will be ready by the time everyone has finished the main part of the meal.

Apple Roll

PREPARATION: 30 MINUTES   COOKING: 45 MINUTES

4 cups sliced apples
2 tablespoons lemon juice
1 cup sugar
¾ teaspoon cinnamon
½ cup chopped walnuts

¼ cup seedless raisins
6 tablespoons butter
½ pound phyllo*
1 cup whipped cream (optional)

Preheat the oven to 350°.

Place the apples in a bowl and add lemon juice, ½ cup sugar and ¼ teaspoon cinnamon. Mix well.

In another bowl, combine the walnuts, ½ cup sugar, ½ teaspoon cinnamon and raisins. Mix well.

Melt the butter in a small saucepan over low heat. When the butter has cooled, skim the foam off the top. Pour the clarified butter into a bowl, leaving the foam in the saucepan and discarding it.

Spread the phyllo dough on the counter top. Lift each sheet of dough, and with a pastry brush, brush some butter on each sheet; stack the sheets. Spread the apples on the dough, then spread the walnut-raisin mixture on top of the apples. Roll the dough into a large sausage-shaped roll. Put it on a floured cookie sheet and brush it with the clarified butter. Bake for 45 minutes, or until the dough is golden brown. Remove to a platter and serve lukewarm. It can be served with whipped cream but it is also delicious served plain.

8 servings

*Thin sheets of pastry dough available at Middle Eastern grocery stores.

Barbecued Bananas

PREPARATION: 5 MINUTES   COOKING: 10 MINUTES

When you are preparing a steak or fish to be cooked over charcoal, here is a simple but delicious dessert that takes only 15 minutes to prepare and can also be put on the grill.

4 ripe bananas
5 tablespoons sugar

4 tablespoons rum

Peel and slice each banana in two lengthwise. Place the bananas on the grill over charcoal. Cook for 5 minutes, then sprinkle with the sugar. Turn them over and cook for another 5 minutes.

Meanwhile, heat the rum in a small saucepan. Transfer the bananas to a heated platter and pour the rum over them. Ignite and serve immediately.

4 servings

Banana Pudding

PREPARATION: 20 MINUTES   COOKING: 40 MINUTES

One day, when walking through the market in Dodoma in Tanzania, Andrea Brandt and I saw some brown sugar for the first time in that town. She was thrilled, and decided to make this pudding. She had hidden somewhere a jar of lingonberries, which she served along with the pudding.

1 loaf (1 pound) white bread	Pinch of nutmeg
6 ripe bananas	¼ pound brown sugar
¼ cup and 3 tablespoons rum	½ teaspoon vanilla extract
6 eggs	1 jar lingonberry preserves

Preheat the oven to 400°. Remove the crust from the bread. Soak the bread for 15 minutes in ¼ cup rum mixed with ¼ cup water.

Peel and mash the bananas. Purée the bananas, bread, eggs, nutmeg sugar and vanilla in a food processor or blender.

Butter a 2-quart mold and fill with the banana-bread mixture. Put the mold in a roasting pan filled with 2 inches of water and bake for about 40 minutes, or until the blade of a knife inserted in the pudding comes out clean. Unmold while the pudding is still warm.

Just before serving, heat the lingonberries in a small saucepan, add 3 tablespoons rum, and pour over the pudding.

6 servings

Cantaloupe with Watermelon and Pine Nuts

PREPARATION: 25 MINUTES

4 cantaloupes
3 pounds watermelon
½ cup dry white wine
1 lemon

2 tablespoons butter
½ cup pine nuts
12 fresh mint leaves

Cut each cantaloupe in two. Remove the seeds, and with a melon-ball cutter, scoop out the flesh. Set aside in a bowl.

Remove all the seeds from the watermelon, and with the melon-ball cutter, scoop out the flesh. Add to the cantaloupe balls and pour the wine over the them. Toss gently and refrigerate.

Remove all the flesh left in the cantaloupe shells and rub with the lemon. Set aside.

In a skillet, heat the butter and add the pine nuts. Sauté for a few minutes over medium heat and drain on paper towels.

Just before serving, fill the cantaloupe shells with the melon balls. Sprinkle with the nuts and garnish each half with 2 mint leaves.

6 servings

Cherry Fondant

PREPARATION: 30 MINUTES   COOKING: 40 MINUTES

4 large eggs
1 cup sugar
½ teaspoon cinnamon
4 sticks (1 pound) butter

1¾ cups flour
Salt
1 pound cherries, pitted

Preheat the oven to 375°.

Separate the eggs. Put the egg yolks, sugar and cinnamon in the container of a food processor and run the machine for 1 minute.

Cut the butter into small pieces. Set aside 1 tablespoon butter for buttering the mold, and melt the remaining butter. With the machine running, add the melted butter in a stream to the egg-sugar mixture. Add the flour and run the machine for ½ minute. Remove the dough to a bowl.

In a mixing bowl, beat the egg whites with a pinch of salt until they are very stiff. Gently fold them into the dough.

Pour the dough into a buttered mold and put the cherries on top (some will sink to the center). Bake for 40 minutes. The cake is done if a knife or a skewer inserted in the cake comes out clean.

Unmold and let cool at room temperature.

6 to 8 servings

Cherry Soup

PREPARATION: 20 MINUTES   COOKING: 15 MINUTES

2 cups red wine	1 tablespoon cornstarch
1 cinnamon stick	1 tablespoon kirsch
2½ tablespoons butter	1 pint heavy cream, whipped, or
1 cup sugar	6 tablespoons Crème Fraîche
1½ pounds cherries, pitted	(see p. xvi)

Put the wine and cinnamon stick in a saucepan and bring to a boil.

In another saucepan, heat the butter and add the cherries. Shake the saucepan for about 3 minutes to coat all the cherries, then sprinkle with sugar. Cook, stirring, for another 3 minutes. Add the hot wine and simmer for 5 minutes.

Drain the cherries over a bowl and discard the cinnamon stick. Divide the cherries among four bowls.

In a small bowl, mix the cornstarch with the kirsch. Add to the wine sauce in the bowl and pour the sauce back into a saucepan. Simmer, stirring, until the sauce is smooth and lightly thickened, and pour over the cherries.

Serve hot or cold with the whipped cream or crème fraîche on the side.

4 servings

Hot Compote of Dried Fruits

PREPARATION: 5 MINUTES   COOKING: 35 MINUTES

1 cup sugar	½ cup prunes
½ teaspoon vanilla	½ cup dried figs
1 cup dried apricots	½ cup Calvados
½ cup dried peaches	1 pint heavy cream

In a saucepan, mix together the sugar and 2 cups water. Bring to a boil and add the vanilla. Reduce the heat and cook for 5 minutes. Add all the dried fruit and the Calvados. Simmer for 30 minutes, or until all the fruit is tender. Serve with the cream.
    4 servings

Date Pudding

PREPARATION: 30 MINUTES   COOKING: 15 MINUTES

When I was growing up in Egypt, one of my aunts would dry dates in the sun, then make a marvelous date pudding that she would serve with very thick Egyptian cream. Today in New York I often make this dessert using pitless dates from California. My mother tells me my pudding is as good as my aunt's even though it lacks the wonderful cream you could cut with a knife.

1 pound pitted dates
½ cup brown sugar
¼ teaspoon salt
2-inch piece cinnamon stick
⅓ cup cornstarch

½ cup coarsely chopped walnuts
1 tablespoon lemon juice
2 egg whites
2 tablespoons sugar
1 cup heavy cream

Put the dates, brown sugar, salt and cinnamon in a saucepan and cover with 2 cups hot water. Bring to a boil, reduce the heat and simmer for 10 minutes. In a small bowl, dissolve the cornstarch with 1 teaspoon water. Add to the dates and cook, stirring, until the mixture thickens. Remove from heat. Remove the cinnamon stick; add the walnuts and lemon juice and mix well. In a bowl, whip the egg whites with the sugar until stiff and carefully fold them into the warm dates. Pour into a 1½-quart mold and chill. Just before serving, whip the cream and serve with the pudding.
    6 servings

Fruit Salad in Frosted Oranges

PREPARATION: 25 MINUTES

This recipe is very simple. The idea is to make shells out of oranges and fill them with fruit salad, which can consist of any fresh fruit in season. The fruit should be flavored with some sugar, lemon juice and any liquor you personally like. The following recipe uses different types of melon and eau-de-vie de framboise, which is a brandy made with raspberries.

4 oranges	1 tablespoon lime or lemon juice
3 egg whites	2 tablespoons sugar
1 cup superfine sugar	1½ tablespoons eau-de-vie de
4 cups melon balls (honeydew,	framboise
cantaloupe, cranshaw or any	Fresh mint leaves
other kind of melon)	1 pound raspberries

Cut off the top of the oranges, and with the grapefruit knife, remove all the flesh. Save the cut-off tops.

Lightly beat the egg whites. Roll the orange shells in the egg whites, then in the superfine sugar. Arrange them on a serving platter and refrigerate.

Prepare the melon balls. Put them in a bowl and sprinkle with lime or lemon juice, sugar and the eau-de-vie de framboise. Toss gently and refrigerate until ready to serve.

Rinse the raspberries and drain. Purée in a food processor and add ½ tablespoon eau-de-vie de framboise. Refrigerate.

Just before serving, fill the orange shells with the melon balls, cover with the tops and place a fresh mint leaf on top of each orange. Serve with the raspberry sauce on the side.

6 servings

Chocolate Sabayon with Grapes

PREPARATION: 20 MINUTES   COOKING: 20 MINUTES

This recipe requires that you peel the grapes. It takes time to peel them, but the results are surprisingly rewarding. My husband always pretends that he married me because I was the only woman he knew who would peel grapes for him. I don't suggest that this recipe is an aphrodisiac, but I do suggest you try it. One never knows!

1½ cups seedless green grapes	8 egg yolks
3 tablespoons brandy	½ cup sugar
¼ pound sweet chocolate, cut	½ cup dry white wine
into small pieces	4 vine leaves (optional)

Peel the grapes. Put the grapes in a bowl and pour the brandy over them. Set aside ½ cup for garnish.

Put the chocolate in the top of a double boiler and stir continuously while it melts.

In a saucepan, beat the egg yolks, sugar and wine with a whisk over high heat until the mixture becomes frothy. Remove the saucepan from heat and slowly add the grapes and the brandy.

Pour the mixture into individual cups, garnish with the extra grapes, and, if desired, serve with a vine leaf under each cup.

4 servings

Green Grape Tart

PREPARATION: 40 MINUTES   COOKING: 35 MINUTES

This pie is not only delicious but lovely to look at. The caramelized grapes are shiny and crisp, and the contrast between the grapes and the filling is a pleasant surprise.

Pâte Brisée II (see p. 235)   2½ cups sugar
1¾ pounds seedless green grapes   1 cup milk
4 egg yolks   ¼ cup heavy cream
2 egg whites   ½ cup chopped almonds
4 tablespoons flour   1 tablespoon brandy

Preheat the oven to 375°.

Make the pâte brisée, reducing the ingredients by half, and roll out the dough. Butter a 9-inch pie pan and dust with flour. Put the dough on the pie pan, press the edges and prick the bottom several times with a fork. Line with waxed paper and fill with raw rice to keep the dough from puffing up. Bake the pie shell for 30 minutes, or until the dough is golden brown. Remove from the oven and let it cool. Discard the rice.

Meanwhile, make the filling. Place the egg yolks, egg whites, the flour, ½ cup sugar, cream and milk in the container of a food processor and run the machine for 30 seconds. Pour the mixture into a large saucepan and simmer, stirring constantly, for about 10 minutes, or until the sauce coats a wooden spoon. Remove the saucepan from heat, fold in the almonds and the brandy. Set aside to cool.

Meanwhile, put 2 cups sugar and ⅔ cup water in a saucepan, mix well, and cook over moderately high heat, stirring constantly, until the sugar has completely dissolved. Continue cooking, stirring from time to time, until the syrup turns a light brown or a candy thermometer registers 265°.

Pour the cooled cream into the pie shell. Rinse the grapes and remove the stems. Place the grapes in circles on top of the cream. With a pastry brush, gently brush the grapes with the caramel. Refrigerate until ready to serve.

6 to 8 servings

Honey Cream with Kiwis

PREPARATION: 20 MINUTES   COOKING: 5 MINUTES   REFRIGERATION: 2 HOURS

My daughter, Cecile, who created this recipe, insists that the choice of the honey is very important. It has to be thick, dark and made from wild flowers. I couldn't find honey made from wild flowers like Cecile's, which came from Spain, but I tried it with regular good dark honey, and the dish was delicious. When preparing dinner, start with this dessert, as it has to be refrigerated.

4 kiwis
3½ ounces honey

1½ pints heavy cream
4 mint leaves

Peel the kiwis and slice them. In a saucepan, heat the honey and add the kiwis. Poach for 5 minutes. Put them in a bowl and refrigerate to help cool them quickly.

In a large bowl, whip the cream until stiff. Purée the kiwis with the honey in a food processor. Then slowly, while stirring, add the purée to the whipped cream. Pour into individual bowls and refrigerate for at least 2 hours.

Serve decorated with mint leaves.

4 servings

Cold Kiwi Soufflé

PREPARATION: 30 MINUTES   COOKING: 5 MINUTES

4 or 5 kiwis
1 cup sugar
4 egg whites

Salt
1 cup heavy cream
1 kiwi, sliced, for garnish

In a heavy-bottomed saucepan (enamel, preferably), mix together the sugar and ½ cup water over low heat until the sugar becomes caramelized and turns light brown. Set aside.

With an electric beater, beat the egg whites with a pinch of salt until stiff, then slowly add the caramel and beat until well mixed. Pour into a bowl.

Beat the cream until stiff. Purée the kiwis. Gently fold the whipped cream into the egg whites, then into the kiwi purée. Pour the mixture into individual glass cups. Garnish each cup with a kiwi slice and refrigerate until ready to serve.

6 servings

Kiwi Sherbet with Fresh Raspberry Purée

PREPARATION: 10 MINUTES   FREEZING: 1½ HOURS

4 kiwis
½ cup lemon juice
⅔ cup sugar
Pinch of salt
1½ cups milk
½ cup heavy cream

6 fresh raspberries
¼ cup confectioners' sugar
1 tablespoon eau-de-vie de
    framboise (raspberry brandy)
1 kiwi, sliced, for garnish

Peel and slice the kiwis. In a food processor, purée the kiwis with the lemon juice, sugar, salt and milk. Pour the purée into ice trays and place in the freezer for 1 hour, or until half set.

Meanwhile, whip the cream until stiff. Remove the purée from the freezer and beat for 30 seconds with a whisk. Fold the whipped cream into the purée and pour into sherbet glasses. Refrigerate for 30 minutes.

Just before serving, purée the raspberries and confectioners' sugar with the eau-de-vie de framboise. Pour some raspberry purée on top of each serving of the kiwi sherbet and garnish with a slice of kiwi.

6 servings

Crème de Marrons au Chocolat
(Chestnut Cream with Chocolate)

PREPARATION AND COOKING: 40 MINUTES   FREEZING: 1 HOUR

This dessert requires a festive occasion, for it is very rich and sinful. The dinner should be light and low in calories so that your guests can enjoy this cream without any feeling of guilt.

2 pounds dried chestnuts* or 2
   1-pound cans chestnuts
1 cup milk
5 ounces semisweet chocolate
1 pint heavy cream

Pinch of salt
2 envelopes clear gelatin
3 tablespoons rum
1 stick (¼ pound) butter
¾ cup sugar

Put the chestnuts in a large saucepan and cover with milk and enough water to cover. Bring to a boil, then continue cooking over medium heat for 20 minutes, or until the chestnuts are done.

Meanwhile, grate the chocolate and set aside. Whip the cream with salt until stiff and set aside.

Drain the chestnuts over a bowl, reserving the liquid and 6 whole chestnuts for garnish, and purée them.

Dissolve the gelatin in a cup with 1 tablespoon cold water. In a saucepan, bring ½ cup of the chestnut cooking liquid to a boil and add the gelatin. Simmer for 2 minutes, then remove from heat.

Add ½ cup cooking liquid to the chestnut purée. Mix well. Divide the purée into two batches in separate bowls.

Add the liquid with the gelatin to the first batch. Mix well, then add the rum and mix well again. Mix together the butter and ½ cup sugar and add the mixture to the purée. Mix well and set aside.

Add the grated chocolate to the second bowl of the purée. Mix well, then add the remaining sugar. Mix well.

Put the chocolate-chestnut purée in a 2-quart mold, then spread the whipped cream, and then the chestnut-butter mixture. Decorate with the whole chestnuts and freeze for 1 hour.

8 servings

*Dried chestnuts are available in most Italian stores in the fall. If you have time, soak them for 1 hour; by doing so, you will reduce the cooking time.

If you are using canned chestnuts, drain the chestnuts and save the liquid. Use ½ cup of this liquid to purée the chestnuts and ½ cup to melt the gelatin.

You can also use fresh chestnuts. With a sharp knife, make a shallow slash in the outer shell, then drop into boiling oil for 8 minutes. Drain, cool, and remove the shells.

Nectarines with Fresh Figs

PREPARATION: 20 MINUTES   COOKING: 20 MINUTES

12 ripe nectarines
½ cup corn syrup
½ teaspoon vanilla extract
12 ripe figs*
6 tablespoons superfine sugar

¾ cup heavy cream
3 tablespoons kirsch
1½ cups strawberries, washed
   and hulled
½ cup slivered almonds

*If you cannot find fresh figs, dried figs can be substituted. Soak the figs in 1 cup hot water for 30 minutes.

Place the nectarines in boiling water for a few seconds. Drain, cool and peel. Heat the corn syrup with ½ cup water and vanilla and bring to a boil. Add the nectarines and remove from heat. Let them stand in the syrup for 10 minutes.

Meanwhile, peel the figs and purée with the sugar in a food professor or blender. In a small saucepan, cook the fig purée over high heat, stirring all the while, for 6 minutes. Remove from heat and, stirring, add the cream. Cool in the refrigerator until ready to serve.

To serve, transfer the nectarines with a slotted spoon to a serving bowl. Pour the kirsch over them, surround with the strawberries, and sprinkle with the slivered almonds. Serve with the purée of figs.

6 servings

Crème aux Pêches   (Peach Cream)

PREPARATION: 25 MINUTES   REFRIGERATION: 2 HOURS

8 ripe peaches
4 tablespoons granulated sugar
½ teaspoon vanilla extract
2 tablespoons superfine sugar

3 envelopes unflavored gelatin
¼ cup brandy
1 pint heavy cream

Setting aside two peaches, peel, halve and pit the remaining peaches. Purée them in a food processor or blender. Remove to a bowl and add the granulated sugar. Mix well and refrigerate.

Meanwhile, plunge the two peaches in a bowl of very hot water with the vanilla for a few minutes. Drain and remove the skin. Cut the peaches in two, remove the pits and dice. Add the superfine sugar. Refrigerate.

In a small bowl, mix the gelatin with 2 tablespoons cold water, then add the brandy. Set the bowl over a saucepan of boiling water until the gelatin is completely dissolved.

Add the gelatin to the peach purée, then add the diced peaches. Mix well.

Beat the cream until stiff. Gently fold the whipped cream into the purée. Pour into a serving mold and refrigerate for 2 hours, or put the cream in the freezer for 20 minutes until it is set.

4 servings

Peach Soufflé

PREPARATION: 20 MINUTES   COOKING: 40 MINUTES

This dessert is easy to make. It is a soufflé, but because of the peaches in the center and the almonds, it does not fall as quickly as a regular soufflé—it has more body. But it is best to bake the soufflé when you are serving the main course so that the soufflé is ready when your guests are.

3 egg yolks	3 peaches
6 tablespoons sugar	2 tablespoons brandy
¼ cup flour	4 egg whites
1 cup milk	¼ cup ground almonds

Preheat the oven to 375°. Mix the egg yolks and 5 tablespoons sugar in a food processor. With the machine still running, slowly add the flour.

In a saucepan, heat the milk (do not boil) and add the egg yolk–flour mixture. Cook, stirring all the while over medium heat, until the mixture thickens and will coat a wooden spoon. Remove from heat and cool by placing the saucepan in a bowl of ice.

Peel the peaches by dipping them in a bowl of very hot water. Cut in two and remove the pits. Place in a bowl and add the brandy.

Beat the egg whites until they form peaks and carefully fold the egg yolk–flour mixture into them. Pour half the mixture into a buttered 1-quart soufflé dish. Place the peach halves on top and sprinkle with 1 tablespoon sugar, and then with the almonds. Pour the remaining mixture on top. Bake for 30 minutes, or until the soufflé is golden brown. Serve right away.

6 servings

Caramel-Cream Pears

PREPARATION: 10 MINUTES   COOKING: 20 MINUTES

6 pears, peeled	1 cup plain yogurt
6 tablespoons sugar	½ cup honey
4 tablespoons butter	

Preheat the oven to 450°.

Halve and core the pears, and arrange them in a shallow baking pan. Sprinkle them with sugar and put 2 teaspoons butter in the hollow of each pear half. Bake for about 20 minutes, or until the sugar is caramelized.

In a saucepan, heat the honey with the yogurt, and stir the mixture into the pan juices. Serve the pears warm with the honey-yogurt sauce poured over them.

6 servings

Chocolate Pears

PREPARATION: 15 MINUTES   COOKING: 40 MINUTES

6 large pears	2 tablespoons butter
¾ cup sugar	1 tablespoon eau-de-vie de poire
1 cup red wine	(pear brandy)
¼ pound semisweet baking	
chocolate	

Peel the pears, leaving the stems on. Insert a small spoon in the rounded end of the pears and remove the seeds.

Place the pears in a saucepan side by side; add sugar, wine and 4 cups water. Bring to a boil, reduce the heat and simmer for 25 minutes.

With a slotted spoon, transfer the pears to a deep serving platter. Reduce the cooking juices by half and pour over the pears. Refrigerate until ready to serve.

Just before serving, melt the chocolate in the top of a double boiler and add the butter. Mix well with a wooden spoon, then add the eau-de-vie de poire. Pour over the chilled pears and serve.

6 servings

Pear Tart

PREPARATION: 45 MINUTES   COOKING: 25 MINUTES

Pâte Brisée II (see p. 235)	½ cup heavy cream
5 ripe Anjou pears	1 egg
1 stick (¼ pound) butter	3 tablespoons confectioners'
2½ tablespoons sugar	sugar
½ teaspoon vanilla extract	

Preheat the oven to 350°.

Reduce by half the ingredients for the pâte brisée and prepare the dough. Butter a 9-inch pie pan. Roll out the dough on a floured board and fit it into the pan, then crimp the edges. Prick the dough with a fork and line with waxed paper. Cover the bottom with enough raw rice to keep the pie shell from rising. Bake for 25 minutes, or until the dough turns light brown.

Meanwhile, peel the pears and cut each into eight slices. Remove the cores. Heat the butter in a large skillet and add the slices of pear. Sprinkle with sugar, add the vanilla, and mix lightly. Simmer for about 10 minutes, or until transparent. Remove with a slotted spoon to a platter.

Beat the cream with the egg. Slowly add the mixture to the skillet and simmer, stirring all the while and scraping the sides to remove any bits of pear or cream.

Place the sliced pears in the pie shell and cover with the cream-egg mixture. Sprinkle with confectioners' sugar and broil 3 minutes, or until golden brown. Serve lukewarm.

6 servings

Poached Pears with Green Grapes

PREPARATION: 25 MINUTES   COOKING: 40 MINUTES

If you have a juicer for making fresh grape juice, you would obtain best results from this recipe, but if you don't, a food processor will serve the purpose almost as well. The pears poached in the grape juice are both refreshing to look at and to taste.

1 pound green seedless grapes   Juice of 1 lemon
4 large ripe pears   6 mint leaves for garnish
6 ounces sugar

Wash the grapes and pat dry with paper towels. Set aside a handful to use as garnish. Extract the juice of the remaining grapes by puréeing the grapes in a food processor, then straining the purée through a very fine sieve.

Pour the juice into a saucepan large enough to hold the pears. Add the sugar, 2¼ cups water and lemon juice. Simmer for 10 minutes.

Peel the pears, keeping the stems on. Add the pears to the syrup and poach for 30 minutes. Let them cool in the syrup.

Meanwhile, peel the remaining grapes. Drain the pears and arrange on a serving platter. Reduce the syrup by half and then pour over the pears. Refrigerate until ready to serve.

Before serving, surround the pears with the peeled grapes and stick a fresh mint leaf on each stem.

4 servings

Fresh Pineapple with Pineapple Sauce

PREPARATION: 15 MINUTES

1 large pineapple
2 tablespoons superfine sugar
Juice of 1 lime

¼ cup heavy cream
2 tablespoons rum
4 mint leaves for garnish

Peel, core and slice the pineapple; set aside 2 slices for the sauce. Arrange the slices on a serving platter and sprinkle with the sugar and lime juice. Refrigerate.

In a food processor, purée the 2 pineapple slices with the cream and rum. Remove to a bowl and refrigerate.

Just before serving, garnish the pineapple slices with the mint and serve the sauce on the side.

6 servings

Raspberries with Peaches

PREPARATION: 15 MINUTES   COOKING: 25 MINUTES   REFRIGERATION: 1 HOUR

4 ripe peaches
1¾ cups superfine sugar
4 egg yolks
½ cup white wine
1 tablespoon kirsch

¼ pound raspberries, rinsed and drained
2 tablespoons confectioners' sugar

Peel the peaches, cut in two and remove the pits.

Place the peaches in a skillet, cover with 1 cup water and add half the sugar. Bring to a boil and simmer until the peaches are translucent but don't fall apart. Carefully transfer with a slotted spoon into a bowl to cool.

In the top of a double boiler, beat the egg yolks and the remaining sugar with a whisk over simmering water until smooth. Still beating, add the wine, then the kirsch.

Pour the sauce into individual glass bowls and refrigerate for 1 hour.

Just before serving, place two peaches in each bowl. Fill each peach half with raspberries. Sprinkle with some confectioners' sugar and serve.

4 servings

Rhubarb Mousse with Strawberry Sauce

PREPARATION: 30 MINUTES   COOKING: 20 MINUTES

1 pound rhubarb
1 cup granulated sugar
1 envelope unflavored gelatin
4 egg whites
1 pint heavy cream

½ cup superfine sugar
2 pints fresh strawberries,
   washed and hulled
1 tablespoon cognac

Wash the rhubarb and cut into 1-inch pieces. Put the rhubarb in a saucepan; add ½ cup water and the granulated sugar. Bring to a boil, then simmer for 15 minutes, or until the rhubarb falls apart. Dissolve the gelatin in 2 tablespoons cold water and add it to the rhubarb. Cook for 1 minute more. Transfer to a bowl and cool in the freezer for 10 minutes.

Meanwhile, beat the egg whites until they are very stiff. Whip the cream until it has thickened slightly and add the superfine sugar, then resume whipping the cream until it is stiff enough to form peaks. Gently fold the egg whites into the whipped cream, then add the rhubarb by folding it in. Refrigerate until ready to serve.

Set aside about 12 strawberries for decorating the mousse and purée the remaining strawberries in a blender or food processor. With the food processor still running, pour in the cognac. Put the sauce in a bowl and refrigerate.

When ready to serve the mousse, decorate it with the whole strawberries and serve it with the sauce.

6 servings

Strawberry Soufflé

PREPARATION: 20 MINUTES   COOKING: 20 MINUTES

6 egg yolks   6 egg whites
½ cup granulated sugar   Pinch of salt
1 tablespoon flour   ¼ cup confectioners' sugar
1 cup strawberries

Preheat the oven to 375°.

Put the egg yolks, sugar and flour in a bowl and beat for 10 minutes with an electric beater.

Wash and hull the strawberries. Purée them in a food processor or blender and add to the egg-sugar-flour mixture.

Add salt to the egg whites and beat with an electric beater until stiff, then carefully fold the strawberries into the egg whites. Pour the strawberries into a buttered soufflé dish and bake for 15 minutes.

Sprinkle with confectioners' sugar and serve right away.

6 servings

Tomato Jam

PREPARATION: 20 MINUTES   COOKING: 50 MINUTES

Last summer I spent some time in the country with my friend Edith Ferber. She had a marvelous vegetable garden, and her tomato crop was so enormous that we ate tomatoes cooked in every possible way. One day she decided to make tomato jam. Served with fresh fruit or kept for the winter to eat on toast, it is not only unusual but delicious.

2 pounds ripe tomatoes   ½ teaspoon cinnamon
1 pound apples   1 clove
2 pounds sugar
Zest (yellow part of the skin) of
    2 lemons

Dip the tomatoes in boiling water for a couple of seconds. Remove with a slotted spoon and let them cool. Peel them, then cut in two and remove all the seeds by squeezing over a strainer set on top of a bowl.

Peel the apples, then quarter, core and dice them.

In a large, heavy saucepan (a copper pot would be ideal), put the tomatoes (plus the tomato juice in the bowl), sugar, lemon zest, cinnamon and the clove. Bring to a boil, then reduce the heat. Simmer for about 30 minutes, or until the jam starts to thicken. Add the diced apples and stir with a wooden spoon. Simmer for another 40 minutes, stirring from time to time so that the jam does not burn.

Sterilize the jars. Pour the jam into them and seal right away.

5 jars

Tarte aux Betteraves   (Beet Pie)

PREPARATION: 35 MINUTES   COOKING: 35 MINUTES

I invented this recipe one night when my husband brought home unexpected guests. What I had in great quantities were cans of beets—I thought that if sugar is made from beets, one should be able to use them for a pie. So I did.

The pie comes out a lovely light purple color. A touch of whipped cream transforms it into a most elegant dessert.

Pâte Brisée II (see p. 235)   3 tablespoons vanilla
16-ounce can beets   3 tablespoons butter
1¼ cups sugar   2 tablespoons flour
4 tablespoons molasses   Juice of 1 orange
4 tablespoons Crème Fraîche ¾ cup confectioners' sugar
   (see p. xvi) or heavy cream 1 cup heavy cream or crème
3 eggs   fraîche for garnish

Preheat the oven to 375°.

Reduce by half the ingredients for the pâte brisée and prepare the dough. Butter a 9-inch pie pan. Roll out the dough on a floured board and lay it on the pie pan, then crimp the edges. Bake the pie shell for 15 minutes (it should be only half baked) while preparing the filling.

Drain the beets. In a food processor or a blender, purée the beets with the sugar, molasses and crème fraîche or cream. Separate the eggs and set the whites aside. Add the egg yolks and vanilla to the purée and run the machine for 20 seconds. Set aside.

Meanwhile, heat the butter in a saucepan and add the flour. Mix well with a wooden spoon. While stirring, slowly add the orange juice. Cook the mixture over medium heat until it thickens and combine with the purée. Set aside.

In a mixing bowl, beat the egg whites until thick but not stiff, and add ½ cup confectioners' sugar, then resume beating until stiff. Fold the egg whites into the purée and pour into the pie shell. Bake for 35 minutes, or until a knife inserted in the pie comes out clean.

Whip the cream. Just before serving, sprinkle with the remaining confectioners' sugar. Serve garnished with the whipped cream or the crème fraîche.

6 to 8 servings

Calvados Cream with Mangoes

PREPARATION: 30 MINUTES   COOKING: 20 MINUTES

4 egg yolks*   1 cup heavy cream
3 tablespoons superfine sugar   2 mangoes
3 tablespoons Calvados

Put the egg yolks and sugar in the top of a double boiler and beat over simmering water for about 20 minutes, or until the mixture thickens and will coat a wooden spoon. Add the Calvados. Mix well and pour into a bowl. Cool by placing the bowl in a bowl of ice.

Meanwhile, beat the cream until stiff. Peel the mangoes and cut the flesh into small cubes; set aside 4 tablespoons for garnish. Add the mango cubes to the egg yolk–Calvados mixture, then add the whipped cream by carefully folding it in.

Pour the mixture into individual stemmed glasses and decorate with the reserved cubes of mango. Chill in the freezer until ready to serve.

4 servings

*Save the egg whites and use later for making meringue or other dessert. Freeze them and defrost in the refrigerator 24 hours before using them.

Coconut Flan

PREPARATION: 1 HOUR   COOKING: 1 HOUR

When my friend Lucy came to New York some fifteen years ago she brought with her some great recipes from Colombia. Her favorite is a coconut flan that is as light as air. She told me that the secret was to buy a fresh, ripe, heavy coconut.

1 cup milk	6 eggs
1 cup grated coconut	2 cups evaporated milk
1¾ cups sugar	

Scald the milk and pour it over the coconut. Cover and let stand for 30 minutes. Pour the mixture through a very fine sieve set on top of a bowl and squeeze out all the liquid. Discard the coconut.

Put 1 cup sugar with ⅓ cup water in a heavy saucepan and bring to a boil. Stir with a wooden spoon until the syrup turns a caramel color. Pour into an 8-cup savarin mold and rotate the mold until the bottom and sides are covered with the syrup.

In a bowl, beat the eggs and slowly add the remaining sugar. Heat the evaporated milk, and while beating, add it in a stream to the eggs. Add the coconut milk and mix well.

Pour the mixture into the savarin mold, and put the mold in a pan with 1 inch of water. Bake for 1 hour, or until a knife inserted will come out clean. Chill until ready to serve.

To serve, invert the flan on a platter.

6 servings

Zabaglione with Fruit

PREPARATION: 10 MINUTES   COOKING: 10 MINUTES

Zabaglione, a kind of soft custard, a traditional Italian dessert. Use your imagination and pick any fresh colorful fruit to serve with it.

6 egg yolks	1 pint raspberries, strawberries,
2 tablespoons sugar	kiwis (diced) or any other
¼ generous cup of Marsala	fruit desired

Put the egg yolks and sugar in the top of a double boiler and beat over simmering water until the mixture is light and frothy. Slowly add the Marsala, continuing to beat until the cream thickens only a little—do not overcook.

Wash the fruit and drain well. Place some fruit in the bottom of individual glass cups and pour some zabaglione on top. Serve right away.

4 servings

Anne's Almond Cookies

PREPARATION: 10 MINUTES   COOKING: 10 MINUTES   REFRIGERATION: 3 HOURS

These cookies are marvelous. They simply melt in your mouth, and are excellent with coffee. The dough has to be refrigerated for 3 hours, so make the dough as soon as you get home from work. A friend, Anne Rubin, gave me this recipe, and she does not like to spend much time in the kitchen!

1 stick (¼ pound) butter	1 teaspoon vanilla extract
⅓ cup sugar	1⅔ cups flour
⅔ cup crushed almonds	Confectioners' sugar
¼ teaspoon salt	

Cream the butter and sugar in a food processor. Add all the other ingredients except for confectioners' sugar and run the machine until they are well mixed. Remove the dough and refrigerate for 3 hours.
   Preheat the oven to 325°.
   Shape the dough into small crescents (they will expand during baking). Bake for 10 to 12 minutes, or until lightly browned. Sprinkle with confectioners' sugar.
   About 3 dozen cookies

Almond Crescent Cookies

PREPARATION: 25 MINUTES   COOKING: 30 MINUTES

Pâte Brisée II (see p. 235)	2 tablespoons cognac
2 cups almonds	1 egg white
1¼ cups confectioners' sugar	1 egg yolk
6½ teaspoons cinnamon	1½ cups granulated sugar

Make the pâte brisée. Wrap the dough in a damp paper towel and set aside.
   Mince the almonds in a blender or food processor. With the machine still running, add ¾ cup confectioners' sugar, 2 teaspoons cinnamon, cognac and egg white and mix for 1 minute. The mixture should be like a thick paste.
   Preheat the oven to 325°.

Roll out the dough ⅛ inch thick and cut into strips 4 inches long. Beat the egg yolk with 1 tablespoon water. With a pastry brush, brush the dough with the egg. Form small crescents with the almond mixture and wrap the dough around it.

Sprinkle a cookie sheet with flour. Place the crescents, ½ inch apart, on the cookie sheet. Bake for 20 minutes, or until they are lightly browned.

Meanwhile, make the syrup. In a saucepan, combine 1 cup water, granulated sugar and 4½ teaspoons cinnamon. Bring to a boil, stirring all the while, then simmer for 10 minutes. Remove from heat and let it cool slightly.

With a spatula, remove the cookies to a platter. Dip each crescent in the syrup, then roll in the remaining confectioners' sugar.

These cookies can be stored for a long time in a tightly sealed container.

50 cookies

Chocolate-Orange Cookies

PREPARATION: 5 MINUTES   COOKING: 15 MINUTES

These cookies are quick to make and excellent for serving with fresh fruit and espresso.

3½ ounces candied orange peel   ¾ cup heavy cream
3½ ounces slivered almonds   ⅓ generous cup flour
¾ cup sugar   8 ounces sweet chocolate
3½ tablespoons honey

Preheat the oven to 375°.

Dice the candied oranges and mix with the almonds. Set aside.

Put the sugar, the honey and cream in a heavy-bottomed saucepan. Cook over medium heat, stirring all the while with a wooden spoon, for 5 minutes. Drop a small amount of the mixture in a bowl of cold water, and if it forms a soft ball, remove the mixture from heat. Add the almonds, orange peel and flour. Mix well.

Oil a cookie pan. Form small mounds with the dough and flatten them slightly with the back of a soup spoon. Bake for 8 minutes. Cool, and with a spatula, transfer to a platter. Grate the chocolate. Melt the chocolate in the top of a double boiler over simmering water. With a spatula, spread some chocolate on each cookie. Cool on a cake rack.

25 cookies

Coconut Balls

PREPARATION: 30 MINUTES

While spending a summer in Tanzania, we decided to take a side trip to the island of Zanzibar. Learning about this trip, one of our Tanzanian friends asked me to bring him back a basket of fresh coconuts. I readily agreed, not knowing that in Zanzibar a basket of coconuts means twenty pounds of coconuts! My husband nearly left me behind. In exchange for the basket and to appease my husband, we were invited to a Tanzanian dinner and I was given this recipe.

2 sticks (½ pound) sweet butter, cut into small pieces
2 cups confectioners' sugar
1 teaspoon coffee extract

1½ cups grated fresh coconut or 7-ounce can shredded coconut
Rind of 1 lemon, grated

Leave the butter out of the refrigerator for 30 minutes.

In a food processor or blender, mix the butter and confectioners' sugar until the mixture becomes a smooth paste. Add the coffee extract. Set aside 1 cup coconut, and add the coconut. Add the lemon rind. Refrigerate for 15 minutes.

When the mixture is firm, make balls the size of walnuts. Roll them in the coconut and refrigerate.

Serve with espresso for dessert.

Mollie's Spritz Cookies

PREPARATION: 20 MINUTES   REFRIGERATION: 2 HOURS   COOKING: 10 MINUTES

Mollie is an old lady full of marvelous cooking secrets that she sometimes, only sometimes, will share with you. Her secrets come from a long way back, from her mother and grandmother. Last summer she gave me this recipe and I made the cookies with lemon extract, my favorite flavoring.

2 sticks (½ pound) butter
¾ cup sugar
1 egg
2 tablespoons heavy cream
2 cups flour
1 teaspoon baking powder

Pinch of salt
3 drops almond, lemon or vanilla extract
1 cup pecan halves for decoration

Preheat the oven to 375°.

In a food processor, cream the butter and sugar. Add the remaining ingredients except the pecans, and run the machine until the mixture is thoroughly blended. Refrigerate the dough for 2 hours.

Roll out the dough on a floured board and cut with several kinds of cookie cutters. Or, instead of rolling out the dough, you can drop it by teaspoonfuls on a buttered cookie sheet. Shape long strips from the scraps of dough left by the cookie cutter. Decorate the cookies with the pecans and place them on a buttered cookie sheet. Bake for 8 to 12 minutes, or until golden brown. Remove from the oven and cool.

3 to 4 dozen cookies

Cecile's Tahini Cookies

PREPARATION: 15 MINUTES   COOKING: 20 MINUTES

One of my daughter Cecile's favorite foods is tahini, or sesame paste. As she is a vegetarian, whenever it was her turn to cook we always had nothing but vegetables with a sesame sauce. After numerous requests for other ways of using tahini, she finally came up with this recipe for cookies. They are simply delicious. Serve them with a good cup of espresso.

5 tablespoons butter
1¼ cups sugar
4 tablespoons tahini (sesame paste)
1½ cups flour

1 teaspoon brandy
4 tablespoons plain yogurt
1 teaspoon baking powder
½ teaspoon baking soda

Preheat the oven to 325°. In a food processor or in a blender, mix the butter, sugar and sesame paste. With the machine running, add the flour, brandy and yogurt, then add the baking powder and baking soda. Run the machine for 10 seconds.

Butter and lightly flour a cookie sheet. With a tablespoon, form small mounds of the dough and put them, 1 inch apart, on the cookie sheet. Bake for 20 minutes, or until golden brown. Let the cookies cool, then store in a tightly sealed jar.

5 dozen cookies

Banana Cake with Raspberry Jelly

PREPARATION: 20 MINUTES   COOKING: 40 MINUTES

1 loaf (1 pound) white bread
¼ cup rum
6 ripe bananas
6 eggs
⅔ cup brown sugar

¼ teaspoon vanilla extract
Pinch of nutmeg
1 jar raspberry jelly
1 tablespoon brandy

Soak the bread in a mixture of rum and ¼ cup water for 15 minutes.

In a blender or food processor, purée the bananas, then add the bread, eggs, sugar, vanilla and nutmeg. Run the machine until all the ingredients are well mixed.

Pour the mixture in a buttered 1½-quart round pan and put in a pan filled with 1 inch of water. Bake for 40 minutes.

Unmold the cake while still warm.

Just before serving, heat the jelly, add the brandy, and pour over the cake. Serve slightly warm.

6 servings

Beggar's Pie

PREPARATION: 25 MINUTES   COOKING: 40 MINUTES

My daughter Cecile jogs four or five miles every day. After jogging she always eats dried raisins, dates or figs. One day, having nothing for dessert, I took all her provisions of dried fruit and made this pie. The pie was so good that she forgave me for rifling her supply of fruit.

Pâte Brisée II (see p. 235)
7 ounces dates, pitted
7 ounces dried figs
3½ ounces raisins

3 eggs
1 cup heavy cream
4 tablespoons sugar
2 ounces slivered almonds

Preheat the oven to 400°.

Make the pâte brisée and refrigerate while preparing the filling.

Cut the dates into two or three pieces and the figs into several pieces. Mix together all the fruit and set aside.

Mix the eggs, cream and sugar in a food processor or blender.

Butter a 9-inch pie pan. On a floured board, roll out the dough and line the pie pan with it, cutting the excess away. Press the edges with a fork.

Fill the pie with the fruit and pour the egg-cream mixture over it. Sprinkle with almonds and bake for 40 minutes.

Serve at room temperature.

6 servings

Les Chichis

PREPARATION: 15 MINUTES   COOKING: 15 MINUTES

In the spring many small towns in France have a fair on the public square that features games and food stands. At a fair in the South of France I tasted a delicious hot fried galette called chichi. My children liked it so much that they kept on going back for more. The women who made them gave me the recipe. Sprinkled with confectioners' sugar, they are marvelous served with a fresh fruit salad.

1 tablespoon yeast	4 tablespoons butter, melted
½ cup hot milk	1 tablespoon brandy or vanilla
3½ cups flour	extract
½ teaspoon salt	Oil for frying
4 egg yolks	Confectioners' sugar

Dissolve the yeast in the hot milk. Put the flour, salt and yeast in the container of a food processor. Run the machine for 30 seconds, then add the egg yolks, butter and brandy, and process until all the ingredients are well mixed. Remove the dough to a bowl and let it stand for 15 minutes.

On a floured board, roll out the dough about ⅛ inch thick. With a 3-inch round dough cutter, cut circles in the dough.

In a deep fryer, heat the oil until it begins to sizzle. Add the circles of dough two or three at a time and fry for 1 minute on each side. Drain on paper towels. Sprinkle with confectioners' sugar and serve piping hot.

Gâteau de Petit Beurre

PREPARATION: 15 MINUTES   REFRIGERATION: 1 HOUR

1 stick (¼ pound) butter
1 egg
⅔ cup confectioners' sugar
2 tablespoons heavy cream
1 tablespoon instant coffee

24 petit beurre or any
  shortbread cookies
1 cup strong espresso
6 walnuts, halved, for garnish

In a blender or food processor, mix the butter, egg, sugar, cream and instant coffee for 1 minute, or until the ingredients are blended and have the consistency of thick cream.

Soak the petit beurre in the espresso for several minutes. Line a serving bowl with a layer of petit beurre or other cookies and spread some of the cream on top of the cookies. Continue, alternating cookies and cream, and finish with a layer of cream.

Garnish with the walnut halves and refrigerate for about 1 hour.

4 servings

Rachel's Cheesecake

PREPARATION: 20 MINUTES   COOKING: 50 MINUTES REFRIGERATION: OVERNIGHT

25 graham crackers
1¾ cups plus 3 tablespoons
  sugar
6 tablespoons butter, melted
3 8-ounce packages cream cheese
3 eggs
1 teaspoon vanilla extract

Juice of 1 lemon
1 teaspoon grated fresh ginger
1 pint sour cream
Rind of 1 lemon
Chopped lemon rind for garnish
  (optional)

Preheat the oven to 350°. Place the graham crackers in the container of a food processor or blender. Run the machine for 30 seconds, or until the graham crackers have turned into crumbs. With the machine running, add ¼ cup sugar and butter, and mix for 10 seconds.

Pat the cracker-crumb mixture firmly into a 9½-inch springform pan. Set aside.

In a food processor or blender, blend the cream cheese, eggs and 1½ cups sugar. With the machine running, add the vanilla, lemon juice and ginger. Run the machine for 15 seconds. Pour the batter into the spring-form pan and bake for 40 minutes.

Meanwhile, mix together the sour cream, 3 tablespoons sugar and lemon rind.

Remove the cake from the oven, spread the sour cream mixture on top, and bake for 12 minutes more.

Sprinkle the chopped lemon rind on top and refrigerate overnight.
8 to 10 servings

NOTE: If you are going to serve this cheesecake the same night you prepared it, you can put it in the freezer 15 minutes before serving it.

Easter Nests

PREPARATION: 25 MINUTES   COOKING: 25 MINUTES

This was my favorite recipe when I was growing up. My mother would make it for Easter Sunday. In the center of each nest would be a small chocolate egg filled with liqueur, and the mixture of the liqueur and the orange was delightful.

NESTS:
2¼ sticks (9 ounces) butter
1¼ cups granulated sugar
4 eggs
1¾ cups flour
Half an envelope of yeast
Juice and grated rind of 2
    oranges

FILLING:
2¾ cups confectioners' sugar
Juice of 3 oranges
5½ ounces candied lemon rind
Chocolate eggs filled with
    liqueur

Preheat the oven to 300°.

Cream the butter in a food processor. While the machine is still running, slowly add the sugar, then the eggs one by one, and then the flour all at once and the yeast. When all the ingredients are well mixed, add the juice and grated rind of the 2 oranges. Mix well and remove to a bowl.

Butter individual savarin molds. Fill each mold halfway with the batter and bake for 20 minutes.

Meanwhile, make the filling. Mix the confectioners' sugar with the juice of the 3 oranges. Pour the mixture into the still-hot nests and refrigerate.

Julienne the candied lemon rind. Arrange the lemon rind to look like the twigs of a nest and place eggs in the center.

6 nests

French Toast

PREPARATION: 20 MINUTES   COOKING: 30 MINUTES

French "French toast" is a dessert made from stale bread. The bread is soaked in rum, brandy or any other liqueur.

1 cup milk	3 eggs
3 tablespoons rum	6 tablespoons honey
¼ cup superfine sugar	4 tablespoons finely chopped
12 slices day-old French or	almonds
Italian bread	Oil for deep frying

In a saucepan, heat together the milk with the rum and sugar. When the milk is hot (do not boil), pour over the bread and soak for 5 minutes, turning the bread over once. Beat the eggs in a bowl. In a deep fryer heat the oil until it sizzles. Dip the bread quickly in the eggs and drop in the hot oil. Fry until golden brown and drain on paper towels.

Spread the honey on the toast. Sprinkle with chopped almonds and serve.

6 servings

Gâteau aux Amandes   (Almond Cake)

PREPARATION: 20 MINUTES   COOKING: 30 MINUTES

This very light cake is good served with a melon salad or with whipped cream.

4 tablespoons butter	Pinch of salt
¾ cup shelled almonds	Confectioners' sugar
⅔ cup sugar	TOPPING (optional):
⅓ cup flour	1 cup shelled walnuts
1½ teaspoon baking powder	½ cup sugar
4 egg whites	

Preheat the oven to 320°.

Melt the butter in a small saucepan. Set aside to cool. Place the almonds in the container of a food processor and run the machine for 1 minute, or until the almonds turn into powder. Remove to a bowl. Add the sugar, flour and baking powder.

Beat the egg whites with salt until stiff. Delicately fold the almond mixture into the egg whites, then fold in the melted butter.

Butter a 9-inch pie pan about 1½ inches deep or use a quiche mold. Spread the batter evenly in the pie pan and bake for 30 minutes, or until lightly browned.

Remove the cake from the pan and cool on a rack. Just before serving, sprinkle confectioners' sugar on top.

If you like, you can add a topping. Melt the sugar with the water and boil at 275°, measured with a candy thermometer. Add the walnuts, mix well and remove to an oiled piece of foil. When cool, lift with a spatula and place on top of the confectioners' sugar.

10 servings

Lemon Squares

PREPARATION: 20 MINUTES   COOKING: 45 MINUTES

Evelyn Gin is my best friend's mother. There is mild competition between us, because Evelyn is as enthusiastic a baker as I am. When I help her daughter Madeline with a dinner party, Evelyn assumes that she will make the dessert. A couple of months ago Madeleine gave a big dinner party where we collaborated on the dinner. Knowing that Evelyn would be making the dessert, I tried to exert some influence by suggesting what it should be. But Evelyn was stubborn as usual and made exactly what she wanted to make. But I had to admit the result was spectacular. Her lemon squares went in a jiffy!

1 cup flour
¼ cup confectioners' sugar
1 stick (¼ pound) butter, cut
    into small pieces
TOPPING:
⅓ cup fresh lemon juice
Grated rind of 1 lemon

2 eggs
1 cup sugar
2 tablespoons flour
½ teaspoon baking powder
1 jar glazed kumquats (for
    garnish)

Preheat the oven to 335°.

In a food processor, mix the flour, confectioners' sugar and butter. Butter a 9-inch-square pan and press the dough into the pan. Bake for 15 minutes.

Meanwhile, prepare the topping. Mix all the topping ingredients in a food processor. Pour the mixture over the partially baked dough and bake for 25 minutes more. Remove from the oven, cool and cut into squares. Garnish each square with half a glazed kumquat.

15 squares

Persimmon Pie

PREPARATION: 20 MINUTES   COOKING: 35 MINUTES

Madeline Gins, the poet, has a great love for persimmons. One day, at her request, I made a persimmon pie, which turned out to be great. I thought I had invented something new, but one of our guests said she was positive that this was an old recipe. I will let the reader be the judge, because I had never encountered or eaten a persimmon pie before I made this one.

Pâte Brisée II (see p. 235)
4 ripe persimmons
1 cup heavy cream
½ cup granulated sugar
2 eggs

2 tablespoons brandy
1 package frozen raspberries, defrosted
¼ cup confectioners' sugar

Preheat the oven to 350°.

Make the pâte brisée and refrigerate.

Cut the persimmons in two and scoop out the flesh with a spoon.

Put the persimmons, cream, granulated sugar and eggs in the container of a food processor. Run the machine for 1 minute, then add the brandy and run the machine for a couple of seconds.

Meanwhile, butter a 9-inch quiche pan. Roll out the dough on a floured board and line the pan with the dough. Cut off the excess and crimp the edges.

Pour the persimmon mixture into the pie shell and bake for 35 minutes.

Meanwhile, drain the raspberries and purée them in a food processor with the confectioners' sugar.

Remove the pie from the oven and spread the raspberry purée on top. Serve at room temperature.

6 servings

Pistachio Cake

PREPARATION: 45 MINUTES   COOKING: 50 MINUTES

In Cairo, where I spent most of my childhood, desserts are often very rich and much too sweet. I was never fond of them except for a pistachio cake that I often bought at a small bakery on my way home from school. Twenty years later in New York I had a sudden longing for that cake. After many failures, I managed to reproduce my favorite cake. It is quite rich, so serve a simple broiled fish or meat and a salad to precede this marvelous cake.

¾ cup shelled pistachios	1½ cups flour
3 eggs	2 teaspoons baking powder
1¾ cups superfine sugar	2 pints heavy cream
1 tablespoon brandy	

Chop ½ cup pistachios coarsely and the remaining pistachios very finely. Set aside.

Preheat the oven to 350°.

Mix the flour with the baking powder. Put the eggs and 1¼ cup sugar in the container of a food processor or a blender and run the machine for 2 minutes. Add the brandy and mix for 1 minute; then add the flour and baking powder and the coarsely chopped pistachios. Mix well. Whip 1 pint heavy cream until stiff. Gently fold the pistachio mixture into the whipped cream.

Butter a 2-quart round cake pan and pour in the mixture. Bake for 50 minutes, or until a needle inserted comes out clean. Cool on a cake rack, then remove from the pan.

Whip the remaining cream. When it is nearly stiff, slowly pour in ½ cup sugar and then the finely chopped pistachios. Spread on the cake.

Refrigerate the cake if you are not going to serve it immediately.

6 to 8 servings

NOTE: Do not use the red-dyed pistachios because they will give the cake a reddish tinge.

Profiteroles Stuffed with Coffee Ice Cream

PREPARATION: 15 MINUTES   COOKING: 30 MINUTES

Profiteroles are delicious puff pastries. The shells are very easy to make and can be prepared in advance.

PÂTE À CHOUX (dough):
1 stick (¼ pound) butter, cut into small pieces
1 cup flour
1 teaspoon sugar
4 eggs

FILLING:
2 pints coffee ice cream
1 pound semisweet chocolate

Preheat the oven to 425°.

Put 1 cup water, butter and sugar in a saucepan. Bring to a boil, then lower the heat. When the butter is melted, add the flour all at once. With a wooden spoon, beat the mixture until the dough leaves the sides of the pan and forms a ball. Remove the saucepan from heat and add the eggs one by one, stirring all the while until each egg has been *completely* absorbed by the dough.

Butter a cookie sheet and fill a pastry bag with the dough. Pipe out 18 puffs, each the size of a walnut, leaving space around each puff, for they will expand. Bake for 25 minutes. Then turn off the oven, open the door and let them puff in the oven for 5 minutes more. Let them cool.

In the top of a double boiler, melt the chocolate over simmering water while stirring with the wooden spoon. Keep warm until ready to use.

Just before serving, make a slit in each puff and insert a tablespoon of ice cream. Stack the puffs and and pour the hot chocolate sauce over them.

18 puffs

Prune Turnovers

PREPARATION: 30 MINUTES   COOKING: 50 MINUTES

Pâte Brisée II (see p. 235)
1 tablespoon tea or 3 tea bags
3 tablespoons granulated sugar
¾ pound large prunes, pitted

1 egg yolk
1 pint heavy cream
3 tablespoons superfine sugar
1 tablespoon brandy

Make the pâte brisée and refrigerate.

Preheat the oven to 400°.

In a saucepan, bring 2 cups water to a boil. Add the tea or the tea bags. Turn off the heat and let the tea steep for 5 minutes. Strain through a fine sieve and pour the tea back into the saucepan. Add the granulated sugar and prunes, and bring to a boil. Reduce the heat and simmer for 20 minutes. Remove the prunes with a slotted spoon into a bowl and cool at room temperature.

On a floured board, roll out the dough ½ inch thick and cut out 6 rounds 5 inches in diameter. Divide the prunes among them, then fold them over. Wet the edges with water and press together lightly.

Beat the egg yolk and brush it on the turnovers. Bake for 30 minutes, or until they are golden brown.

Meanwhile, whip the heavy cream until stiff. Fold the sugar and brandy into the whipped cream. Put in a bowl and serve with the turnovers.

6 turnovers

Strawberry-Rhubarb Pie

PREPARATION: 30 MINUTES   COOKING: 50 MINUTES

PIE CRUST:
3 tablespoons sugar
2 eggs
9 tablespoons butter, cut into small pieces
1½ cups flour

FILLING:
1¾ pounds rhubarb
1 cup sugar
1 lemon, thinly sliced
2 pounds strawberries
1 egg white
1 pint heavy cream

Preheat the oven to 375°.

In a food processor, mix the sugar, eggs and butter. Add the flour and run the machine until the dough forms a ball. Remove to a floured board and roll out the dough.

Butter a 9-inch pie pan and line the pan with the dough. Press the rolling pin around the edges to cut off excess dough. Bake for 15 minutes.

Meanwhile, wash and cut the rhubarb into 2-inch pieces. Put the rhubarb in a saucepan and add 1 cup water, 1 cup sugar less 4 tablespoons, and lemon. Bring to a boil, then simmer for 20 minutes.

Remove the pie crust from the oven. Wash and hull the strawberries.

Whip the egg white with 4 tablespoons sugar and slowly add to the rhubarb.

Whip the heavy cream. Pour the rhubarb into the pie pan and spread the whipped cream on top. Decorate with the strawberries and serve slightly warm.

6 servings

Tarte au Sucre

PREPARATION: 15 MINUTES   COOKING: 25 MINUTES

This is a quick pie that is delicious with fresh strawberries or fruit.

PIE CRUST:
2 cups less 4 tablespoons flour
1 egg
1 tablespoon yeast
¼ cup granulated sugar
1 stick (¼ pound) butter

FILLING:
6 tablespoons dark brown sugar
3 tablespoons Crème Fraîche
  (see p. xvi)

Preheat the oven to 400°.

In a food processor, mix the flour, egg, yeast, sugar and butter. With the machine still running, add 3 tablespoons water. Stop the machine and make a ball with the dough. Set aside in a cool place for 30 minutes.

Butter a 9-inch pie pan. On a floured board, roll out the dough—it should be thick. Line the pan with the dough and firmly press the center with the palm of your hand to make a depression.

In a heavy-bottomed saucepan, melt the brown sugar over low heat. Add the crème fraîche and mix well. Immediately remove from heat and pour into the pie shell.

Bake for 25 minutes. Serve at room temperature.

6 servings

Brioches with Ice Cream

PREPARATION: 10 MINUTES

This is an emergency dessert when you are suddenly faced with unexpected guests and no time to prepare something special.

6 brioches   1 quart coffee ice cream
½ cup rum

Remove the top of each brioche. With a spoon, remove some of the inside. Pour some rum into each brioche and fill with ice cream; put back the top and serve immediately.
   6 servings

Chestnut Ice Cream

PREPARATION: 15 MINUTES

Many years ago in Paris after I had met my husband, he told me one night about a young Frenchwoman he had once known who had invited him for dinner. The dinner was delicious, but she served him chestnut purée for dessert. My husband barely touched it and, as soon as possible, left her house, never to return. Needless to say, I never served him chestnut purée for years after hearing the story. But last winter, when I made this light elegant dessert, he loved it.

2 pints coffee ice cream   SAUCE:
½ pint heavy cream   4 1-ounce squares semisweet
1-pound can chestnut purée   chocolate
                                    ½ cup strong espresso
                                    2 tablespoons cognac
                                    6 marrons glacés (optional)

Let the ice cream soften at room temperature for 10 minutes. Meanwhile, beat the cream until stiff. Then gently fold the chestnut purée into the cream. Add the chestnut purée to the ice cream, mix well and freeze until ready to serve.
   In the top of a double boiler over simmering water, melt the chocolate with the espresso and cognac. Mix well with a wooden spoon and set on the corner of the stove to keep lukewarm until ready to use.
   Put the ice cream into individual glass cups. Pour some chocolate sauce over the ice cream and garnish with a marron glacé. Serve immediately.
   6 servings

Beer Batter for Crêpes

PREPARATION: 5 MINUTES   COOKING: 20 MINUTES

The standard crêpe batter must stand for at least 1 hour before making the crêpes. This recipe allows you to prepare the crêpe batter and use it immediately.

6 eggs
½ cup milk
½ cup beer
6 tablespoons flour

⅛ teaspoon salt
1 tablespoon sugar*
4 tablespoons butter, melted

In a food processor, blend the eggs, milk, beer, flour, salt and butter.

Heat 1 tablespoon butter in a crêpe pan and add 3 tablespoons of the batter. Rotate the pan until the batter covers the entire surface. When the edges are lightly browned, turn the crêpe with a spatula and cook on the other side for a few seconds. If the crêpes are to be filled, don't cook the second side. If they are to be eaten as is (with sugar or jam), cook the second side a bit longer.

Without buttering the pan again, continue to make crêpes until all the batter has been used.

12 to 16 crêpes

*Omit the sugar if you are using the crêpes for an appetizer or the main dish.

Index

About the Author

COLETTE ROSSANT grew up in Cairo and Paris and came to the United States in the late 1950s. Now the chairman of the language department at St. Ann's Episcopal School in Brooklyn, she is also the English translator of *Paul Bocuse's French Cooking* and the author of *Cooking with Colette,* a children's cookbook, and *A Mostly French Food Processor Cookbook.* She lives in Manhattan with her husband, an architect, and their teenage children.